Adventures of a Suburban Boy

JOHN BOORMAN

faber and faber

First published in 2003
by Faber and Faber Limited
3 Queen Square London WC1N 3AU

Published in the United States by Faber and Faber Inc.
an affiliate of Farrar, Straus and Giroux LLC, New York

This paperback edition first published in 2004

Typeset by Faber and Faber Limited
Printed in England by Mackays of Chatham, plc

Photos from John Boorman archive
and from *Positif* magazine, courtesy of Michel Ciment

Copyrights in film stills are held by the following:
Catch Us If You Can © Warner / Anglo Amalgamated-Bruton Film;
Deliverance © Warner Bros; *The Emerald Forest* © Embassy Pictures
Corporation; *Excalibur* © Warner Bros; *Exorcist II The Heretic* © Warner Bros;
Hell in the Pacific © ABC-Selmur / Cinerama; *Hope and Glory* © Columbia Pictures;
Leo the Last © United Artists; *Point Blank* © MGM;
Where the Heart Is © Buena Vista Pictures; *Zardoz* © Fox

A CIP record for this book
is available from the British Library

ISBN 0-571-21696-X

2 4 6 8 10 9 7 5 3 1

For my children –
Telsche, Katrine, Charley, Daisy, Lola, Lee, and Lili-Mae –
a record.

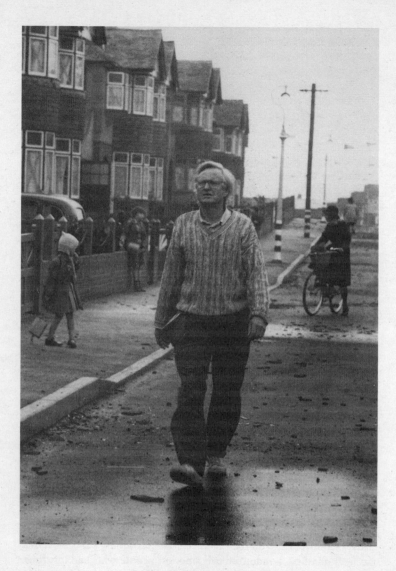

On the set of *Hope and Glory*,
recreating the suburban street of my youth

Light and Shadow

If you plant oaks you necessarily take a long view. As with children. Both are acts of faith in the future of a precarious planet. When I came to this simple Georgian house in the Wicklow Hills of Ireland some thirty-four years ago, the ancient oaks I inherited cast their spell on me. They rooted me to the place. Although I was drawn away to distant forests and wild rivers, making movies, I have returned to raise my children and tend my trees.

The great pioneer film director, D. W. Griffith, believed that film was the universal language promised in the Bible that would herald the Second Coming; and so it must have seemed in the glory days of the silent era. In the first twenty years of the last century, film swept the world, effortlessly crossing barriers of class, race and nation. A measure of the speed of this revolution was that scarcely five years after his arrival in Hollywood, Chaplin was the most famous man in the world, and probably the highest paid.

In *The Lost Girl*, D. H. Lawrence describes Nottingham miners watching those early films: while they looked at the live music hall acts out of the corners of their eyes, embarrassed, uneasy, they *stared* at the movies, unblinking, mouths agape, like men in a trance, mesmerised.

The power of film lies in its links to the unconscious, its closeness to the condition of dreaming. In my dreaming youth, like so many others, I was as entranced as those miners, coming to believe that film was the ultimate art form, that it could include everything and everybody, reconnect us to all that had been taken from us. I was born in a faceless, mindless London suburb amongst people who had lost their way in the world, who had forgotten who they were, and had fallen from grace.

*

In the Arthurian legend, the Grail was lost because men had sinned against nature. The world became a wasteland. The Fisher King's wound would not heal. Only by finding the Grail could wholeness, harmony and oneness be restored, and the King be healed, and grace restored.

I have sought that lost grace in the film-making process, where the material things of the world – money, buildings, sets, plastic, metal, people – disappear into a camera and become nothing but light and shadow flickering on a wall: matter into spirit, the alchemists would say. Memories are even more shadowy and insubstantial . . .

1933: Semi-Detached Lives

I was born in a snowstorm, according to my mother. My father set out on foot to fetch the midwife and by the time they struggled back through the blizzard, my head had already ventured into the world.

In the morning, my father left for work as usual. My sister had been parked with grandparents. In the meantime my mother was alone with the newborn child. She recalled those few hours of solitude as the happiest of her life. The house was muted by the silence of snow. Exhausted from the storm, the earth lay quiet. Rosehill Avenue, the suburban street she detested, was transformed, its banality concealed for the arrival of her son. The husband to whom she was never reconciled was conveniently absent. She fell into a reverie of perfect grace and I was enfolded within it.

So my first memory is not mine but my mother's. What I do remember is her face and voice as she told that story, the memory of a memory.

The poignancy of lost perfection, the long shadow that exquisite happiness casts over ordinary pleasure, can make for a life of discontent. For soon the snow melted and the street reappeared, nude and nasty, and her life needed to be lived.

Fifty-five years later I set out to make *Hope and Glory*, a film of my childhood in the London Blitz. I began by putting down the incidents and episodes that had hung in the memory, but film has its own imperative: as I started to shape these recollections, imagination asserted its function, and I began to invent scenes between my parents and Herbert, who was my father's best friend and the man my mother loved all her life.

I also embroidered my fifteen-year-old sister's relationship with her French-Canadian lover. When I showed the script to my mother and my sister Wendy, they were shocked. How could I possibly have witnessed and recalled these intimacies? Some of the scenes I thought I had invented had occurred in reality, it turned out.

We define ourselves in the stories we tell of ourselves. We hone them; repeat them until we no longer remember the memory, but only the story of the memory. Especially if one is involved in transforming experience into fiction, the functions of imagination and memory become conjoined, but just as we recognise truth in fiction, we can also sniff out the fake in fact.

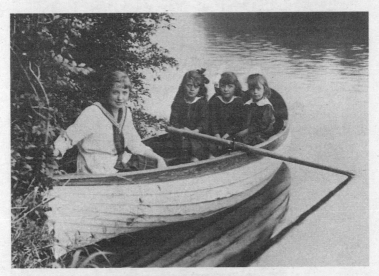

My mother Ivy in the bow, with her three sisters
Jenny, Billie and Bobbie (1920s)

When I brought my mother and her three sisters to the film studio to inspect the set that reproduced our Rosehill Avenue sitting room they were delighted with its accuracy. They had only minor caveats: 'The wireless was in the other corner,' and 'Your mother always had a vase of flowers in the window.' Working on the designs with Tony Pratt and in the act of writing, long-buried memories were exhumed. In a book of period

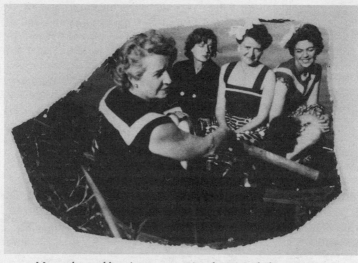

My mother and her sisters, re-creating the original photo (1950s)

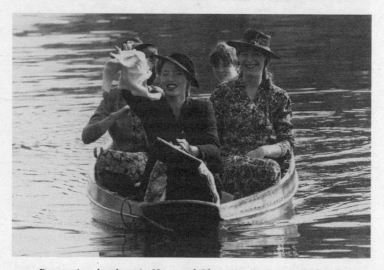

Re-creating the photo in *Hope and Glory*: Katrine Boorman (front),
Amelda Brown and Jill Baker as my mother's sisters,
and Sebastian Rice-Edwards as myself

wallpaper samples I found the very design we had in our living room. It was profligate, but I had new blocks made and reproduced it. After the four sisters had made their small adjustments to the room, they pronounced themselves satisfied. My Aunt Billy said, 'It's almost perfect. What a pity you got the wallpaper wrong.' Was it her memory at fault or mine?

I reconstructed Rosehill Avenue for *Hope and Glory* on a disused airfield at Wisley in Surrey for a cost of three quarters of a million pounds. When I went back to the real Rosehill Avenue I found it did not resemble my memory of it. It was too small, not long enough and had a bend in it. I built the memory – an endless, dead-straight street stretching to the very centre of London, where St Paul's Cathedral could be seen festooned with barrage balloons.

The film of *Hope and Glory* is now a patina, overlaid on my memories, and writing this memoir becomes an archaeological dig. Movies exist only frame by frame; the rest is memory and anticipation. As in life, *now* is the only reality. A film can be rewound and be seen again, but in life the past is a murky place where imagination may be more reliable than memory.

I was born in 1933 at 50 Rosehill Avenue, Carshalton, a monotonous street of semi-detached houses similar to four million others that were built between the wars. My father bought the house with a deposit of fifty pounds and paid off the mortgage at seventeen shillings and sixpence per week. The purchase price was £676.

As home-owning members of the new lower middle class, my parents were dismayed when council estates began to spring up around Rosehill Avenue, rehousing London's slum-dwellers. Like other owners of semis, they had only a murky view of their place in the class system, but they aspired to a vague gentility, which was affronted by these invading hordes. They noted with mounting horror that Wendy came home from school swearing and talking 'common'. She caught doses of working-class diseases like scabies and scarlet fever, and eventually tuberculosis. She also absorbed an incipient socialism from these fugitive kids from Bermondsey.

She argued incessantly with our father. He was not a snob, certainly never disdained those he considered below him, but he deeply respected his superiors and felt threatened if things and people were not properly in their places. He had fought in the First World War and was a sentimental patriot, a passionate royalist, a dogged Tory. He insisted that whenever the National Anthem was played over the wireless we all stood rigidly to attention, chin in, chest out, shoulders back, fists clenched with thumbs pointing down the seams of the trousers. He once caught me lying in bed with the National Anthem playing on my crystal set. 'On your feet,' he commanded. It was a cold wartime winter night and there was no heating in bedrooms then.

I whimpered a rather inventive excuse: 'If I stand up, the lead on the earphones is not long enough, so I wouldn't hear it anyway.'

'You don't have to hear it, son,' he said in his paternal imparting-of-wisdom voice. 'As long as you know it's playing, you stand up. You don't need to hear it.'

'But Dad, it's freezing.'

He weakened, his manner softened. 'Just this once, then. But *lie* to attention. Remember, thumbs pointing down the seams of your pyjamas.'

His views were thinly thought out and, when challenged by Wendy, he would go white with rage, tremble and bark out inarticulate defences of his besieged positions. His anger would cause him to mangle his usually immaculate platitudes into gloriously surreal non sequiturs: 'I will not stand by and listen to you insult the country I fought and died for.' He had to choke back barrack-room insults he would dearly have loved to hurl at Wendy to refute her political heresies. Red in the face, words twisted and strangled in his throat, he would bowdlerise some savage curse into monumental ineffectiveness.

'You don't know your . . . your . . .' (Oh, to find a euphemism for arse, yet preserve the alliteration) '. . . your apron from your elbow.'

Wendy would argue that being a Tory was against his own interests, that he was sustaining the class that oppressed us. But voting Conservative was a way of reassuring himself that he would not slip down into the dreaded working class. Thus was England's class system shored up.

My mother inculcated in me a horror of the semi, and later I was ashamed of my origins because of the disdain heaped upon the suburbs by architects and intellectuals. The middle classes mocked the aspirations of this new lower middle class – 'Come, friendly bombs, and fall on Slough!' wrote John Betjeman shortly before the war.

Four million built between the wars! The semi was neither a detached house standing in its own grounds, nor a unit in a working-class terrace of joined-up cottages; it was a half-hearted, halfway house to respectability. Four million of them! So twelve, sixteen million people lived in them? Where did they come from, these multitudes? Where are they now? Many, like me, have never admitted to being semi-dwellers. I grew up wishing I had been higher born; then in the sixties, wishing that

I could claim to be lower born. Ironically, sixty years on, most of those houses are still cared for, pampered with double glazing and cherished with patios, unlike the Radiant Cities that came later, the new towns, the tower blocks that have fallen into dismay. The great Le Corbusier's manic followers came like shock troops bringing more destruction to England than Hitler, just as the Victorians demolished more Wren churches than the Blitz.

Was there ever such a stealthy social revolution as the rise of this semi-detached suburbia? They all missed it, or got it wrong – the academics, the politicians, the upper classes. While they worried about socialism and fascism, the cuckoo had laid its egg in their nest and Margaret Thatcher would hatch out of it.

In London the Underground system pushed out spokes from the smoky and grimy hub and the new semis clustered around each station or rib-boned along the new bypasses. Where did they come from, these millions? Some had slipped down from the middle class, losing their money in the Depression; most were dragging themselves up from the working class. They came from all parts and stations, disowning their lowly past, anaesthetising it, so that most of the children I knew had no notion of where they came from, no memory of family history. We were wary of each other, kept ourselves to ourselves. Privacy protected our uncertainty about how to behave. In the thirties we were enjoying a new prosperity. There was a garage for the Morris 8 or the Austin 7. On Sundays the car was ceremoniously wheeled out from the garage, washed and polished, and the parents, with their two little tots in the back, would motor off to the seaside or to Box Hill or to the zoo at Whipsnade. They were home-owners, and they had the freedom of the road.

The private, inward-looking world of the nuclear family was taking shape. These dormitories, ten minutes' walk from the tube, with no roots and no past, were home to a new phenomenon, as yet unnamed: the Commuter.

With the bonds of traditional society severed, they found themselves in a comfortably snug void. Filling that emptiness was the wireless. It played all day, banishing the dread silence, yet I never heard a reference to the semi-suburbs in those BBC programmes. The broadcasts came from a distant land where people spoke in alien accents as remote as the universe that unspooled each week at the Regal or the Odeon in American movies or snobbish English ones. We never imagined meeting such people or sharing their experiences, which isolated us still further.

7

We lacked the skills to reflect on what we had become. We could not fathom ourselves. We took on the daft, foolish looks of institutionalised people, never certain how to speak or walk or behave. Grief embarrassed us; we shrank from gaiety, turned our faces from any kind of public display of feeling.

As yet, in these streets, there were no shops, no churches, no sport, no pubs. During the day the men and the young were siphoned out to work and school; the wives were left to clean and polish, listen to the wireless. Down these deserted streets, trading on the dreams and loneliness, came men knocking on doors selling sheet music, magazines, vacuum cleaners, brushes, the man from the 'Pru' collecting the weekly insurance premiums, the hire-purchase payments on the furniture, and on and on. My mother would dig anxiously into her purse and sniff, seeking both money and sympathy, one of the many things that filled me with shame. It was worse when she was sniffing out money to buy *me* something. I determined that I would free myself as soon as I could from her brave self-sacrifice, fill her purse with money so that she would never again have to scrimp and scratch.

Architects were contemptuous of the semi, not least because they were totally uninvolved in its design and construction. Those tasks fell to 'spec' builders, who surely expressed the deep unconscious fantasies of a people oppressed by the patronising values of their betters.

The past was wholly annihilated. Everything must be new and newly made, preferably in chrome and Bakelite. Oh, how they broke free of the weight of tradition! The sun rose in stained glass over the front door, its rays splayed out on the garden gate; even the settee was shaped like a sunbeam. The 'spec' builder lured us with promises of fresh air and sunlight, flowers and lawns, a refuge from the sooty cities and smoky slums. They offered us Tudor gables, leaded panes, bow windows – eclectic fragments from pre-Industrial Revolution England. We had a teapot that was a chromium globe reflecting the whole universe, or at least the whole of our semi. The china, the cutlery, the carpets and curtains – all new, all in novel shapes and patterns. Clocks, vases, electric fires, cookers, streamlined and gleaming, all machine-made, banishing the craftsman, untouched by human hand.

Health and hygiene were all the rage. Hitler and Mussolini were much admired before the war for their initiatives improving fitness and encouraging sport. Health usurped religion in this churchless but not godless world. We were convalescents from the Industrial Revolution and needed several generations of fresh air and proper food to recover. Oh, what the English inflicted on the English: misery, deprivation and bondage on a scale quite equal to that visited upon their colonial vassals. Half the population was wrenched from the land and into city slums where its past, its ways fell out of mind. And now here were the survivors fleeing to those new suburban streets, fugitives from the shocks not only of the Industrial Revolution but also of the unspeakable horrors of the First World War and the privations of the Depression. Forget all that. Don't look back. Reach forward into the smiling new world of semis and sunshine, lawns and indoor lavatories. If you got through the Great War, escaped the mines, the foundries, the mills, then take comfort in amnesia and embrace the new fantasy, Arcadia for all.

We wore collars and ties now, and bowler hats. This was a new army of clerks, pen-pushers, a legion that leapt up to man the new 'service industries', and who, after but a few years, would be made extinct by the button-pushers, the computers.

It was a massive migration. This was a new land and the England of old was gone for ever. Its passing went unremarked because of the deceptive way it kept up appearances: church-spired villages watered by tumbling streams, wood smoke rising from the thatch, a place of honour for the dead, the country wisdom of old men purchased for the price of a pint. The English country villages became, in truth, little more than movie sets, museums with working models. They pleased the eye, beguiled the heart; and the sham fed the folk myth. It was perhaps these faint echoes, like the impaired instincts of domestic animals, that sent us groping our way into those monotonous streets of semis, lured by a handful of cunning design metaphors that evoked a bucolic English past – yet paradoxically broke free of it, and pointed to a shining future.

A Brief Family History

What little I know of my family origins begins at the outbreak of the First World War. My father, George, and his best friend, Herbert Brooks, were seventeen in 1914. They joined the East Surrey Regiment, which for some bureaucratic reason was diverted from France to India. His school friends, most of the boys he knew, became subalterns and were sent to

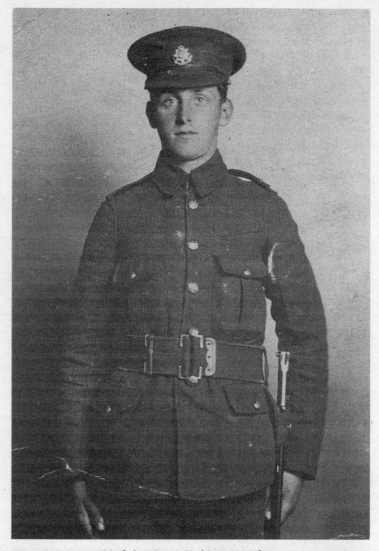

My father, George, in his army uniform

France. Scarcely any of them came back. In due course, young George, who looks fourteen rather than seventeen in that first proud photograph in army uniform, was commissioned, transferred to the Indian Army and ended as a Captain commanding Gurkhas. In a story he never tired of telling, young George, who lived to see a man walking on the moon, rode into battle against the Turks with a drawn sword on an Arab mare: 'It was a suicide mission, a charge against a Turkish artillery position.'

They found the Turks had withdrawn, the Gurkhas' reputation preceding them – and that was as close as he ever got to action! He was never again required to draw his sword in anger. A million of his fellows perished in the mud of Flanders. His survival was a fluke, the stroke of a pen. I owe that penman my existence.

He was offered a Regular Commission in the Indian Army and stayed on after the war, to the dismay of his doting mother. He was having what he would later come to recognise as 'the time of his life'. While his peers perished in France, he stuck pigs, played polo and fell in love with an Indian princess. From the stories he told of those times, one image lingers in my mind:

> When we were sleeping under canvas, an Indian servant would sit cross-legged in the tent and fan me all night. I became so accustomed to this flow of cool air that if he dozed off and stopped fanning, I would instantly wake up and give him a tongue lashing.

I wondered about the thoughts of that Indian of long ago, faithfully fanning the face of an English boy of nineteen, the two of them in a tent under the stars in a subcontinent so heavy with history and mystery, about which my father knew little and cared less.

Apart from stories, he brought back the usual elephant's foot umbrella stand and carved ivories, which were powerful icons for me as a child and held out the promise of exotic worlds beyond the banalities of suburban London. He had an annual bout of malarial fever, and I would stand at his bedside listening to his delirious ramblings in Hindi – probably berating that poor man for not fanning him. As he tossed and turned, an occasional wave of body heat would escape the bedcovers. It seemed to me that its moist and musky smell was the real palpable India that had stayed with him, and which escaped like a genie into our semi.

Our house, straining for middle-class status, like most in our street, had a name on the gate as well as a number: 'Bhim-tam'! I faithfully reproduced it on the set for the film without knowing or wishing to know what it meant. I harbour the romantic hope that he named it for that Indian princess, but I fear it is just a Hindi equivalent of 'Mon Repos' or 'Dunroamin''.

George may have been unscathed by the war and untouched by India, but rude shocks awaited him back in Wimbledon when he finally succumbed to his mother's anguished pleas and returned in 1920. His family was ruined.

His father had inherited a prosperous family laundry. He stole a march on his competitors by inventing the first washing machine, a large hexagonal wooden drum with diagonal ribs that superseded washerwomen at tubs. So successful was it that he started to manufacture the machine and sell it to other laundries. Horse-drawn vans delivered the laundry, so substantial stables were kept – the horses being the only aspect of the business that interested my father. As a boy my father was indulged with fine horses which stood him in good stead when it came to riding into battle; indeed, young George's promotions probably came in part from his prowess in the chukkas.

Grandfather was essentially a happy-go-lucky inventor, and apart from making the washing machine, had as little interest in the laundry as his son, and left his wife and mother to look after it. He devised complicated clockwork toys and started a factory to make them, but never put enough effort into marketing. They were too complex and too expensive to succeed (like my movies, some would say).

He told me with gleeful amusement how his famous washing machine had helped him secure an army contract to wash blankets during the First World War. The laundry was soon overwhelmed by the ever-increasing volume of military blankets that arrived each day. He solved the problem by employing people simply to shake out the blankets, fold them, and send them back. One day he was summoned and arraigned before the Quartermaster-General. He was charged with sending the blankets back – not properly dried! He was stripped of the contract and a heavy fine was imposed. He could so easily have proved his innocence of the lesser crime by admitting a greater one.

'It proves there *is* justice in this world,' he said, drawing a moral, 'you just have to hope it doesn't come your way too often.' And his laugh rang out. He could laugh anything off. He saw the world as a huge joke – he just could not take it seriously.

He was a compulsive spender and giver of gifts. His house was always full of friends and relations, and within minutes of their arrival he would have demonstrated to them just how trivial were their troubles. His was a laugh full of music, like runs on a clarinet – not the explosive barking laugh that belonged to my maternal grandfather, but full of notes and tunes that could play all day without repetition.

'If you're having fun,' he confided, 'you've got them fooled.'

'Who are *they*?' I wondered.

'You'll know them when you meet them,' he laughed. And not too many years later I met them and knew them. He did allow himself the occasional serious interlude. He would take me aside and extract a solemn undertaking: 'Promise me you'll never wear anything but silk next to your skin,' or 'Never eat salmon unless it is smoked' – and this during wartime austerity.

One day my grandfather found himself in a train sitting opposite a young widow. She was in great distress: she had been left penniless and was obliged to go into domestic service. Having lost her husband, she was now on her way to give up her three-year-old son for adoption.

Grandfather told her she was too distressed to take such an important decision. He had a son of the same age. 'You go and take up your position and I'll look after the boy until you're settled.' Grandma was quite accustomed to her husband arriving home with chance acquaintances who would stay for weeks at a time, and took it in her stride. The widow would visit on her day off, and the boy was brought up as my father's brother, went to public school with him and was married out of my grandparents' house – yet no formal arrangement was ever made. If the subject was raised, Grandpa would laugh it off and away. The young widow became a midwife and we called her 'Nursey'. She was one of many who were always present on Sundays at Grandpa's.

By the time George returned from India, however, the laundry was gone, the horses and land were lost, and the solid Victorian villa sold up. Even the money he had saved and sent home from India was spent. All that was left was a 'trading company', a yard full of junk: items that chums had left as security against loans from Grandpa; he was the softest touch. George, whose every boyhood desire had been met by an adoring mother, an indulgent father and the largesse of the family business, who was fawned upon and celebrated in India – an India in which he had yearned to remain – came home to penury and ruin. Grandpa never explained, dismissing it with a peal of laughter: 'The joke's on me this time.'

All he left when he died was his laughter ringing in our ears. I can hear it still. My sister's son Robert, whose birth is the climax of *Hope and Glory*, inherited that clarinet laugh, in the way genes have of jumping generations. Like my grandfather, Robert too can see the joke. My father, however, could not, and the iron entered his soul. Added to his private dismay was the public post-war catastrophe: a million servicemen thrown on to a depressed economy, many of them shell-shocked, wounded, crippled. I can recall as a child that if one went into the street or on a bus it was rare not to see an amputee. The year 1919 brought the pandemic of influenza which killed more people than the war, some twenty million throughout Europe.

What Grandpa always had, however, was an abundance of friends. One of them was starting an oil company, which became Shell-Mex. Grandpa told my father that oil was the coming thing and wangled him a job. 'The oil business is boring,' he used to say with glee. There was nothing like a good pun to get the tunes coming from the clarinet.

So my father had a job, but poor Herbert, his friend, just could not find one, even though he had left the army earlier than George. Most of their school friends had been killed in action, so George and Herbert stuck together, were never apart. Word reached them that the new landlord of the Alexander Hotel at the foot of Wimbledon Hill had four beautiful daughters. When they arrived at the pub it was jam-packed with young fellows come to worship at the shrine. Henry Chapman, destined to become my maternal grandfather, had thoughtfully covered the walls behind the bars in mirrors. Only three of the daughters were in evidence but the reflections seen through a beer glass suggested an infinity of loveliness. The mirrors caught their every movement, their graceful backs, their Lillian Gish profiles. My father, looking up, could observe the tops of their blonde heads floating in mirrors cunningly placed on the ceiling.

As George and Herbert downed their pints of mild-and-bitter, swooning in that delirium of delight, they both fell in love with Ivy, the eldest of the Chapman girls. Each night they returned to gaze and eventually exchange a little badinage. One night the door of the pub burst open and there stood a striking figure in a long fur coat, smoking a cigar and flanked by two prize-fighters complete with cauliflower ears and potato noses. This was Ted Chapman, Henry's brother and deadly rival, who owned the much larger and more fashionable hotel at the top of Wimbledon Hill, the Dog and Fox. Insults flew back and forth between the brothers and soon Ted was able to provoke an affray. George and Herbert were quick to defend the honour of the house. How they welcomed the fists of the prize-fighters, for the pain assuaged the greater pain of their unrequited love for Ivy. Soon they were to discover that the antagonism of the brothers was Sicilian in its intensity. Ted's foray was a reprisal for a recent visit by Henry to the Dog and Fox that had climaxed in a lot of smashed glass and broken furniture. Henry had been registering his displeasure at Ted's attempts to lure his daughters to work behind *his* bars at the top of the hill. Henry's mirrors and daughters had severely dented Ted's takings. Furthermore, it seemed that Henry had procured the Alexander for the sole purpose of incommoding his brother. Their rivalry knew no bounds and no end: Ted's Rolls-Royce trumped Henry's Daimler; although Henry strongly disapproved of my father, he gave Ivy a lavish wedding, bigger than the one Ted had given *his* daughter.

George and Herbert courted Ivy, took her out, were invited to the Thames-side bungalow at Shepperton that Grandfather Henry kept as a weekend retreat. She was attracted to them both. She found it hard to separate them in her heart. Her father glowered disapproval. Neither was grand enough for his beautiful daughter. Just penniless opportunists, he told Ivy, but she was inclined to escape her overbearing and tyrannical father. She and her sisters had spent an incarcerated childhood in a gin palace, the Kingsbridge Arms, on the Isle of Dogs in the heart of London's dockland. Nannies and tutors tended to the four girls, but they scarcely left the fortress that blazed with light and the promise of oblivion in cheap gin or porter. Outside it was dangerous, dirty, brutish. This was before the First World War. Grandpa owned the only car in the district, a Unic. Mother remembered the swarms of barefoot urchins that would pursue them as they came and went. Some of them would leap on to the running board and Grandpa would swat them off. So isolated were they that my mother was seven years old before she realised that other people's parents did not drink a half-bottle of champagne for breakfast each morning.

Each morning hundreds of pints would be pumped and lined up on the bar counters. As the hooters signalled the short midday break for the dockers, the doors of the pub would be flung open and the men would surge in, throwing a shower of pennies over the counters and grabbing their beers. After the rush, Mother would sweep up the coins from the floor and set them out in neat piles of twelve (to the shilling), then in columns of twenty (shillings to the pound).

Then came the Great War. Mother described watching the Zeppelins winding their stately way up the Thames, navigating by it. As each one reached its target, the gargantuan dirigible would drop a tiny little bomb. With casualties and damage all around them, Grandfather Henry decided it was time to evacuate his young daughters. As a child, son of an East End coachman, he and his brothers were mudlarks playing and scavenging at the river's edge. He loved the river. Further up the Thames, on the rural middle reaches, prospering merchants and tradesmen were building riverside bungalows as weekend retreats. The motor car put it within reach.

India was the influence and they built in the style of Simla or, more particularly, Kashmir. They were built of wood and set up on stilts against flooding, and had fretted, decorative verandas. Henry bought one (or perhaps built it) on Pharaoh's Island, which divides the river just above Shepperton Lock. The particular conceit of this community was that each bungalow would be named for things Egyptian; there was a Pyramid, a Sphinx, and so on – they are there still. Grandpa's was called 'Philae'. So my mother and her sisters were taken to the riverside to escape a war, just as she would flee there with her children in the war that followed twenty-one years on.

When my father arrived on the scene, Philae had been exchanged for Chestnuts on the towpath, the Kingsbridge Arms for the 'Alex' in Wimbledon. George did not impress at rowing or punting, but he was a strong swimmer, which scored him some points with Henry. It was about this time that my mother's affections began to veer towards Herbert, but Herbert still had no job, so how could he propose marriage? He loved her deeply, but felt obliged to step back and give his friend George a clear field. My father began turning up at Shepperton without him. George made the running and Ivy waited in vain for Herbert to declare himself.

It was the twenties. George took Ivy to the Danse de Thé where her eyes would search in vain for Herbert. Mother and her sisters were great exponents of the Charleston. They became flappers, had their hair bobbed. There were eligible young men. It was gay, gay, gay. They had river parties after regattas. They tied several punts together and drifted downstream. They danced on the boats to a wind-up gramophone, and Chinese lanterns lit their way. They grew up with a passion for river life and a horror of conventional living.

There is a photograph of me at six months, sitting naked on a chocolate box, the picket gate of Chestnuts in the background. The picture

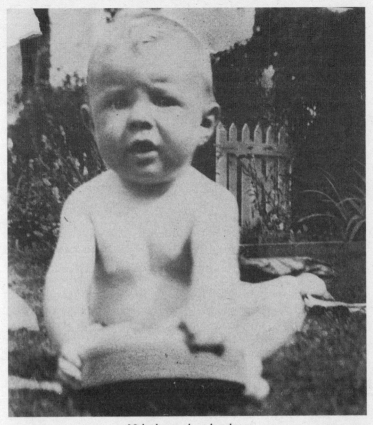

Naked on a chocolate box

was hand tinted by my Auntie Billy, the third Chapman sister. My earliest memories, in the extreme close-up lens of infancy, are of the sheen of varnished boat mahogany, green-tinged brass fittings, the tinkle of coloured-glass wind chimes hanging from verandas, the addictive tang of creosoted wood, and my Grandfather Henry, an ogre in rope-soled canvas shoes, padding and pacing his veranda, the floorboards squealing under foot like squashed mice.

On one such visit, I remember the empty terror I felt as voices were raised, my father white-faced and trembling, mother snatching me away from those rapturous river textures, the taste of her tears mingling with the consoling smell of the pleated leather car seats on the way home.

It was almost certainly a row about money. After giving them a lavish wedding, Henry had no interest in Ivy and George, and was not about to alleviate their poverty.

Father toiled for years at the clerical job he hated. Mother was trapped in the suburban wastes of Rosehill Avenue. She pined for the river. My father's pleasure was the sea. As a bachelor, he and his pals would race their belt-driven motorbikes down the Brighton road. Now, with a young family, he liked to follow the same beloved route in his gleaming Austin 8. Herbert was married too now and doing well, ironically, better than George. He ran a slightly superior, Union-Jack-flying Standard 10. His son, Peter, was my best friend.

Herbert and George would race their cars down the Brighton road as they had once raced their motorbikes. 'The kids need a run down to Brighton for a good blow,' Dad would declare. This was his panacea for all ills, especially hacking coughs and runny noses. 'A good blow' meant striding along the promenade taking deep bites out of the icy wind, its cutting edge of salt stinging our scabby noses. This cure-all air was called 'ozone'. It was the patent medicine of 'Dr Brighton': 'Bright, Brighter, Brighton', ran the advertisement. It perfectly expressed my father's philosophy. It was all to do with escaping the sulphurous pall of coal pollution that hung over London and reached out to our 'sunny' suburbs: combined with the heavy mists of the low-lying Thames valley, this produced those sickly yellow 'pea-souper' fogs, now happily banished.

So we would lean into Brighton's 'ozone', a thirty-mile-an-hour wind that would 'flush out' the bad air and 'blow through' us. The cleansing of the lungs was not the end of it. The flesh was also to be purged by plunging into 'the briny'. My father would lead us into the surly grey sea. The angry waves dashed the pebbles, foam-borne, to pummel our pale and skinny legs. 'A quick dip', my father called it, and we were required to endure it winter and summer.

Mother, on the other hand, always longed for the river, more particularly the Thames at her beloved Shepperton, and so we children were shuttled from one to the other, respective parents extolling the virtues of river and sea.

War to the Rescue

How wonderful was the war! It gave common cause, equal rations, community endeavour, but most delightful of all it gave us the essential thing we lacked: it gave us a myth, a myth nurtured by the wireless, newspapers, the cinema, that allowed us semi people to leap our garden gates, vault over our embarrassments into the arms of patriotism.

Chamberlain's speech announcing the onset of the Second World War is the beginning of *Hope and Glory*. It was one of those rare momentous occasions that is carved into the memories of all who experienced it. I rendered every detail, every word, in the film. For both my parents it represented the possibility of deliverance. My father had lived out a twenty-year hangover from the intoxication of his Indian Army days. Although he was nearly forty, he could not wait to join up. It was a blessed escape from the dull drudgery of his clerical job, and perhaps vague and unarticulated dissatisfactions with his marriage. My mother found herself trapped in that suburban street, exiled from the Thames and married to a man she was deeply fond of but did not love.

So there we were, marooned in this unformed fantasy, drowning but too polite to wave, when along came the war with lifelines for all. All our uncertainties of identity and dislocations could be subsumed in the common good, in opposing Evil – in full-blown, brass-band, spine-tingling, lump-in-throat patriotism. We had found our heroes – ourselves.

When my father went off to war he left a six-year-old boy with a house full of women. I had two sisters and no brothers. My mother's three sisters were ever present and there was no male to curb their excesses: the sudden inexplicable tears, the conspiratorial laughter at some sexual allusion, the mysterious bleeding, and the stifling embraces when a boy's face was pressed into that infinite bosom softness, falling, falling, inhaling layers of odour only superficially concealed by Lily of the Valley – acute, knotted, scarlet-blushing, shameful embarrassment.

The women of the street were rampant with purpose. It was their war. The men were marooned in army camps in quiet country places while the bombs dropped on us. We kids rampaged through the ruins, the semis opened up like dolls' houses, the precious privacy shamefully exposed. We took pride in our collection of shrapnel. Most of it came from our own anti-aircraft shells, which also did more damage to roofs

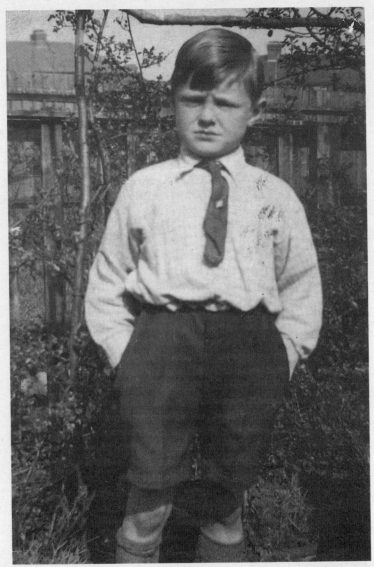

Me, aged five

than the Luftwaffe. I often picked up fragments that were still hot and smelt of gunpowder. Much more valued were bits of German bombs. We learned to recognise each type. The commonest were the incendiary bombs, easily identified by their smell and narrow diameter. The bigger German bombs had beautiful internal ribbing and an oily odour. The most prized acquisition of all was live ammunition. We would lock bullets in a vice and detonate them by hammering nails into their heads. Even at night we could recognise our own and enemy planes by their sounds – the deep throaty roar of the Spitfire's Rolls-Royce Merlin engine, the 'wow wow' of the Messerschmitt.

One winter's night when my father happened to be home on leave, with no air-raid warning, a bomb fell on the house next to our own. It was a 'blockbuster', which would have demolished the street had it exploded. It went through the roof, cut a hole in the floor at the foot of the bed where an old woman lay, and buried itself deep in the earth. It was found some fifty years later and the street was evacuated while it was recovered and defused. My father went in and rescued the old woman and brought her to our house. It was raining heavily. It was just before Christmas. My younger sister Angela and I were making paper chains and had them spread out across the living-room floor. My father arrived with two ARP men and three Home Guard volunteers. They trampled all over our paper chains with their muddy boots. I recall that as the most painful moment of the war.

A little girl across the street, Pauline, was awkward and unpopular. One night her mother was killed. The next morning she stood at her front gate. We were deeply impressed. We watched at a distance, and then little by little got closer to her. With the cruelty of children we questioned her about how it felt to lose a mother. We pressed for all the details. We needed to prepare ourselves. She revelled in the attention which seemed to outweigh the loss of her mother. We invited her to play with us, which we would never have done normally. She declined and kept her vigil at the gate with the rubble of her house behind her. I reconstructed this scene in *Hope and Glory*.

The unexploded bomb severely damaged the structure of our house, giving my mother the excuse to gather up her children and make her escape back to Shepperton and the river. My father begged his friend Herbert to watch over us while he was away, so my mother was thrown together with the man she had always loved. She did part-time war work in Herbert's factory. He was an important man in a reserved occupation.

He had a petrol allowance. He used to drive her home each afternoon, a rare luxury. He would park his car by the river in front of our bungalow and I would watch them talking, mute behind the glass. I knew something important and disturbing was happening, but she looked so happy with Herbert that I felt it must be a good thing. Somehow I entered into an unspoken conspiracy with my mother that we would not mention Herbert in front of my father.

Enter God, English and Irish Versions

As she and her sisters had fled to Shepperton to escape the Zeppelin raids in the First World War, so my mother took her children to the same magical stretch of river two decades later. The lock lay at the centre, and through it passed the skiffs and punts and dinghies, the pleasure steamers. There was not one, but two weirs where we could frolic dangerously in the cascading waters. Another river, the Wey, fed into the Thames at Shepperton. There were backwaters and streams to explore and three islands to circumnavigate.

My sister and I were put into the local Church school, and I was also sent to Sunday school and recruited into the choir. This meant Friday evening practice, Sunday Matins at 11 a.m., Evensong at 6 p.m. and often a Saturday wedding.

St Nicholas in Shepperton is a Thames-side church, unassuming, but harmonious and pleasing to the eye. Its tower is a mixture of brick, stone and flint, a reflection of the mild, eclectic folk it served. The stained glass is bland, but as a boy I got an ecstatic charge from the shaft of dusty coloured light from the West window, which seemed to pick out the choir like the finger of God as we piped out those thumping old hymns. Our reedy little voices bounced off the grey limestone and the brass plaques commemorating dead vicars and forgotten squires whose momentary eminence had gained them proximity to the altar.

Mr Rosewell, organist and choirmaster, was a solemn man who unexpectedly also played the piano in the King's Head pub next door. He had an infallible ear for the onset of puberty, which would fracture the innocence of the voice. As we assembled for each service, he would run his intense eyes across our faces then choose one of our number to

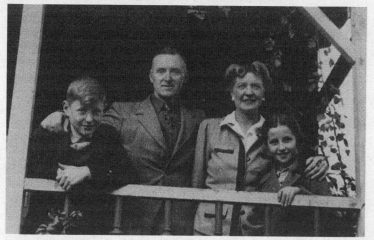

Escape to Shepperton

pump the organ. We never understood how he made this choice. We searched for deeper meaning. Was it a reward or a penance? Had he heard the signs of a breaking voice? Was this the limbo that would lead to expulsion?

I would sometimes see my mother in the congregation watching me with a proud smile on her lips. I would avoid her eye and desperately hope that the other boys would not realise that it was me she was looking at. I would feel the blush rising from my neck. Realising that the all-knowing Mr Rosewell could see this in his organ mirror was enough to make the blush flush deeper. After the service, if he demanded to know who had sung out of tune, out of time or not at all, and why, I would admit to each and every crime, for how could I deny anything with a red face, how could I convince Mr Rosewell that my only sin was acute, chronic embarrassment?

Our voices reached out each Sunday to a sparse congregation, voices that curled around the frayed regimental flags, bounced off the mournful lists of the war-dead, expired against the unyielding walls. Our vicar, the Rev. Sheppard Smith, dull and doleful, tall and stooping, seemed always to be on the point of collapsing under his own height. His droning sermons were so soporific that it was as if he cast a spell over the church. At the sound of his voice, heads would sink on chests or fall back against pews, eyes glaze over. Feverish fantasies invaded my young mind as the faithful fought their weekly battle against sleep. Would ivy and briars grow up and engulf the church, would we be discovered a hundred years hence – village folk, river people, market gardeners – as rescuers hacked their way through the foliage to find the sleepers preserved in the aspic of the Rev. Sheppard Smith's sermons?

He had a method of rousing the congregation by suddenly raising his voice in violent emphasis on a random word. It was the unexpectedness that jerked them awake. Only once do I recall him showing real passion. A parishioner had complained of us choirboys that we whispered and fidgeted. The Reverend responded like a vengeful God. How many in the congregation, he thundered, attended twice, three times on Sundays, as did the choir? Anger spent, he sunk back into neo-narcolepsy. All the vigour of our hymns crashing against the stone were nullified by that mordant monotone.

Years later, I was devoted to Evensong at Salisbury Cathedral. Each day, for eight hundred years, voices of praise and supplication have rung against those walls. Can the ephemeral wring a response from the implacable? Voice against stone, man's cries to God, a fine metaphor for the human predicament. In the Middle Ages it was a vivid symbol of the struggle of the spiritual to overcome the material. The genius of the cathedral builders was to make stone seem light, even weightless, to suggest that it could be transcended. All those prayers, all those psalms, all those centuries. Could they bring a God into being? By faith, by need, by the weight of worship, perhaps man can evolve a God. Perhaps everything happens in reverse? Instead of starting with a lonely God, it starts with nothingness, the void, then life develops, the higher forms emerge, man's yearning for God finally brings God into being.

Now and then we were invited to tea in the vicarage, a graceful Georgian house far too grand for the modest church. There was a croquet lawn; Mrs Rev., worn and put upon, showed us how to play while the vicar sat apart, fixing his look on some distant place, above our heads, perhaps on the vacant throne of God.

I walked in to St Nicholas' Church one morning a few years back, and I was pleased to see that an inner vestibule door to exclude draughts had been built as a practical memorial to our organist, Mr Rosewell. A young priest was alone by the altar. I told him that I had sung under Mr R's tutelage. He was very courteous, and we spoke for several minutes before he begged to be excused as he was in the middle of saying Mass.

I was as acutely embarrassed as when Mr Rosewell had caught me blushing. But Mass? What would the Rev. Sheppard Smith have made of that, High Church in our lowly temple?

The local Church of England school was two miles from our wooden riverside bungalow on the towpath. Angela and I plodded up Ferry Lane with its parade of poplars planted (according to my mother) by my grandfather, past the square where St Nicholas' Church is flanked by two pubs, the posh Anchor hotel and the olde worlde King's Head – all low-beams, polished mahogany counters, brass beer pumps, pewter tankards. On through the village we wended, past fields of cabbage and turnips, past the walls hiding the mysteries of Ladye Place, the great house I dreamt of owning when I was grown up and rich. On to the war memorial, which divided the road as well as reminding us of the fallen of 1914–18. A left turn down a sandy lane brought us wearily and fearfully to the primary school. A dearth of teachers, of course, as all Christian soldiers had marched off to war. Which left the terrifying Mr (Whacker) Wakefield, who had a remarkable resemblance to Hitler, both in appearance and character.

Bible stories were banged into our heads. I remember the lurid colour illustrations in our school Bibles. When the air-raid sirens sounded we ran, cheering, to the shelters. There Mr Wakefield would command us to put on our gas masks and recite the times tables. That scene and Mr Wakefield himself found their way into *Hope and Glory*.

On Empire Day we had to form up in the schoolyard holding red, white or blue pieces of cloth to create a Union Jack for the benefit of Spitfires and Hurricanes flying past above us. It must have been 1943.

Since most of us were destined to become artisans, there were wood- and metalwork classes. We had to make model planes so as to feel vicariously involved in the war effort. Whacker looked beadily at my inept attempt at a Flying Fortress, sighed, and told me to read a book. As the others carved and glued and painted, I bent over my book, deeply humiliated. Failure then and since has always embarrassed me, and confessing it to others is even more painful than the failure itself. Thus began the vice of dissembling, concealing my shortcomings. The root of this was not, as is often the case, the fear of not being loved, but the terror I had of the sneer on my father's face. He knew he was a failure in my mother's eyes. Her love and hopes were diverted from him to me. My failures were therefore as satisfying to him as my successes.

I don't think he knew this or understood it. But thus the revenge of ambition is hatched.

A greater shame was awaiting me. I failed the eleven-plus exam. I have no memory of sitting it, but I can vividly recall the shame of telling my parents. Even now, my palms are sweaty as I type this confession. At that time a very small number passed and went on to grammar schools to learn Latin and Greek; the rest went to technical schools to learn crafts. At fourteen they left to take up apprenticeships. My mother went to see Mr Wakefield for advice. Should she try to scrape up the money to send me to a private grammar school? Mr Wakefield thought that my prospects as a craftsman were not good. If I could get a private education I might aspire to be a clerk.

My mother cast about for possibilities. In Chertsey, the next town up the river, there was a Catholic school run by Salesian priests of the Order of Don Bosco. Priests were exempt from war service, especially the neutral Irish, and Irish they mostly were despite the Italian origins of the order. In her sweet way my mother did not share the casual prejudices of her class against Catholics and the Irish. She simply calculated that this was a school that, unlike so many, would not have surrendered most of its teachers to the war.

It was my first contact with Irishness in all its glory and grim horror. How the oppressive rule of Rome crippled an anarchic, poetic people! Ireland was to have an insidious influence on my life and work, drawing me and keeping me there for thirty years almost against my will.

I was terrified by the ambience of violence, both threatened and overt. The young brothers and priests seemed pent up, over-wound, their only release the infliction of pain. I saw no evidence of the paedophilia that was to explode into the open years later. I was a day boy – there were hints and rumours from the boarders of boys being invited up to a priest's room and given cigarettes and altar wine. It went on, of course, and there was a complicity that protected the priests, the belief that somehow doing those things with a priest gave instant absolution. Secrecy was guaranteed. No boy had the courage to betray a priest. The Salesians were much more alarmed when one of the Brothers started an affair with a senior girl at the neighbouring convent. They fell in love and met clandestinely and probably innocently, but it resulted in a scandal that shook the College to its foundations.

In 1998 I made a film, *The General*, about a Dublin crime boss, Martin Cahill. In a seminal scene, one of Cahill's gang, Gary, has been

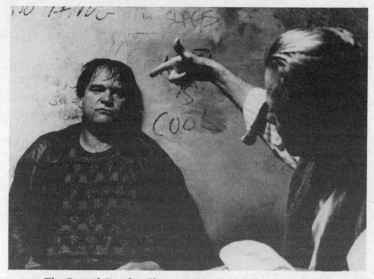

The General: Brendan Gleeson as Martin Cahill with Jon Voight

accused of raping his own daughter. Cahill is disgusted but feels obliged to help, since loyalty given and exacted is at the root of his power.

CAHILL That priest, he done you when you were an altar boy, didn't he?

GARY Yes. He done all us boys.

CAHILL That can be your defence. You can say it screwed up your sex life, some shit like that.

GARY I wouldn't like to grass on him. He was a nice old boy. It didn't hurt too much. He enjoyed it, and he let us drink the altar wine.

I wanted to show that Gary had no sense that he was passing on the abuse that he had suffered.

At the school, corporal punishment was inflicted mercilessly and remorselessly. Knuckles were rapped with rulers, ears pulled, faces slapped as well as the more formal canings. When being caned on the hand, it was vital to keep your thumb pressed low: the pain was endurable when confined to the fleshy part of the hand, but if it caught the thumb knuckle and bruised the bone the agony was prolonged.

In *Hope and Glory* I showed the boy, my surrogate, clutching his hands after a caning. It was difficult to hold a pen steady for an hour or two afterwards, which could lead to further punishment for poor hand-writing.

Fr Dalton was the priest we dreaded most of all. He set us work in the classroom and then prowled between the desks peering over shoulders at our efforts. He would come up silently behind us and if he detected slovenly penmanship or a daydreamer, he would strike without warning, with the flat of his hand, on the side of our heads. The ringing ears, the galaxies of stars spinning across the classroom, the giddy nausea were as nothing compared to the silent dread of sickening apprehension as we awaited the next inevitable blow.

As a non-Catholic, I was excused chapel and religious instruction, and no attempt was made to convert me, except by one boy who was my best friend at the time. He was concerned that when I died I would not qual-ify to join him in Paradise but would, at best, be confined to limbo (that indecisive theological twilight zone that has been quietly dropped by Rome these days). He had learnt that, *in extremis*, any Catholic can bap-tise, a concession from the Church to comfort the parents of babies dying at birth. Since we needed privacy and water, the deed had to be done in a lavatory cubicle. I was squeamish about using water from the toilet bowl, but he cleverly scooped up water in his hand as it was flush-ing and I submitted to the ceremony. Thus it was that I became, in a manner of speaking, a closet Catholic.

While religious instruction was being conducted, I was banished to an empty classroom so that there could be no accusations of proselytising. I felt alienated. I could be observed by all, sitting alone, shut off from the truth, from the grace of God. A longing, an ache grew in my heart. It was curiosity masquerading as spiritual fervour. I wanted to know the differ-ences between the Protestant and Catholic faiths, what it was that divided them so absolutely. Finally I asked if I could join the class. I was admitted.

Our old vicar, the Rev. Sheppard Smith, was very much at home in the bloody, vengeful stories of the Old Testament. He was keen on the 'begats': the repetitious monotony appealed to him. Of course, his desic-cated manner took all the juice out of whoever-it-was who 'lay' with his own daughters, and made God's instruction to Abraham to kill his own son seem no more remarkable than when he asked his wife to pass the sugar at one of the vicarage tea parties.

On the other hand, the Catholics were concerned only with the

Gospels. The Old Testament was too Jewish. Not that we got much New Testament in the first couple of years. It was all catechism, chanting the responses, branding the hot truth of the Church into young flesh. Give me a child until he is seven and he is mine for life, say the Jesuits. I escaped that one. The Salesians were a blander, less intellectually rigorous version of the Soldiers of Christ. The focal point of the school was the chapel, a temporary, temporal building with a corrugated iron roof. I would complete my homework during the service, which preceded each day's lessons. The endlessly repeated Hail Marys would drift out on a whiff of incense. To a schoolboy these repetitions were unendurable, but years later in the Amazon I witnessed how the primitive power of repetitive chanting could induce ecstatic trance. Perhaps this explained why so many boys fainted and had to be brought outside for air. The incense was blamed, but maybe they had entered some mildly altered state.

This faint echo of a once potent ritual was as wearisome as Sheppard Smith's bloodless blood sacrifices. We learned by rote, we memorised. The religious repetitions extended to include all subjects; we entered the marbled halls of abstractions and traipsed from empty chamber to empty chamber. Pain inflicted and received was the only reality, the only touchstone to life.

Routine, repetition. The priests would parade briskly up and down the *ambulacarum*, a covered walkway, reading their in breviaries a passage from the scriptures assigned to each day of the year, to be repeated until death.

As the priests and my fellow pupils left the chapel each morning, I watched them dip their fingers into the holy water and make the perfunctory sign of the cross. Another stale ritual stripped of meaning. How special, how holy was that water? One morning during the service I ventured into the vestibule. The chanting swelled, the incense leaked out. The holy water was in a white enamel bowl screwed to the wall. I peered at it. It looked like ordinary water, odourless, tasteless and transparent – nothingness in liquid form. The movement of water, in rivers and streams, was my element – swimming in it and under it, falling into trance watching the sun agitate its surface – but the holy water, captured in its anonymous bowl, was static and sterile, the magic of flow removed. Just as religion itself, once ecstatic revelation, was now tamed and institutionalised, safely in the hands of Sheppard Smith and these Salesian priests. Like us, they had had the devil beaten out of them as boys and probably God got knocked out as well.

Hardened to the daily indignities, coarsened by pain, palms calloused, ears stinging from plucking priestly fingers, the catechism hammered into our heads, we were beaten into pliant submission – until the faintest rumblings of rebellion were heard. The priests, sniffing the air for the odour of dissent, detected the advent of puberty as it rioted through the class. With the perfect timing honed over countless generations, a priest, hitherto unknown to us, appeared in the classroom: the Devil's Advocate.

The Jesuits invented mass education on theological grounds so that the faithful could read the Gospels. It meant they could also read philosophers of other persuasions. Descartes and the Reformers were the direct result of this initiative, a disaster for the Church. The priests quickly realised that this dangerous questioning of the Word of God began in puberty when doubts and fantasies of all kinds swirl in the brains of boys fevered by testosterone.

So before we had a chance to challenge the truth of the catechism, the Devil's Advocate appeared. We were twelve years old. He systematically ripped out the whole fabric of our belief system. It was shattering for the boys who were devout. He tore down the whole rickety structure with the application of ruthless logic. The boy next to me wept. Then, surveying the wreckage, the DA led us into the realm of Apologetics. He began to reconstruct religion on a logical basis. Certain truths were held to be self-evident and axiomatic: that God existed, that He created the world, that He sent his Son to save it from its sins, and so on. We learnt of St Augustine and Thomas Aquinas. I found it exhilarating and disturbing.

Being a Protestant at the weekends and a Catholic at school, I was troubled that they each claimed to be the one true faith. I wrestled with this, back and forth, and I prayed for guidance. Sometimes the coloured light from the West window swayed me over; sometimes the chanting and incense seemed to carry the mystery.

One day when I was drifting dreamily on the Thames in our punt, watching the reflections of sky and trees move to the rhythm of the river's deep purpose, a thought struck me with all the unexpected force of Father Dalton's hand from behind – there was a third possibility! Either one of them was the True Church in which case the other was in error, or else . . . *they were both wrong*. A great joy swept through my being. It lifted me up and I hovered over the water. A heavy burden had dropped away and I was weightless and free to worship that which was my nature – nature itself.

Breathing the River

The biblical stories had always felt alien to me. The desert landscapes, olive trees, burning bushes, Gadarene swine were impossibly remote from my experience of oak woods, willow banks, rain and rivers. Judaeo-Christianity seemed so landlocked, so hot and dusty; and apart from Moses parting the waters and Jesus walking on the stuff, there is scant reference to watery things.

Water was my element. With my father away 'typing for England' and my mother cooking in Herbert's factory canteen, Angela and I spent our days on the river, in the river. Water was (and still is) utterly mysterious to me – without form, invisible, yet ever-present, essential. Why does it alone expand instead of contracting when it cools? How does it defy gravity by travelling up trees? Capillary action, the science priest explained, surface tension draws it upwards. Pin a name on a mystery. Transubstantiation: the bigger the mystery, the bigger the word needed to obfuscate it.

The focal point of river life in Shepperton was the lock. Because of petrol rationing there were mercifully few mechanical craft, only the Salters' passenger steamers and the occasional electric 'slip' launch whose slender bows and flattened sterns were designed to minimise wake so as not to discommode the punts and skiffs.

The lockkeeper, Dick Young, would have been long retired but for the war. The gates and sluices were all operated by manpower and it was heavy work for him. At ten years old I was able to work the lock alone and I loved it. I would pull the wheels that opened the four sluices then watch entranced as the water exploded up in beautiful volcanic patterns, an entropy that was always the same and always different. As the rising water found its level, the patterns would soften and ease and finally come to rest. Only then could the gates be opened. I would put my skinny back to the great weight of the gate and astonish onlookers by opening it unaided. Of course, a boy can pull a laden barge. Even a slight steady pressure will move a great weight in water. In water the rules are different. The weak shall inherit, if not the earth, then at least the water.

The waiting downstream boats would row or paddle into the lock and hold themselves steady on the chains that hung down the deep, green-slimed walls. We would close the gates, close the sluices – no resistance now, so we would spin the wheels with one finger while Dick collected dues from each boat with his butterfly net on a long bamboo pole. Then we would go to the other end, the upstream gates, and pull at those sluices, repeat the whole thing. I would work at it for hours on end.

One fine summer's day, I was in the familiar daydreaming trance induced by the spiralling water erupting from the sluices and the heady ozone aroma it gave off, when I fell into the water above the lock. The sluices were open, sucking water down. I was dragged under. I fought against the pull of the sluices but I could not struggle to the surface. I had heard Dick's stories of similar incidents. The correct thing to do was to go with the flow, swim down and through a sluice gate and come up on the other side.

Dick saw me fall, as did others. They urged him to close the sluices and so stop the downward pull. Dick said no. If I was being dragged through a sluice I could be crushed if it was closed.

I fought against the flow and held my breath until I could hold it no longer. I let the air escape slowly. I opened my eyes to a turbulent green world. I watched the air bubbles race away from my mouth up to their own element. The lock must have been almost filled now for the downward pressure had eased. The body commands its functions involuntarily. I breathed in, and the sound of water as I drew it roared like the wind. I exhaled and sucked water in again. No longer struggling, I felt a perfect ease as I breathed my beloved river. I was the river.

Dick, probing with his long boat hook, finally yanked me out. I resented the violent intrusion into my communion with water. Then came nausea. Dick pressed hard on my back and belly – this was before mouth-to-mouth. I spewed out a stomach full of river. I never told my mother.

The river was a solace from the harsh disciplines of school and the marginal horrors of war, and this experience forged an even closer union. On bad nights when the black dog is on my back, I still summon the consoling river from my childhood and let it flow through my mind, soothing fears and washing away anxiety. My own Irish river that flows past my house offers the same comfort. In the summer, I bathe in it each day, alone and naked, and try to recapture the grace I knew as a child.

The air raids diminished. The Battle of Britain was won. There were doodlebugs – or V-1s to give them their correct name – but these seemed almost ludicrous to us who had survived blockbusters and raining incendiary bombs. We no longer ran for the shelters as the daytime siren sounded, but instead scanned the skies and listened for the pulsing beat of the engine, for when that engine cut out, the flying bomb would glide gently to earth. We would watch its trajectory and if necessary, run away from where it was headed. It was the bomb you could outrun!

The benign and blessed neglect of a working mother and an absent father allowed us the freedom of a perfect summer on the Thames. We caught and cooked fish. We ate moorhens' eggs. I never tasted a banana or an orange until 1947, but we scrumped apples and pears from neighbours' gardens. I went back to school sick at heart. As I reached the high walls that enclosed our misery, I heard cheers ringing out. The school was in ruins. A doodlebug had struck an hour earlier. Caps were thrown in the air, joy was unconfined. That scene was the climax of *Hope and Glory* and on the soundtrack I said, 'In all my life nothing has quite matched the perfect joy of that moment as my school lay in ruins and the river beckoned with the promise of stolen days.'

I tore off the school uniform and fell back into the embrace of the Thames: varnished mahogany, the hypnotic drip of water from the punt pole, the sound of oars feathered, and one of those wartime Indian summers. Autumn brought the healing smell of creosote as the fretted wooden verandas were painted against the winter. War rumbled on. School threatened to reopen, but the river cocooned us in its grace. My friend Peter, son of my mother's lover, Herbert, appeared one day with an air gun. The polished wooden stock and sleek black barrel aroused atavistic excitement. He showed me how to look down the sights, how to focus on a single object, how to block out the world but for that. Swimming and boating were about expanding into the world, losing one's self in the allness, the pleasure of being part of a larger nature. Now my eyes – no, eye – was narrowed by the gun. We shot fish as they basked in the shallows. We searched restlessly for targets, anything alive, anything that moved. One day I sat in the boat, gun cradled in my arms, when I caught a flash of blue speeding through the air above me. I pointed the gun up and fired. All the harmony, all the connectedness acquired during that magical summer, all the grace accumulated, came together in that moment. The lead pellet was me. It reached up and improbably, impossibly, struck the kingfisher as it raced across the river. It fell stunned into the water, its fluttering feathers throwing off turquoise signals of distress. I rowed over to it, picked it up, tried to revive it, prayed to all my gods and both religions, but it soon died. I was consumed with shame and remorse. I had killed the spirit of the river, god's messenger: the kingfisher. Something broke in me. I became the Fisher King whose wound would not heal until the grail was found and harmony restored.

Years later, alone in my house in Ireland, a kingfisher, pursued by a hawk, flew against my window. It too died. I had it mounted in a glass case, a symbol of my loss of grace, the end of childhood, the beginning of endings.

Shortly after, school resumed, and one afternoon I came home to find our beloved bungalow consumed by fire. The ration books were burned too. We possessed only what we stood up in. It took weeks to get emergency clothing coupons. We fell on the mercy of friends. I remember the sensation of lightness, the giddy delight in having no possessions, of being pure spirit. With the burning of the family photos, the burden of the past was erased. I recall my mother's face, twisted in pain, as she broke away from Herbert's embrace, as he tried to console her, believing the fire to be punishment for her infidelity. My father felt guilt too. He knew he was too old for the army, need not have joined, and could have been at home protecting his family. I hid my secret knowledge that the river had demanded a sacrifice for the death of the kingfisher. Fire for water.

The agony for me was having to face the sympathy of the priests, and worse, the way my school friends backed away from me, left a vacant zone around me, isolated me in what they imagined was my grief – as I had done to the little girl who lost her mother in Rosehill Avenue.

We found a bungalow further up the towpath, which we rented – Weir View. Friends made a collection of kitchen utensils and old clothes. We managed just fine. 'At least we have each other,' my mother sniffed.

The two years after the war were bleak – food and clothing were still rationed, and without a patriotic purpose to sustain us, it was a miserable time. I was six when the war started and eleven when it ended. I was twelve before I saw the first banana I could remember, and thirteen before I tasted one.

My father was demobbed from the Army in 1945, thoroughly disillusioned. He had hoped for a commission and had completed officer training. However, they told him he was too old since he had his fortieth birthday during the course. When he asked them why they had allowed him to take the course, they said that he wasn't too old when he started the course, he was too old when he finished it. So far from escaping his pen-pushing job, he pushed a pen and tapped a typewriter in the RASC. What a comedown from sticking pigs in India!

After the war, Herbert and George went into business together, but there was tension between them. Sensing the love that had grown between them, my father forbade my mother to see Herbert. I used to wish, secretly and treacherously, that Herbert had been my father, and wondered how different I would have been, pondering the mysterious nature of chance. Why had my father been spared through the accident of his posting to India?

In 1949, Herbert became very ill. My mother announced that she was going to nurse him. He was in constant pain and she refused to abandon him. Her presence was the only amelioration for his suffering. She sat at his bedside luminous with love, her eyes of the palest blue, caressed him. I remember feeling that whatever brought about this radiant grace could not be wrong. She eased Herbert's last days and he died knowing that a great woman had loved him greatly. My father brooded in the shadows; I was disappointed that he could not make his peace with Herbert. Perhaps he did. I only remember his hurt, as my mother grieved at the death of the love of her life.

Father made Mother do penance. The source of his discontent was that although she loved him, she did not love him enough. He had seen the way she looked at Herbert in those dying days, a look which had never fallen upon him. Having the moral advantage, he wrested her away from the river and bought a bungalow near Brighton where he ended his days. In his late seventies he still took his regular 'quick dips' and went for his daily 'blow' along the front. He and Ivy bickered and when he was angry his clichés got even more tangled than in the past. He complained that the tides were becoming irregular, rushing in and out at ever shorter intervals. One day as I was walking with him he looked up at a gull perched halfway up the sheer face of the chalk cliffs. 'That bird is in a very precarious position.'

He would glare out at the English Channel: 'The sea is our destiny.'

'In what way?' I asked.

'In every way. Atlantic convoys, the Armada, fish and chips.'

After he died my mother sold up and bought a flat facing the Thames at Kingston. Her sister, Jenny, lived there with her. The other two sisters,

Billy and Bobby, were just around the corner. They had all buried their husbands and were back together. They loved the Thames of their childhood and picnicked on its banks in their favourite places, and on a warm day they would slip into the water and swim across and back. A ritual.

1948: A Turbulent Priest

In the fourth form, the thrashings abated. However, I was accused of fighting in the street whilst wearing the school uniform – a cardinal sin. My accuser mistook me for someone else. I was caned in front of the whole school, and to my enduring shame I could not hold back my tears. I wept not for the pain, but for the unfairness of it.

I was playing cricket for the First XI, the youngest in the side, so I took on heroic status amongst my fellows. It encouraged me to stand up for myself. The priests were unnerved by my new self-belief. How puny now seemed their reign of terror. We formed a small swaggering coterie made up of sporting heroes and a couple of clever boys, Vince and Mellot, who devoted themselves to exposing the intellectual weaknesses of our teachers, whilst we others challenged their authority.

Then a new priest arrived to take charge of the fourth form, Father John Maguire. We eyed him with scepticism. He was a Scot from the Gorbals but of Irish descent, as were many Scottish Catholics. There was something intense and dangerous about him. We were calloused and cynical, having survived three years of beatings and humiliations. Nothing could touch us. We offered him what the army used to call 'dumb insolence', a concerted passive resistance. We had learned to regard our teachers as the enemy, since they clearly took that view of us. Fr Maguire began to gain our grudging respect when he displayed his ability to dribble a tennis ball in the schoolyard, a skill honed on the mean streets of Glasgow. His feet twinkled under the flying cassock, but like most Scottish footballers of the day, and many a day, he was not a team man, was loath to pass the ball.

We soon discovered that his mind and temper were as quick as his feet. In fact he was far more brilliant than the dull donkeys in dog collars around him. He drove us with a fierce passion. If we failed to respond to his teaching, his wrath was terrible to behold. He was biased and partial. He doted on his favourites; he was a scourge to those he took against. He introduced us to medieval disputations, debates in which an argument could only be advanced through strict logic. He sent us out of the school on quests to discover the larger world, to law courts, film studios, Parliament. He took us to a mortuary and challenged us to lie down in a coffin. We were to write accounts of these trips and he encouraged me to keep a journal, which I have done fitfully ever since and which provides most of the substance of this memoir. He told me that I saw things differently from other people and told me I could be a writer.

His passionate curiosity was always straining against the confining strictures of life in a religious order. He loved to travel, preferably in borrowed cars, which he drove with furious ineptitude. He often set out on foreign journeys without money, hitchhiking and relying on charity, staying at monasteries and religious houses. In fact, poverty was perhaps the only vow he kept. He agitated our imaginations with stories of his exploits in foreign places. He gained access to a hospice in France where human freaks were cared for. He told us that there was an inner sanctum where the most monstrous were kept. It was a forbidden place, for even priests might baulk at a God who could make such blatant errors. He pressed his case to be allowed into this unholy of unholies. He had credentials. He wrote papers on medical ethics, such as when it was permissible for a Catholic doctor to perform a lobotomy. He was insistent, and was eventually admitted.

There was something else behind this burning curiosity. I believe he was searching for some evidence of the hand of God. He wanted a sign. I begged him to tell us what he had seen in that place. He described some of the monstrous creatures he encountered on his way to the inner sanctum. What could be worse than that, I asked, what did you find at the forbidden centre? His face darkened, his voice quietened. Blobs, he said. *Blobs*. It was the lack of detail that so fired the imagination, that and the crack in his voice, which seemed to come from a deep fissure inside him. A moment later he recovered himself and gave the party line. He described how saintly, how beatific were the nuns who cared for them. He told us of the radiance that comes with the grace of God, how it is instantly apparent. His own eyes burnt feverishly as he spoke and I assumed that must be evidence of this grace. Wasn't it unfair, I said, naively, that there had to be blobs so that the nuns could find grace? 'Grace is especially available to those who care for the least human of humans,' he told us, 'which is why

I teach Form Four.' Was it the sins of the blobs' fathers that were visited on the blobs, I wanted to know? The other boys tittered. He glared at me.

Sin is everywhere, ready to ensnare us, and – he implied – to deform our progeny. A girl who wore provocative clothes was an occasion of sin, he was fond of saying. The flinty glint in his eyes softened when he spoke of girls. He was always falling in love, usually with the sisters of us boys, mine included. He loved the company of women; he loved to hear their confessions. He liked to test his celibate resolve by their proximity. He would then quench his ardour by hurling himself into his teaching with renewed fury. There was still volcanic energy left over and at night he studied for degrees, of which he had quite a collection.

Some years later he was appointed Prefect of Studies (headmaster) of Salesian College, Oxford. He saw the proximity of the university as an opportunity to take another degree. He asked permission of the Provincial Superior, who refused on the grounds that running a school should leave no time to attend university. Whatever spare time he had, the Superior said sniffily, should be spent on his devotions. He took the degree secretly, breaking his vow of obedience. An envious colleague turned him in. Despite making a great success of the school, he was to be banished to the theological seminary in Rome, a place of punitive discipline where he would be denied all privileges – particularly those of travel, indeed of any contact with the secular world. He fled. He jumped the wall.

I was living in a house buried in the New Forest at the time and working for Southern Television. He sought sanctuary with me. It was a perfect refuge for a runaway priest, shrouded in high yew hedges and overhung with oak and beech, a secret place. This privacy was only violated by the village idiot, a boy of eighteen who wandered freely in and out of all the houses and gardens. He would often come in the front door, walk through the house and out of the back door without so much as glancing at the occupants. I was working long, stressful hours and rearing two small children. Father John and I talked into the night. He could not, would not go to Rome, yet he was uneasy in the secular world. He saw me struggling with my responsibilities – a demanding wife, needy children, a harrowing job, bills and taxes. It appalled him. He was institutionalised. The Order provided, and despite its restrictions, everything was taken care of. He could go off on his wild excursions and then slip back into the safety of the religious community. Paradoxically, what he saw in my life was an unendurable lack of freedom. He wrestled with his conscience but could not come to a decision. One day, as he was saying his Breviary, he glanced up and there was the idiot looking at him through the window. Their eyes met and the boy pointed a finger and cried out. I had the uneasy suspicion that this *idiot savant* could look into our souls and see the stain of sin. What fascinated me was that this did not disturb the priest in the least. I suppose that if you have seen blobs, you are inured to a retarded boy.

He finally decided to make his superiors an ultimatum. If they persisted in their determination to send him to Rome he would leave the priesthood. It worked. A compromise was reached. He would be expelled from the Order but remain a priest. A job was found for him as Chaplain to Reading University. It suited him well. I asked him once what sort of problems the students brought to him. He said that ninety per cent of student difficulties could be expressed in the following algebraic formula: A loved B but unfortunately B loved C and C might very well love A. He had many female students in his care with whom he could fall in love, and the long vacations to indulge his world travels. There were plenty of opportunities for him to preach, and he was in great demand. He was a virtuoso. He had a formula. A couple of stories from his gag book, some personal anecdotes, extrapolate the moral, give it substance with some references from the Gospels – and all presented with fire and dramatic delivery. He was like a skilful barrister arguing a case. He held a brief for God, and like a good lawyer, the innocence or guilt of his client was irrelevant. What a contrast to Sheppard Smith, yet they had one thing in common: the grace of God was sadly missing.

The tensions, the dynamics of community life had kept him on his toes. Now he was alone, a condition alien to him. Something was lost, the fire went out. He became complacent, fat. He published two volumes of reminiscences, which were dull and careful. He took great pride in my celebrity (rather than my work) and liked to visit me on film sets and tell risqué stories to actresses. When he stayed with me in Ireland, he said Mass every day in the local church. I would sometimes assist him, an ancient altar boy, and as he went through the ritual in a businesslike way I had the feeling that he was disappointed in God, that he had put in an enormous effort for scant return.

At the end, he was in hospital in Hammersmith. My sister, Angela, one of those he had loved with such devotion, visited him. I had sent him a copy of the book Michel Ciment wrote about my films, in which I acknowledged his inspiration and encouragement. He showed it proudly to the nurses.

Angela found him angry and bitter. I put off seeing him. I was disappointed in him. He taught me to observe and record, to discriminate, and to search out truth. He loved language, its roots and derivations, its idioms, and this led him into Latin and French and across all the Romantic languages. He had, so to say, the gift of tongues, yet as a pedagogue and a preacher, even at his fiery brilliant best, he lacked something – poetry, insight. Poor old Sheppard Smith could draw on the soaring glories of the King James Version of the Bible and even in his most soporific voice they carried hints of wonder and mystery, intimations of God. But there is no poetry in the prosaic Catholic translation of the Bible, and Father John was bound to it and it kept him earthbound.

1949: Epiphany

My love of cricket was nurtured by my father. He had played the game but never excelled. He wanted me to play for England, or at the very least, for Surrey. He trained me from an early age. I was never more than an average player. However, by diligence and concentration I achieved some success. I was a good reader of the game and became the captain of the First XI. In that early summer of 1949, studying for matriculation, we travelled the home counties, playing our matches against other schools, and I lived in a state of ecstasy and anxiety – the smells of bruised grass, of linseed oil applied to bat, the exquisite terror of standing alone, facing eleven others seeking to depose you, with guile, with hostility, in six different ways. To be out there in the middle, to remain there, to score runs, seemed like the very purpose of life, an apotheosis.

In *Hope and Glory* I have a scene where the father, with a kind of religious solemnity, is teaching the boy the secret of the googly, how to deceive the batsman with a ball that appears to spin one way, but in fact does the opposite. The boy says, 'It's like telling fibs.' The father replies: 'That's it. When you tell a lie, you hope to get away with it. When someone else does, you want to find them out. A good batsman will spot a googly. A good bowler will hide it. Always remember that, son.'

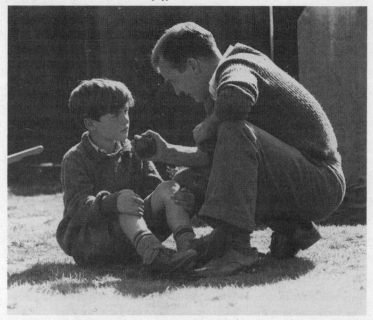

Hope and Glory: the father teaching the secret of the googly

This attitude of my father towards the game was a great joy and a burden to me. Although it was a bond between us at first, it was also the cause of rupturing that bond. I was twelve at the time and came home from a match in which I had been ignominiously bowled out first ball. My father asked me how I had fared. I lied. I told him I had scored twelve runs. He made me recount each shot. I improvised – an off-drive, a square cut. I even admitted to a lucky edge through the slips to give it authenticity. He let me go on. Then he told me that he had watched the match. Too embarrassed to admit failure, I suffered the humiliation of being caught in a lie. I ran off and hid myself away. How I hated him for that triumphant sneering smile. He yearned for me to succeed, yet he revelled in my failures. I was both his surrogate and his rival.

I was sixteen, sitting the exams, but cricket was my hermetically sealed universe, and I gave no thought to the future. Then it all stopped. Exams were done. School was over. Cricket was finished. I fell into a desultory limbo as I awaited the results, not that there was any prospect of university. It was not something my parents would contemplate. They could not afford it. They had lost everything in the fire that destroyed our home. They were ludicrously under-insured, but had put what money they had into a small hotel in Kingston. They bought it in partnership with Herbert, who stepped in to help them out. It offered a home as well as a business. My father, demobbed, had gone back to his old job at Shell, but was desperate to escape it. My grandfather's influence had groomed my father for preferment, but he had got mixed up in some sort of scandal in the company. His fellow miscreants were fired; he was demoted and exiled into a dead-end job. I had always been given to understand that my father had been led astray, that he did nothing wrong, and while not brilliant, was certainly honest and loyal and diligent. Near the end of his life, I raised the subject. 'You were always straight, weren't you, Dad?' With a crooked smile he said, 'As a corkscrew.'

My father told me to find a job. I thought I wanted to be a writer. Father Maguire had encouraged me to believe that this was possible. I confessed this to my mother. She bought me a second-hand portable Corona typewriter. 'Don't tell your father.' It was my portion, my total inheritance. Furtively, I began to write stories, which I picked out with one finger on this magic machine that I hoped would transport me to another life away from the suburbs. I nurtured dreams of greatness. I applied for jobs as a cub reporter on local papers, but to no avail. I took one of those phoney correspondence-writing courses. The tutor told me my writing was too poetic and overheated (he was quite right), that there was no market for such, and I should be thinking of articles for *Woman's Own* and the *Lady*. I wrote and wrote. It was a race. Would my talent as a writer be recognised before I was forced to take a job? How desperate I was.

I did have a job of sorts. While I was still at school I had been selling ice cream at a riverside café at the weekends and I went full-time once school was over. I got the job through my mother's youngest sister, the tall and glamorous Bobby, who worked there. She had married Danny, a man much older and shorter than herself, on the rebound from a love affair with an Italian hairdresser, Giuseppe. She confessed to me in her seventies that she still had romantic and erotic dreams about Giuseppe. Danny, another man insufficiently loved by a Chapman sister, made her life a misery with his jealousy. Even I fell under suspicion, which was not as ridiculous as Bobby imagined. I watched her out of the corner of my eye as we worked together, unable to shake off a shameful incestuous lust. At night, I would be distracted from my attempts to write a nice piece for *Women's Realm* by fantasising situations which would allow a sexual liaison with my aunt. One of these involved her rewarding me for killing her awful husband. I was also strongly attracted to my cousin, her fourteen-year-old daughter, June. And sometimes I would end up betraying Aunt Bobby with June, which left me in a tumescent shambles of moral turpitude.

Also working in the café was a twenty-one-year-old Italian girl who had rashly married an English soldier at the end of the war. At eighteen she was plucked out of Naples and set down in a cold London suburb. She caught my sly looks at Aunt Bobby and gently teased me. One day she asked me to take her out in my canoe. She sat back as I paddled. She flirted away, amused by my confusion and blushes. There were pleasant places where we could have had our picnic but she insisted that we stop underneath Kingston Bridge. We moored up, hidden on a slope of grass under the shoreside arch, her black eyes and olive skin all the more mysterious and exotic in this shadowy place. The light on the water dappled the arch above us, and in turn danced dizzying patterns across her face. It was late afternoon. She looked at her watch. 'Don't you want to kiss me?' I managed to mutter that I did. Although I didn't. I fervently wished to be elsewhere. Anywhere but here.

As I moved towards her, she held me off, playfully. 'I'm an old married woman. What would your aunt say about this? Did you ever take her out in your canoe, you naughty boy?' (Oh, God, what if she tells Aunt Bobby about this?) She closed her eyes, offered me her open mouth with total abandonment. I had no idea how to kiss an open mouth. Lips were kept pressed firmly together in the movies of that era.

She clutched me to her. I was engulfed in a swamp of that oh-so-familiar Lily of the Valley, and under that, something more acrid. It reminded me of the whiff I had once caught of a fox's lair when I was evacuated briefly in Somerset. Whispering in my ear, she launched into a tirade against her husband. She hated him. He was stupid. He disgusted her. She hated England. It was damp and cold, like the English. She pressed her pelvis against me. I was surprised there should be a bone there. I expected it to be soft. I was sixteen! How innocent we were! She pulled me on to her, moved under me. I concentrated on trying to stay on top and not be ignominiously bucked off. She was writhing. Her face was turned away, her eyes closed. She seemed to have forgotten about me.

Suddenly she lay still. I prised myself off. She opened her eyes and looked at her watch again.

'When we did that,' she said, 'my husband was crossing bridge. Coming home on bicycle.'

My ineptitude must have made it a hollow vengeance. The thought of her husband's proximity filled me with dread. I paddled the canoe back as fast as I could, with nervous glances at the towpath, my heart skipping a beat at every glimpse of a cyclist.

It never occurred to me to write about these experiences. I could only write about abstract things, events remote from my own dull and shameful life.

It was the river that seduced me and consoled me as it had my mother. We had left the landlocked and earthbound suburbs and embraced the flow of river life. Our lives were fluid. As the dread prospect of a job far from water drew closer, I took off in my canoe with a sleeping bag, a Primus stove, and my dog, and set off upriver from Kingston. It was a burning hot day. The sun lay under the river; the water became molten magma roaring up at me.

I had taken a vow of silence. In the absence of language, objects became more vibrant and vivid: water dripping from the paddle, each drop a perfect universe; the trembling leaves of a quaking aspen mesmerised me, they became musical notation; the humblest blade of grass asserted its nowness, uniqueness. Above all, the silky surface of the water enthralled me. I would fall into a rhythmic trance as I paddled past Hampton Court, beyond Penton Hook, and made camp on the island of Magna Carta at Runnymede.

Instead of a tent I had a waterproof tarpaulin, which I lay on and then folded over my sleeping bag, and Briggy the dog crept under it. I slept fitfully, the dog barked at water rats and the rustling of moorhens in the rushes. The island tossed and turned, coughing and whispering. I was burnt from the day's heat and a little feverish. Wild dreams, fragments of a deep past, contended with the night noises of the island.

I awoke from fathoms deep and hauled myself up from the blackness to a private dawn of fragile stillness. Senses acutely sharpened, I felt a oneness with that place and aware of its power, not chosen by chance for the Magna Carta ceremony. I entered the river with reverent care and infinite slowness so as not to disturb its perfect smoothness. If I could swim out into it without causing a ripple, I would live for ever and the

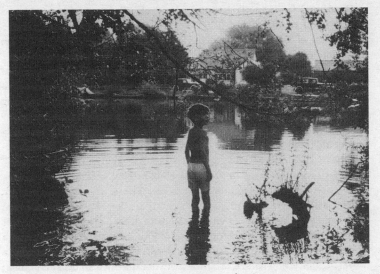

Hope and Glory: entering the river

great mysteries would be revealed to me. I succeeded, a boy's head moving across a mirror where the liberties of man had been won. I knew myself to be in a state of grace, the grace I had lost at the death of the kingfisher. That experience, so profound, sent me on a quest for images, through cinema, to try to recapture what I knew that day. And occasionally, in the course of my life, I did.

1950: Friends and Lovers

David Young was a year older than me and lived in a neighbouring riverside bungalow. His father was an inventor of gadgets that nobody seemed to need; he made a precarious living with a gambling system that involved backing second favourites at the racetracks. David's brother Lionel was a cameraman and we doted on his extravagant stories about the film business. At the time he was working on the Boulting Brothers film, *Seven Days to Noon*.

David and I swam in the river early each morning throughout the summer and we didn't feel like stopping when winter crept up on us. The winter of 1947–8 was one of the harshest on record. We just kept going and never missed a day. The river was swollen and the heavy current prevented it freezing over, but ice would reach out several feet from the bank and we would have to dive out beyond it. As I hit the water the first sensation was of scalding heat, the nervous system confused by such extremes. Despite the pain, we could not give up on communion with the river. Neither of us caught a cold that year – bacteria couldn't deal with the Thames at zero. However, getting up the nerve to plunge in took longer and longer each day. Two skinny kids in woollen bathing trunks shivering on the river bank talking in funny voices. We developed several imaginary characters. The one most loved was Willie, a slow-witted lethargic who went to any lengths to avoid effort. He would come up with inventive reasons to delay our morning plunge: 'Wait, there's warmer water on the way.' Our laughter was convulsive, epileptic. We were in fits and it kept us warm. It was odd that we should admire an Oblomov, since we were destined to be such hard workers.

David wanted to follow his brother. He had aspirations to be a clapper-loader, but was having no luck at all. What could we do to avoid taking a mundane job? How could I make some money fast, to buy me time to write, and to let David enjoy the luxury of waiting for a job to come up at one of the studios?

I took David to see my paternal grandfather to seek his advice. After the collapse of his laundry he had kept right on inventing things. He made vacuum cleaners and rented them out by the hour, but at that time voltages varied from district to district and the motors kept burning out. I don't know what went wrong with his patent ice-cream machine. He told me it made ice cream so delicious that children stole money from old ladies to buy it. There were even cases of kids clubbing their mothers to death when they were denied it. He had to stop making it, he said, before the country fell into anarchy.

My favourite of all his innovations was a remnant of his bankrupt toy factory – a jack-in-the-box. You had to press certain spots in a particular order to get Jack to jump. You tried this, and tried that, the whole time in a state of unendurable apprehension, for at any moment the silent, impenetrable box would burst open and Jack would leap out at you grinning and wagging on his spring.

Grandpa was finally living in tamed domesticity, his last fortune won and lost. It had been some years since he was allowed to handle money, although as a boy he had taught me how to steal coins from my grandmother's purse, which he and I would gleefully and secretly spend. 'You have to keep it in circulation,' he said. Although it wasn't circulating back to him any more.

He was living in Marlow Drive, Cheam, a dismal suburb later lampooned by Tony Hancock. There were two pictures in the hallway – *The Laughing Cavalier*, which I suppose was him, and *The Sinking of the Lusitania*, which must have been a metaphor for his fortunes. As he opened the door, his mischievous laugh spilled out together with the pervasive smell of TCP which my sickly maiden aunt, Lily, employed to thwart the legions of bacteria that stalked her.

We explained our predicament. What kind of business could we get into? We were seventeen and eighteen with no capital and no skills. He suggested dry cleaning. Very big in America. Must catch on here. Remember, it was he who spotted a good future for oil. He said that, in a manner of speaking, he could claim to have invented dry cleaning, and with a torrent of laughter he repeated the story of how, in the First World War, overwhelmed by the thousands of army blankets to be laundered, he had simply folded them and sent them back. I loved the story but David was hearing it for the first time. He did a laughing duet with Grandpa. They had an immediate rapport. Life was ludicrous.

The launch of our endeavour was delayed for two months while David served a prison sentence in Wormwood Scrubs for refusing his two-year term of National Service. He claimed to be a pacifist, but he had no religious affiliations. Quakers, for instance, were generally excused military service, although the less strict would agree to serve as ambulance drivers or stretcher bearers. Other protesters were considered shirkers or skivers. An examining board would consider the cases of the refuseniks and would take the view that if you were prepared to go to prison rather than join the Army it proved your convictions were genuine. This was practical but illogical, since by going to prison the conscientious objector thus proved that he should not have gone to prison.

I took my place with the weeping wives and the distraught mothers on visiting day at the Scrubs. David had me rocking with laughter as he described his fellow felons. The warders remonstrated with us angrily. Tears were in order but not levity. The regime David described was so innocent by today's standards. No drugs. The tobacco barons ruled. Old lags were maudlin over sparrows they had domesticated. Only child molesters were beaten up. David worked in the library and played chess with one of the 'screws', who gave him the odd 'snout' which, as a non-smoker, he could sell for chocolate or girlie magazines. We discussed our plans for the dry-cleaning business. I produced a street map with our proposed routes which I pressed against the thick glass that divided us. The prisoners on either side of David and the watching warders were convinced we were planning 'a job' and David's stock shot up. The greater the crime, the higher esteem a prisoner enjoyed. 'Conshies' were only a peg up from child abusers on this scale, so the news that David was planning a life of crime helped his cause considerably, and his panache in planning a heist in full view of the law on visiting day was greatly admired.

When David got out we set ourselves up in business. I had saved a bit from selling ice cream. He scraped up a few pounds. We bought an implausibly romantic van, a big Hudson Terraplane with sickeningly soft suspension, a pre-war American import that nobody wanted. We rented a basement, printed pamphlets and launched Y&B Cleaners. We found a dry-cleaning factory that would accept our business and we set out to canvass the suburban streets around Twickenham and Isleworth. I was back in those hated streets from which my mother had fled. We joined those plodding legions that were 'on the knocker' – selling insurance, brushes, vacuum cleaners. We worked all day and every evening. The marginal discount that we got from the factory just about paid our costs and a few pounds to keep us alive. We quickly realised that we were working for the factory. We were factory workers! We borrowed more money and bought an old steam press. We poached a presser from the factory to work it and did our own 'spotting': applying chemicals to various stains. We would do this every night when we came in from the rounds from ten to midnight. Our margin shot up and we began to make profits.

I rented a bedsitter on Richmond Hill. My landlady was a large dis-traught woman who had inherited a number of houses mostly occupied by non-paying sitting tenants. One evening she had a call from the fire brigade announcing that a house of hers was on fire. 'Thank God for that,' she said. She lived at her wits' end, terrorising her tenants and ter-rorised by them. When confronted with a problem she either ran away or attacked wildly.

The gas meters had to be fed with pennies, but she always forgot to empty them. Our gas fires and cookers would give out when no more coins could be stuffed in. I went round one night to ask her to empty mine. I waited patiently for her arrival, as the room got colder. She burst in, hair flying, wild-eyed like a deranged Brünnhilde. She unlocked the box of pennies and hurled it on the floor. The coins cascaded across the room. She stood panting and staring belligerently at me, then turned on her heel and stormed out. From then on I needed only one penny, which would drop through. I caught it and I reinserted as required. I kept a tally at first but soon forgot and so did she.

One of my fellow lodgers made a deep impression on me. He smoked a pipe and spoke in a soft hypnotic voice. He was a mystic. He introduced me to John Cowper Powys and gave me a copy of his delirious version of the Grail myth, *A Glastonbury Romance*. I had loved the stories of King Arthur as a child and I had read Eliot's *The Waste Land* with enormous excitement. The fact that I understood it so poorly made it even more thrilling. I fell into the arms of Cowper Powys. His universe consumed my nights. Sleep-deprived, I trudged the streets with David in a trance-like state. The housewives were pale phantoms, the streets of semis stretched to infinity and I was destined to walk them for eternity. But the deeper Arthurian England – an England that lay under the numbness of suburban life – held me in thrall, alerted my imagination, promised deliverance. One day, as I trudged from door to door – knocking, ringing, soliciting dirty clothes – I had an X-ray vision of these people pressed together in serried rows, or lined up in bedsitters as was I; a vision that they, we, were leaking into each other, that an osmosis was afoot, that we were becoming the cells of a single monstrous creature. Surely my landlady knew this. It was the source of her panic. I was under the influence of Cowper Powys's notion that all thought, all ideas, all pain, circulated endlessly in the ether.

There were no books in my parents' home. I read the *Dandy* and the *Beano*. As I got older I became fascinated by comic books, with those lurid smudgy colours, the cross-hatching and the superheroes. Anxious to feed my habit, one of my aunts bought Shaw's *Man and Superman* for me in the belief that it was a comic book. I was eleven. My aunt turned out to be right. It was a kind of comic book. Shaw did to me what he was best at: provoke, excite, subvert. David and I called ourselves Shavians, fancied ourselves as Fabian socialists. I had read all the plays and prefaces by the time I was seventeen. It was a great solace to us as we trudged the streets that we smugly shared Shaw's scathing views on Christianity (it is Paulism), the medical profession, politics, big business, colonialism. As we slaved away and observed the increasing leisure and affluence of the working classes, we were consoled by a fatuous superiority.

During my last term at school, I found a book in the library, picked up by chance, that was like a blinding light – Newton's *Optics*. The vivid poetic writing, the sense of discovery was such a contrast to the dry science textbooks through which we were obliged to trudge. The behaviour of light was to become my life. It sprang from here. Newton made me conscious of seeing, aware of imagery. Light and Water, my related mysteries.

I saw Bertrand Russell skulking about in Richmond leering at young girls, the same girls I furtively watched and craved. Atheism was dangerously daring. I was so soaked in God, marinated in religion, I could not altogether deny Him. I admired Russell's arid response to an interviewer's question, 'What would you say if, when you died, you found yourself in the presence of God?' 'I would say, "Sir, what possible reason could you have for concealing all evidence of your existence?"' How courageous to acknowledge both your base nature and certain oblivion. Having seen him, caught his eye in the Maids of Honour café, I tried to read his *Principia Mathematica*. I found it hard to reconcile the man and his ideas – and harder still to understand either.

David and I both began to collect our little shelves of orange Penguins – Aldous Huxley, Thomas Hardy, Richard Aldington. David made fun of D. H. Lawrence and I pretended to, but in truth I was terribly taken with that 'language of the blood'. *Sons and Lovers* was *the* book until *A Glastonbury Romance* came along. My head swirled with turbulent cosmic currents and vague plans began to form in my mind of great works, of books and films that I might forge. I nursed these thoughts and they comforted me as I trudged the streets, knocking on doors, soliciting custom, having them slammed in my face. I lacked guidance, and like many an autodidact before me, I vacillated between overweening ambition and despair – a pattern that would pursue me throughout my life, reaching too high and falling short.

As we developed the business, it became apparent that the people who could afford to have their clothes cleaned and pressed were not the middle-class mortgagees in the semis but the residents of council estates, particularly households with grown children where there were several wage-earners paying a low rent between them. There was a new prosperity and it expressed itself in pride taken in clothing. This was 1950 and clothes rationing had just ended. We cleaned a lot of demob suits and woollen dresses with sweat stains under the arms (impossible to remove), the staple post-war clothing. We did repairs. Shirt collars were turned when they frayed. Patches were sewn on to the worn elbows of jackets. Rips in cloth were 'invisibly mended' – labour-intensive, microscopic work. Ladders in nylon stockings were repaired on a special machine.

My mother, like most housewives, darned the holes in our socks. Until I was bought a school uniform, I had never had an item of clothing from a shop except shoes. My shirts and pants and jackets were cut down from my father's and grandfather's, everything else was knitted – socks, underwear, even bathing trunks that sagged to the knees when wet. But the affluence that would produce the Teddy Boys and the Mods and Rockers was on its way, and the evidence was in the back of our van.

After a year we had made a little money and paid off our debts. I lacked David's courage and convictions, and with my eighteenth birthday approaching I sold my share of the business to him for £100. Still only seventeen, then, I had retired and was living on my capital. This was the intention and I had achieved it. In the six months before I was called up, I devoted myself to writing and exploring London and spending the money. It seemed such a vast sum that I thought it would last for ever.

Washing his hands of the painful Herbert episode, my father sold his share of the hotel and bought a pub in the City of London, the Plough in Fore Street. It stood gaunt and alone in a wasteland of bomb sites around London Wall. I gave up my bedsitter and lived in a tiny eyrie at the top of the pub where I pounded my typewriter. The *Manchester Guardian* published my impressionistic account of living there; the sounds of rush-hour footsteps, the melancholy of the bomb sites at the desolate weekends when the City is deserted. It was a newspaper that tolerated high-flown poetic writing now and then, and subsequently published several of my pieces.

My friend Barrie Vince and I devoted ourselves to sampling the aesthetic pleasures of London. Barrie had been top of the class in just about everything, everything, that is, except what really counted: he was hopeless at cricket and football, whereas I was the lord of the playing fields. He was spared the kind of bullying and beatings such a swot would normally attract, partly because he was under my protection but also because he did not really swot. It all came so easily to him. He could not help but get everything right. Our bond was a mutual admiration for Bernard Shaw and a passion for chess.

He often visited us by the river at Shepperton and I tried to teach him to swim. His lack of coordination was prodigious. It was as though he had a brain in each limb that intellectualised every movement and debated its function with all the other limbs and organs. He even intellectualised breathing. He did not trust his body to breathe without specific instructions. He was nervous that his breathing would stop while he was asleep. Teaching him was a tortuous process but I persisted since I could not conceive of having a friend who could not swim. He was equally determined. He went to the library and studied books on swimming technique, which inhibited his progress even further. Finally he got the hang of it, albeit doing it by numbers. One afternoon, after school, we set out to swim across to the weir at Chertsey, a wide stretch of river. Halfway across he announced that he could go no further. His eyes rolled and he sank. I dived after him, got his head above water and swam him towards the shore. He did not struggle. He had absolute confidence in me. He just went limp and concentrated on drawing air into his lungs and, once oxygen had been suitably extracted, expelling it.

I was exhausted and half drowned myself by the time we got to the river bank. As soon as Barrie's feet touched the bottom he made a total recovery, while I lay panting in the shallows, too weak to clamber ashore. A woman on a bicycle stopped as Barrie offered me a hand and hauled me up the bank. She said she had watched the whole thing and she warmly congratulated Barrie on saving my life. He accepted the compliment graciously as I lay gasping on the grass.

Barrie had a dark, fat Jewish mother and a thin blond Catholic father, and they bickered incessantly. Barrie was desperate to leave home. With his record-breaking examination results he had his pick of universities and disciplines, but he placed no value on anything he was good at. Among the very few subjects that he had no talent for was music, so he decided to study that, while registered for a law degree which provided a grant to buy books. He never attended law lectures but swotted on borrowed books for a week or two at the end of each year and got a reasonable degree. His book grant was spent on tuition at the London School of Music.

There he met a piano student, Patricia Gray, and the three of us went around together, a *Jules et Jim* set-up. We went to all the Promenade concerts at the Albert Hall. As music students, Barry and Patricia were admitted to the final rehearsals, and I would sneak in with them, and all three of us would ostentatiously follow the score. Sir Thomas Beecham made a deep impression on me in the way he used his sardonic wit to terrorise and amuse the orchestra. Furtwängler was the most electrifying – his violent jerky movements felt like the death throes of the Third Reich, but what sublime music he drew from those players. Barrie wanted to be a conductor and after these concerts he would bear the imprint of whoever had been waving the baton that night: he would assume the bland stiffness of Adrian Boult, the avuncular panache of Beecham, or the charming modesty of John Barbirolli.

To be able to play or compose music is the most sublime of all vocations. 'All art constantly aspires towards the condition of music,' according to Walter Pater's famous dictum – how pitifully short movies fall from that. I would have traded all my films for musical talent. But this modicum of musical education I acquired helped me communicate with film composers to the point where Hans Zimmer could write, on the sleeve of the *Beyond Rangoon* soundtrack recording, 'Each piece of music owes as much to the director as it does to the composer. John is very knowledgeable in respect of music.' Gilles Jacob, director of the Cannes Film Festival, told me the score vulgarised the film, however.

The three-way friendship between Barrie, Patricia and me was forged in the shadow of great music. We were earnest people hell-bent on high culture, but we were young: it was all too intense, too much for us. There was an erotic charge between us that played havoc with our concentration. We started to indulge the guilty pleasures of watching trashy films and listening to popular music. 'How potent cheap music is,' as Nöel Coward's character observed; how alluring is American cinema. How easily we fall from grace, recoil from the sublime and guiltily embrace the spurious. I neglected my writing, Barrie his music, and Pat her piano as we spent afternoons at the movies, evenings up in the gods at the theatre, and down with the devil in murky wine bars.

Barrie and I were both in love with Pat. She was a country girl from Somerset, plump with rosy cheeks, budding and ripe. She would mediate with a judicious word in our clever-clever arguments. Looking back, I can see that she was just rather down-to-earth and we were silly and pompous and full of ourselves, but we admired her mind as we bounced her like a ball between us, because she was so delighted with our insights.

Pat watched us while we played chess. She would comment on our moves with a little silvery laugh or a prettily raised eyebrow. We both assumed she could see a move or two ahead of us, yet she always declined to play, said she preferred watching. Barrie was a better player than I was, but more often than not, I beat him. He could see so many options and possible traps that he ended up making obvious mistakes. I lay in wait, ever opportunistic. A Grand Master once said that he had never had the satisfaction of beating a thoroughly fit opponent. So it was with Barrie. If the game was going against him he would develop a streaming cold before he was mated. Barrie's huge brain was constantly striking blows at his body – cramps, indigestion, dizziness, fainting fits. They were at war. Would it work in reverse, I wondered? If Barrie had a cold and beat me would the cold disappear?

It was put to the test one day. He arrived with the flu. His fevered mind inspired him to a brilliant game. As he gained advantage, there were definite signs of recovery. His sinuses were clearing. I was reeling from his daring moves. He was usually such a defensive player. As he pressed home his advantage, he seemed to be shrugging off his sickness. Then I saw a glaring error he had made and knew I could mate him in three moves. Should I let him win and possibly effect a cure? Compassion vied with pride. My hand reached out of its own volition, without my consent, and made the killer move. Barrie saw his mistake immediately. He resigned and took to his bed for three days.

It was early in 1951, the Festival of Britain. The country was still hung over from the war and hardly ready for a party. Barrie and Pat and I stood on the Embankment and watched the Royal Festival Hall rising across the river. Barrie dreamed of wielding his baton there and my hopes lay next door in an arch under Waterloo Bridge where the National Film Theatre was opening for the first time. At first, the NFT mostly showed a repeating repertoire of great classic movies. My love and admiration for silent cinema began there during those few months, as I lived on my capital and waited for the call to arms.

Barrie and I had made a short film while we were still at school. A friend had a 9.5 mm camera but could not think what to do with it. I wrote a script and Barrie composed the music. It was about a girl lost in a threatening city. She was being pursued. It ended with everyone dancing. I can't remember why. Barrie's dissonant chords made no concessions to the content of the images. I was enthralled by making images and juxtaposing them.

Film directors will often tell of the indelible impression their first visit to the movies made upon them, how that film is seared into their memory. I reproduced mine in *Hope and Glory*. I was horrified, not by the film, of which I have no memory, but by the audience: seven hundred children screaming and fighting at a Saturday morning matinee. By contrast, at the NFT, the audience was as respectful as churchgoers. We watched the great silents – *Greed, Battleship Potemkin, Intolerance* – and any Chaplin, Buster Keaton or Harold Lloyd that came along. The essential mysteriousness of movies gave substance to the vague sense of destiny I had felt at Runnymede. I imagined that it was possible to achieve, through film, a radiance, a transcendence.

Pat and I began to see each other without Barrie on occasions. We finally confessed our love for each other, but we did not want to hurt Barrie, who also loved Pat, nor did we wish to fracture the magical *ménage à trois*, so we kept it secret.

All the pain and confusion of first love was exquisitely intensified by the subterfuge, the guilt of betraying our dearest friend. How Pat and I tortured ourselves with the moral dilemma. If we told him, we would surely lose him, yet this lie would poison our perfect triumvirate. We wallowed in it. I was reading Nietzsche and came across the famous forgiving aphorism, 'Whatever is done in the name of love is beyond good and evil.' I showed it to Pat and it gave us comfort.

My mother's open declaration of love for Herbert during his dying days had made her hostage to my father. He had used his moral advantage to drag her away from Kingston and the Thames. This grim pub in the City was a metaphor for their marriage: a tottering building standing precariously amongst the ruins. However, he was dependent on her to run the catering which was the core of the business, so she was able to make some demands. Her price was a weekend bungalow on the Thames in her beloved Shepperton.

On one of the weekends when my parents were at the bungalow, Pat and I made love, the first time for both of us. I am appalled that I can remember so little of it. Afterwards she said, 'I'm so glad you knew what to do.' I didn't, but she was very generous. I wrote some words in my journal at the time. The style was code rather than poetry in case of prying eyes: 'I have lived my life outside the walls, and now the gates have burst open and I ride in triumph into the city, banners flying, drums beating. The siege is over.'

Our secret was now even more shameful and we lay there in the weary Sunday silence of this battered city and decided to give ourselves up.

Barrie must be told, she said. To my relief she decided it would be better if she broke it to him.

In a state of permanent tumescence and moral turpitude with only that slogan from Nietzsche to sustain me, I waited for Pat's report on Barrie's reaction. Gravely, she told how he had fallen apart, limbs collapsing separately in all directions. He was suicidal, she said. I had a flash, a revelation. I knew exactly what he would do. I could see him swimming out to Chertsey Weir and simply, limply, hopelessly sinking. I hurried to his house. I would save him. Again.

My heart was heavy when I knocked on Barrie's door. When he opened it I was shocked to find him in fine fettle. His nervous breakdown had lasted less than four hours. The scales had fallen from his eyes, he said. He realised now how shallow and banal Pat was. He rejoiced in his deliverance. He thanked me for helping him see the light. He suggested a game of chess. He played with uninhibited flair and beat me in three straight games. He showed no sympathy for the cold I was developing.

I went back to Pat, guilty at not having defended her more vigorously, and with a dishonourable suspicion that he was right about her. As soon as I saw her – the softness, the drenched eyes, the quivering mouth – I fell back into a swoon of love, not only beyond good and evil, but also beyond thought, beyond reason. We spent many nights on the damp grass of Kensington Gardens re-entering the city gates. The truth was that in the absence of Barrie we had less to talk about, and since he was no longer an issue, we no longer talked about him.

Pat lived in a hostel run by fierce nuns in Notting Hill Gate, and after seeing her home I would catch the tube back to Moorgate and sit with my hands cupped over my mouth and nose inhaling the residue of her perfume. It was, of course, Lily of the Valley, the very scent favoured by the Italian girl. It seemed to me to be the very essence of sex, to emanate from the deepest, darkest, moistest centre of womanhood.

Just about then, her mother died. I comforted her, as I had comforted my mother when our house burned. I had the same wrenching, sinking sensation I had felt when I saw her break away from Herbert's embrace, her face twisted in pain, tears streaming. Pat's grief prolonged our relationship. I wasn't sufficiently self-aware to realise that she and Barrie and I had been replaying my parents' relationship with Herbert, a pattern I was to repeat more than once during my life.

1951: Auntie Calls

I was eighteen, waiting for call-up, waiting for the letter that would summon me to His Majesty's Service, but it was another letter that called me to another place. It bore the crest of the BBC: 'Nation shall speak peace unto nation.' My articles in the *Manchester Guardian* and a piece I did for a teenage magazine (I don't think the term 'teenager' had been coined yet) called *Heiress* had come to the attention of the producer of a radio programme called *Under-20 Parade*.

There was no television then to speak of. The wireless was the thing, the expression of nationhood. It had got us through the war: the newsreaders, the war correspondents, solemn and pompous with their plummy Oxford accents. We were weaned on *Children's Hour* – Toy Town, Uncle Mac. We graduated to the action-packed special agent, Dick Barton, and the suave detective, Paul Temple, whose wife was called Steve – I thought girls with boys' names incredibly sophisticated. The BBC came to be known as Auntie and she fed us the right music and literature and nourished our minds. It was a much greater influence on us than the cinema. The comedy shows were the cultural cement that connected and bound us together – Tommy Handley's *ITMA, Much Binding in the Marsh, Take It from Here*. The catchphrases, the topical references became the lingua franca of everyday life. For David and me, a little later, it was the Goons. They taught us the language of the Absurd so that we had a weapon, however feeble, to beat against the implacable Establishment. The bastion of the BBC was breached by Spike Milligan and his pals, the stern keeper of the nation's morals was ravished by anarchy, at least for half an hour each week. It made it a little less daunting to this nervous boy who arrived much too early at Portland House and was led through those curving corridors into the labyrinth.

Did I have any ideas for youth programmes? Well yes, I did. I saw a way of penetrating the film studios that had refused entry to David and me. What if I did a series interviewing film technicians and found out exactly what they did?

I soon found myself sitting in a big Humber Super-Snipe recording car, driving through the guarded gates of Elstree Studios. I was in! The recording equipment replaced the back seats of the Snipe and the interviews were recorded directly on to gramophone records, cutting spirals of wax, which curled up magically into the air. This technology was soon to be superseded by the tape recorder, a German wartime invention, its patent appropriated as war reparations. Tape, with its facility for easy editing, saved my subsequent radio career, since my pauses, hesitations and stutterings could be removed. I have always suffered from a condition where a quite ordinary word will suddenly elude me in the middle of a sentence. If I am in a public situation, panic sets in and the word refuses to emerge. I hunt through my inner thesaurus for a synonym, and eventually, after an agonising wait, some approximation will present itself.

These excursions to film studios taught me a little of how movies were made and I had my first, but alas not my last, encounter with the monstrous ego of a producer. I was visiting the set of a picture directed by Terence Young called *Tall Headlines*. The producer was a flamboyant, hugely vain man, Raymond Stross. He gave me lunch at his private table prepared by his personal chef. He bombarded me with accounts of his great achievements, always triumphing against impossible odds. He listed his possessions, his daring deals, the beauty of his current wife, his unerring judgement. I began to realise that he was under the mistaken impression that I was there to interview him. How could I break it to him? He lit his cigar from a book of matches, which he tossed over to me with a proud smirk. The cover read 'TALL HEADLINES' in an elongated typeface. He urged me to open it. I flipped the cover up and saw that on the inside was printed '. . . LIGHTS A NEW FLAME IN MOTION PICTURE ENTERTAINMENT.' He waited eagerly for my approbation, but miserably all I could blurt out was, 'Mr Stross, I came to interview the Gaffer.' He went very pale and left the table without a word.

My name was in the *Radio Times*, I was in love, and still no word from His Majesty. Could it be possible that they would forget me? Seeing less of Barrie, I saw more of David. We both missed our companionship of funny voices, the doubled-up, gut-wrenching, helpless mirth that punctuated and consoled our dry-cleaning days on the 'knocker'. Most Saturday nights David and I would go to 100 Oxford Street to listen to traditional jazz played by Humphrey Lyttelton and others. No dancing for us. We sat still in our polo-neck sweaters and listened with earnest attention.

David had discovered a new comedian and urged me to go with him to the Kingston Empire to witness this phenomenon. We became avid devotees of Frankie Howerd and followed him on the music-hall circuit from Finchley to Streatham and back to Kingston. We had discovered 'camp'. Like 'teenager', it was a word yet to be coined. We certainly had no idea Frankie Howerd was gay. David had been in prison, I had been in a Catholic boys' school and yet we barely knew that homosexuality existed. What we saw on the stage was a man entering into an intimate complicity with an audience in which he revealed his pettiness, his envy, his cowardice, his monumental triviality, his pervasive lust. A man admitting weakness – something we had been taught never to do. How it liberated us from the masculine severities of the time – at least while we watched him. It was comedy that was causing fissures in the implacable class system and we glimpsed the possibility of slipping through them. The drabness, the dreariness of the forties had ended. The fifties, the Festival of Britain beckoned.

None of the comics we loved – the Goons, Frankie Howerd, the ineffable Jimmy James – was overtly political. There was no direct threat to the Establishment, yet it encouraged an ambience of mockery. Only in Shaw did I encounter and thrill to the subversive. One of the great experiences of that time was seeing *Man and Superman* with John Clements as John Tanner. Once a week they played it with the Hell scene, and I wallowed in a glorious five-hour glut from the Irish tongue-lasher. But it was class, not politics, that inhibited us and possessed us, more than we knew.

Enter a Scarlet Woman

My sister, Wendy, was a mother before her seventeenth birthday. I depicted the birth of her son, Robert, in *Hope and Glory*. She followed her French-Canadian soldier husband, René, to Montreal at the end of the war. She had another child there, Linda, and in that fateful year of 1951, she came home for a visit, bringing her three-year-old daughter, but leaving Robert with his father. She slotted into the cramped accommodations of The Plough and proceeded to turn our lives inside out. My mother was nervous of the return of the prodigal daughter. She guessed correctly that Wendy had no intention of returning to Canada. She had outgrown her husband and hated his family of dim alcoholics. She claimed that several of René's many brothers had attempted to rape her.

Wendy was as confrontational as she had been as a child. Her vociferous socialism had survived her North American experience intact. She heaped praise on the Soviet Union, either from conviction or simply to infuriate my father. She forced us all to face issues we were more than content to cover and smother with evasion. She derided my mother for allowing my father to drag her back to the pub life she had hated in *her* youth when *her* father obliged her to serve in *his* bars. She chided my father for spending hours counting the money and poring over the accounts. 'You do that to avoid having to talk to customers.' She said I was pathetically weak to retreat to my parents' home after gaining my independence. I argued that since I was about to go into the army for two years I had to give up my flat. 'So you sacrifice a principle for a matter of convenience?'

Her arguments were excessive, but there was always enough truth in them to cause damage. She said I wasn't facing up to my feelings towards my parents and I shouldn't be with them until I did. I was outraged and scared because she was right. Deep down, I hated my father for incarcerating my mother in this gaunt castle. By living there, I was acquiescing in her captivity. I angrily accused her of the same sin. After all, she had come home to the nest herself. There we were, all of us. Even Angela was still at home. She had just left school and was taking a course in hotel management. None of us really wanted to be there in those cramped rooms where the cigarette smoke and beer fumes seeped up from the bars below.

I had carried in my mind, through her absence, an idealised image of my exquisite Madonna-like sister nursing her baby, a victim of the lust of this Canadian soldier. She laughed in my face. She told me that she had been screwing since she was twelve. She told me how she had been impatient with boys who wanted to kiss for hours, and urged them to get on with the real business.

She was twenty-six, sophisticated, wild, blonde, wearing the glamour of America like perfume. Barrie, David and I were soon besotted with her. After the blandness of René's Canadian family in Trenton, Ontario, she was hungry for stimulation, and we avidly took her into our circle; we made her our queen and proudly exhibited her at our symphony concerts, 100 Oxford Street, the theatre, galleries, parties. It amused her to wield power over us pups. We wagged our tails when she noticed us. We whimpered when she kicked us. We went belly-up when she scolded.

Pat was no match for her. Wendy told me I needed someone with fire, a girl who could challenge me intellectually. The person she was describing sounded a lot like her.

It became clear that she would not go back to Canada. She told René. He responded by putting her nine-year-old son on a plane. He was pining for his mother. We picked him up at the airport. He refused to speak. He said not a word for three months.

My mother became concerned on several counts. She had always clashed with Wendy, who had been an only child for eight years before my arrival, and her provocative behaviour stemmed from that unwelcome event. She demanded attention. Her direct, challenging manner was stimulating, exciting but also disruptive. What did she propose to do, my mother asked. There were two children who needed to go to school. Where was she going to live? How would she support herself? I can see now that Wendy must have been desperate for help.

Mother also accused Wendy of dominating me and trying to seduce me. I was excited and troubled by the way she talked about sex and love. She said that the highest level life offered was to have total intimacy with another person, which must include sex. Falling in love was to be avoided because you lost judgement, it bred jealousy, you became foolish; and since it was a delusion, it made the all-important intimacy fake. That incest was a taboo would have recommended it to her. There were electric moments when we came close, but she probably felt the situation was complicated enough. And I held back, not wanting to betray Pat. I already felt guilty for neglecting her in favour of my sister.

Wendy needed something more than we boys could provide and she solved this by getting involved with the West Indian community. She described it as her brown period. She loved the vitality, the ease, and the sense of celebration that was so lacking in our pinched little lives.

There was another youth radio programme, *Under-20 Review*, in which four young people, aided by a distinguished adult, played at being critics. I took part in a couple of these and the producer, Richard Keen (known to his colleagues as Mad Keen) asked me to take on the role of chairman. So I had a regular spot and the world of the arts was prised open for me. Each week I would receive a novel or biography to read, passes to the press shows of movies, tickets to the opera and theatre. No longer perched up in the gallery, I took my place in the stalls.

My propensity to blank out in the middle of a sentence made the weekly sessions quite stressful. I never understood why the producer persisted with me. Nevertheless it gave me a sense of being involved in the arts, and there was a fee, which was important, as my vast fortune from the dry-cleaning business had somehow been frittered away.

The call to arms finally came, though several months later than expected. I was seeing less of Pat and more of Wendy, and Wendy was seeing more of David, although that did not diminish her delight in all things Caribbean. One night she took me to a West Indian club, The Sunset, in a basement off the Tottenham Court Road. I met her black friends. London was not the multiracial city it is today: a few Poles left over from the war, some central European refugees, mostly Jews. The West Indian community in Notting Hill Gate was unacknowledged. Few knew they were there at all, much less the culture they brought with them and that flourished in clubs like The Sunset.

The warmth, the welcome, the laughter overwhelmed me but beneath the bonhomie there was something dangerous and unpredictable. Wendy's West Indian friend was courteous and slightly condescending about my ignorance of the Caribbean. I had never been abroad, nor had any of my friends. The war had consumed all our geography: ask me about Minsk or Monte Casino, Normandy, Iwo Jima.

We drank a lot of rum and I smoked hash for the first time. The cellar was hot and smoky and airless. I broke out in a cold sweat. I felt the urgent need to get to the toilet. It was up some rickety wooden steps. I got to the top and looked down. The dancers, crushed together, seemed to sway like one being. It made me dizzy watching them. And sick.

A friendly black hand was gently shaking me as I lay on the floor of the urinal. I got up, but all solid surfaces had liquefied. I staggered out of the treacherous toilet and stood at the top of the stairs. I was concentrating all my will on staying conscious and upright until I could find Wendy. Swaying at the top of the steps I looked down at the roiling black faces. I took a deep breath of the sweet and sickly scent of sweat and pot smoke that rose to meet me. It was not hard to spot Wendy, the only white, the only blonde. She looked up and saw me. I reached out. I stepped off the platform and floated down to her, an elegant swallow dive. I drifted towards a phalanx of outstretched arms and grinning faces. I landed softly. They passed me hand over hand across the bobbing, laughing heads, to the door. As I swam across them, I observed the subterranean life beneath me as though through a face mask. I snorkelled across the dance floor. Through the laughter and jeers, a voice cried out, 'Old rocking chair got him.' Wendy was furious. She had to take me home and abandon who knows what delights.

Shortly after this our adult guest on *Under-20 Review* was Colin MacInnes and we discussed his book, *City of Spades*, which revealed to a startled nation the mores and manners of London's West Indian community. My stock rose when I was able to describe (and exaggerate) my familiarity with the subject.

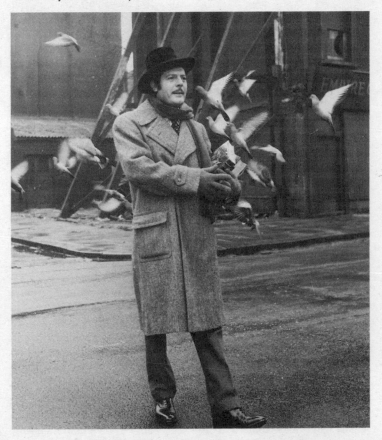

Leo the Last: Marcello Mastroianni in Notting Hill

Eighteen years later, inspired by that experience, I made *Leo the Last* in a street in Notting Hill Gate. Marcello Mastroianni played a fastidious ornithologist who inherits a grand mansion and finds that his comfortable life watching birds around the world has been financed by rents from a slum inhabited by immigrant West Indians. In the intervening years there had been much change – more political awareness, more bitterness and resentment, more integration – but the enviable ability of the West Indians to see life as a celebration has remained intact.

March 1951: Conscripted

I was drafted into the Royal Fusiliers and reported for basic training at Shorncliff Barracks in Kent. I was eighteen years and two months. Like every man reaching this age, I had to serve two years in the armed forces. The Nissen-hutted camp was perched on a cliff top, and the bitter sea winds bounced off the cliffs and struck upwards, grit-laden and malevolent. The food was such disgusting swill that we all refused it for the first couple of days. The usual indignities: shaving in cold water at 5 a.m., drilling, route marches, humiliations. The NCOs were all war-hardened regulars and we were nig-nogs, sacks of shit tied in the middle, lily-livered scum. We learnt how to shoot our 303 Lee Enfield rifles and how to bayonet sandbags. They ran us ragged and we soon wolfed down every morsel of swill we could get our hands on. We were paid twenty-one shillings a week, a guinea. At the end of our six weeks' infantry training, we were to be shipped out to the distant and perplexing Korean War. We were mostly drawn from London and predominantly working class. There was not a single black among the thousand or more rookies in our intake.

In the evenings we blancoed our webbing, buffed up our brasses, rubbed our boots with spit and polish until the toecaps reflected our not-yet-soldiers' faces. We folded our blankets into perfect box shapes at the end of our beds, we buffed the floor, and in the last moments of the day before lights out I would write to Pat or Barrie or my mother – mostly catalogues of the horrors and black humour. And when I could, I put down impressions in my journal.

The nation was mobilised to combat the Communist threat. Besides the men who had fought in the Second World War and stayed on, there were now hundreds of thousands in training. This enormous social upheaval has passed unnoticed into history. Where are the novels, the poetry, the films of National Service? It was seen as a chore – unromantic, unheroic, drudgery, to be done and forgotten. Yet it brought young men from all classes and places together. It coarsened them, shipped them around the world, yet there is almost no residue.

Meanwhile David, though seven years younger than Wendy, was taken by her as her lover, and she filled my place as his partner in the dry-cleaning business. Pat was seeing more of Barrie in my absence: they had me to talk about. Barrie's National Service would be deferred until he had completed his law studies.

After our very basic training, we were adjudged to be infantrymen and fit to fight on foreign soil. Preparations were made for the move to Korea. I recall no mutinous anger or even questioning of the situation. All resistance had been crushed. In *Full Metal Jacket,* Stanley Kubrick spends the first hour of the film detailing the brutal training of Marines. Behind it is Kubrick's civilian voice saying, 'Is this not the most extreme degradation of the human body and brain ever endured by men in any army?' The answer in my head was no. Our training was more brutal, our NCOs more sadistic, our deprivations even more severe than the Kubrick version. As with Kubrick's Marines, it was designed to break the will, to make men obedient killing machines. It derived from the First World War and the need to persuade men to get out of their trenches and advance against German machine guns. A million met their death in this fashion, proving the success of the system. Yet when the Marines in *Full Metal Jacket* finally go into action they panic, fall apart and are shot up by a Vietcong girl sniper. The implication is that a lack of conviction about the purpose of the Vietnam War overrides the training. In our case, we saw Korea as America's problem, but since they came in to help us in the Second World War, it was up to us to support them. Ill-equipped and ill-informed, these men went out and fought obediently and well. Their discipline held. Coming hard on the heels of the Second World War, it was as though we were all too weary to think out the implications.

Preparing to cross the globe for this remote conflict, we all became very close, with the fierce loyalty and concern for each other that comes from shared adversity. We would die rather than admit it, but there was an exhilaration in marching drill, in being in step, in harmony, like a single organism, a platoon.

A couple of the boys were illiterates and dictated their letters to me. One of them, Lofty, found it painful to admit his feelings for his girl-friend in front of me, and especially in earshot of the others. He would say, 'Tell her I toss off every night thinking of her tits.' I would write, 'I think of you every night as I lie in bed.' Then he would be off again in a loud voice for the amusement of the others, 'Ask her if her Dad's still banging her.' I would write, 'Give my regards to your Mum and Dad.' Afterwards he would ask me to read it back to him, which I did quietly and discreetly. He would nod and his eyes became moist and he would say, 'You can be, you know, a bit more loving next time.'

Lofty was killed in Korea. Being so tall, he stood up in an entrenchment and one of his own nervous officers shot him. The rest survived but suffered terribly from frostbite due to a lack of proper protective clothing.

I had refused the option of Officer Training so as to stay with the platoon, but at the last moment I was informed that I was being transferred to the Educational Corps, and ironically, one of my tasks later on was to lecture to troops being posted to Korea. My pals jeered and cheered as I went off, but I felt bereft – the atavistic death that comes from exclusion from the tribe.

The training centre was at Beaconsfield, close enough to London. I harboured the hope that I could sneak off to do my weekly broadcast. It would surely be easy-going. Not so. Sensitive to a cissy reputation, the Educational Corps plunged us into even more rigorous training. NCOs from the Brigade of Guards drilled us, constantly reminded us that we were fighting men before we were instructors and teachers.

Another tin hut, another platoon, another set of forced intimacies, friendships, loyalties. Our purpose was to raise the level of skills in an army that was becoming more and more technical. We were to teach literacy, mathematics, engineering, map reading – all aimed at making more effective soldiers.

The perverse pleasure I took from drilling in basic training was intensified here. We did advanced stuff: diagonal turns, counter marching, fancy formations. It was like being a shoal of fish or a flock of birds. We were many and one, absolved from the burden of individual identity.

We were paid our twenty-one shillings on Thursdays. Everyone was broke by Wednesday and the last cigarettes long since smoked. On one such day we came back exhausted after a long route march and although I, alone, did not smoke, the corporate craving of my comrades was so intense that I began to share it. There was not one cigarette among them. Mail was delivered to our beds. A scattering of letters awaited us, but on one bed was a parcel. We gathered around as the blessed recipient ripped it open. He discarded the letter, the cake and whatever else in a frantic quest for the cigarettes that would surely be included. A pot of home-made strawberry preserve had broken in transit. He found the packet of Players under it, drenched in jam. A groan went up, a terrible despair fell upon us. He lifted out the soggy pack. With infinite care, we cut the card-board packet open with a razor blade. The cigarettes were bloated, sod-den. Surgically, we lifted them out one by one. They were threatening to burst out of their swollen pink skins. We dried them carefully by the stove, slowly, so as not to traumatise them. As we waited, the craving intensified and I, who had never smoked, was dizzy with desire.

Twenty men. Twenty cigarettes. We lit them up with a ritual solemnity I was not to see exceeded until I lived with a tribe in the Amazon. So my first cigarette was a pink, strawberry-flavoured Player. I smoked with passionate addiction for the next fourteen years.

My special friend in the barrack room was Pierre Butt. He was witty and fastidious with a disdain for all things military. His permanent state of unhappiness cheered us all up, but his popularity plummeted when he started to wake us up in the night screaming. He had a recurring dream that a rat was walking over his face. We would shout at him, throw things at him to wake him up from his nightmare. One night another fel-low woke to find a real live rat crawling across his bed. His yells woke us all. From that night on we began to suffer a collective nightmare – a fear of rats. The barrack room at night was a cacophony of whimpers and cries, with occasional screams jerking us all out of fitful sleep. Only Pierre slept soundly, the sleep not of the just, but the justified.

At the end of the training, those who passed were promoted to Sgt-Instructors; the failures were RTUed – the ignominy of being Returned To Unit was the threat hovering over us throughout the course. The post-ings went up on the Company noticeboard and we were summoned for briefing and told we would be shipped to a transit camp to await our various postings. Any questions? I raised my hand. I had volunteered for Korea in the hope of joining up with my Fusiliers pals. Needless to say they planned to send me elsewhere. I pointed out that my name appeared twice. I was to be sent to both Germany and Gibraltar. I said I was anxious to obey orders, but could the major offer me guidance as to how I could comply with these conflicting demands? What a cocky little prick! He responded that if they knew what they were getting, both postings would surely be more than happy to relinquish my services to the other. And perhaps they were, for I languished for weeks in the transit camp. One by one my comrades moved on to the many theatres of the Cold War where Britain still held sway: Malta, Cyprus, Egypt, Gibraltar, Malaya, Kenya, and of course, Germany.

Hammered and welded into part of a unit, I was now alone. The numbing indolence of a transit camp felt like grief. There were no duties, nothing to do, nothing required of me. The months of rigour and discipline were abruptly removed. A heaviness descended on me. It became an effort to move my limbs. When I could muster the energy, I dragged myself in slow motion to the canteen and slumped down with a mug of thick tea. Reading became much too tiring. I lay on my bed for long stretches, smoking and staring at the damp patches on the ceiling. Even masturbation required an effort of imagination which was beyond me. Each night as I fell asleep, I promised myself that the next day I would go up to the office and beg them for a posting, and each day I never quite made it.

During the course, I had managed a few hasty trips to London to record radio broadcasts and to see David, Wendy and Barrie. Pat and I wrote to each other assiduously, but when we met it was like entering a previous incarnation. I felt coarse in her company. Now I lacked the will to make the journey. I was Oblomov. Or the version of the archetype David and I had invented, Willie.

The Posting Clerk came looking for me one day. A sergeant working on the army newspaper in Korea had been killed. They needed an urgent replacement. I had managed to find a bathtub and soaked in it for a couple of hours, lacking the will required to climb out of it. Failing to find me, they sent another. Our lives turn on such casual accidents. I was bitterly disappointed. I had never set foot outside England, not even in Wales. The wheel of chance turned and they sent me to, of all places, a Royal Engineers' basic training camp – a grim, closed-off, fenced-in, impenetrable compound, which lay under the mystical beauty of the Malvern Hills.

There were three other sergeants and a captain in the Education Centre. I was given a desk in a room where all the sergeants sat. When I attempted to speak, I was silenced by the senior man, Sgt Yeomans, a severe figure who stared at me with burning eyes magnified by thick lenses.

I was assigned duties by Capt. Adlam, whom I later overheard describing me as 'innocuous-looking', which I suppose I was. I met him forty-five years later at the opening night of Tom Stoppard's play, *Arcadia*, at the National Theatre. He recognised me as I stood talking to Tom. He had followed my career. He told me he had spent his life working for the British Council. He said he always felt Stoppard was writing for him alone. This distant authority figure seemed pretty innocuous himself now.

All recruits had to attend instruction and pass basic tests in English and maths. Illiterates, of whom there were many, were separated for special intensive classes. In military style we drilled and drummed the words into their heads for hours on end. We had a very high success rate. One of our failures was a big, strong, weak-minded boy called Atkins. We kept him at the Centre doing odd jobs since he was incapable of managing any part of the training. He was so lacking in will that I realised I had finally met Willie, the character David and I had amused ourselves by inventing. He was vacant, without purpose, his only characteristic a low cunning. One day I sent him with my big army mug to fetch me tea. He arrived back holding only the handle. He had banged into a wall or something and the mug of hot tea had broken off. When I brought this to his attention he looked puzzled. He knew there should have been something on the end of the handle, but what was it? To him it was just another example of the perplexing nature of life. Did I detect the slightest glint of wit in his eyes? Willie, after all, had a murky subterranean malevolence. Was Atkins having me on? The suspicion rankled. Although my colleagues had given up on him as a hopeless case, I persisted, making him trace out letters over and over again.

We taught typing. Thirty men would sit at thirty typewriters staring at a finger chart on the wall. There was a gramophone record with a voice that dictated the letters: E-V-E-R-Y-SPACE-G-O-O-D-SPACE-B-O-Y-SPACE-D-E-S-E-R-V-E-S-SPACE-F-A-V-O-U-R-RETURN CARRIAGE. It was drill in another form. Thirty hands would shunt back the carriage and advance to the next line. The sound came pounding through the flimsy walls of the Centre like rifle shots, as each letter was hit in unison. Again, I recalled my father's bitter words, as he went from commanding Gurkhas in the First World War to being a clerk in the Second: 'I'll be typing for England.'

I taught map reading. As one who always takes wrong turnings, gets lost in cities, on ski slopes, in rainforests, maps to me were like Braille to the blind. Here at last was a means of finding my way in the world. I came to appreciate the beauty of those Ordnance Survey maps, and admire the men – military engineers – who had set out to measure the world, to domesticate its topography. Early maps had been pictures, miniature renditions of landscapes. The OS maps were metaphors: elevations became colours; the shape of hills, contour lines.

Sgt Yeomans was a regular soldier around forty years old. He had a celibate, monk-like devotion to the service. He lived according to the letter of the Army law; the Army Act was his Bible. The rest of us were National Service rabble, hoping to skive off whenever we could. Yeomans made our lives a misery. He organised our work and insisted that everything was done according to the book. He was forever putting us on charges for being incorrectly dressed – a tunic button undone – or not addressing him by his rank, for swearing, or failing to face the flag and stand to attention at the sounding of the last post, and so on and on. He would march us down to the Company commander, who was exasperated by all this and would sometimes challenge Yeomans on the validity of the offence. Yeomans would quote chapter and verse of the Army Act. One day when I was arraigned before him, the CO said, 'Sgt Yeomans, if everyone lived according to the book, the Army would grind to a halt.' Yeomans responded, 'My duty is to obey the rules, sir, not to challenge their efficacy.' 'Don't you ever transgress?' 'No, sir, never.' And he never did.

King George VI was fading away. In *Hope and Glory* there is a scene with the family sitting around the dinner table listening to the King's Christmas message on the radio. The feeble stuttering of our afflicted monarch seemed to reflect the pathetic weakness of England in the face of the mighty German war machine. It needed the rich rotundity of Churchill's voice to set things to rights.

One day, walking back to the Centre from lunch in the sergeants' mess, a cook went by in his grubby whites. He was whistling the Gilbert and Sullivan song, 'We're soldiers of the Queen, my lad . . .' We knew the King was sick. So this was it. I got to the Centre and announced the death of our monarch. Yeomans said, 'You are on a charge for spreading malicious rumours concerning our sovereign, detrimental to morale.'

I told him angrily that it was a fact, not a rumour.

'What is your evidence?'

It sounded very weak that my only corroboration was a whistling cook.

'Just a whistle, not even words,' he said scornfully.

'I know the words. Everyone does.'

He had an insane logic that always left you feeling helpless and foolish. He looked out of the window at the flag flying on the regimental pole.

'Is the flag at half mast, Sgt Boorman?'

I had to admit that it was not. A bitter little smile of triumph. He stood there at the window watching the flagpole for half an hour until it was finally lowered. He turned away and removed the picture of the King that hung over his desk and replaced it with one of Elizabeth. He then marched me down to face the charge.

The CO, while acknowledging the correctness of the offence, dismissed the charge on the grounds that my intention had not been malicious and that he doubted that morale could fall much lower in the Education Centre than it already had. Yeomans stood to attention throughout, his face a mask; only the eyes glinting through his spectacles hinted at insanity. He said, 'If Sgt Boorman happens to hear a cook whistling "Deutschland Über Alles", sir, are we to expect an invasion and go on war alert?'

Capt. Adlam, our leader, was cowed and intimidated by Yeomans' insistence on absolute adherence to the letter of the law. It was wreaking havoc with our work. Obeying all the rules left little time for anything else. We were all trapped in this claustrophobic construct and it somehow sapped all our energy. It was all we could talk about.

We had an orderly at the Centre, Private Durrant, a wily old sweat who had married a girl from Malvern and kept deserting his regiment, the Borders, to be with her. You can't beat the Army, they said. But he did.

He was punished, did his jankers, and went AWOL as soon as he was released. They finally gave up on him and posted him to us where his duties included lighting the stoves and generally clearing up. However, he was such a skiver and malingerer that he managed to avoid all physical work. He claimed to have a hernia so he got a 'chitty' from the Medical Officer excusing him from lifting heavy weights. Durrant interpreted this as anything heavier than a mug of tea. He was also excused boots, claiming flat feet. Later, in his greatest coup, he succeeded in bamboozling a young army doctor into excusing him from saluting. He said he had to keep his right hand in his pocket to press the protrusion back into the abdomen. He would walk nonchalantly past officers with his hand stuck deep into his pocket. When hysterical young officers demanded their due, he waved his chit in their faces. All in all, he achieved a higher level of excusable insolence than anyone thought possible.

Yet he too feared Yeomans. Try as he would, he could not best him. He found himself charged and convicted on several trivial offences. Yeomans would ensure that he was confined to barracks, well aware of Durrant's passion for being at home at night with his wife. Durrant had met his match. From time to time, he even found himself in the humiliating position of lighting Yeomans' stove, although always contriving that it would go out after ten minutes. It was his bitterness over this chore that led to his great plan.

Durrant was thick with another of our sergeants, Tim Bradshaw. Tim had worked on nuclear fuels at Aldermaston before being drafted. He was a compulsive liar and an amateur criminologist, so he and Durrant were soulmates. They had a secret corner of the storeroom where Durrant had an armchair and a kettle. Atkins was always to be found there too. He adored Durrant and did his bidding, happy to be his serf. He hoped to learn such cunning, and aspired to be such a man.

Here it was that they plotted the downfall of Yeomans. Tim and Durrant called us together and briefed us. It was vital that we were all co-conspirators. We agreed, all but Sgt John Baker. He was a person of great goodness and compassion. He was also, in his quiet way, as self-disciplined as Yeomans – who probed away at John, searching out his tender spots, but could never fault him. John declined to be part of the plot. He contrived to be absent by conducting a class at that time.

On the appointed day, we sat silently working at our desks, the room thick with tension. We knew that Durrant was outside listening at the door. Yeomans looked at the unlit stove. He called for Durrant, who failed to appear. He then turned to Tim.

'Sgt Bradshaw, as the junior NCO, you will light the fire.'

'Light it yourself,' said Tim.

Yeomans rose with the cold, white-faced rage that we all recognised as a prelude to a charge.

'Sgt Bradshaw, I am giving you an order.'

Tim ignored him and went on marking exercise books. Quivering with ire, Yeomans launched into one of his tirades.

'Sgt Bradshaw, we know you are slovenly and devious, but it appears that you are also insolent and stupid . . .'

As Yeomans faced Tim, it meant that his back was to the door. That gave Durrant the opportunity to sneak silently into the room. He tiptoed across until he was standing closely behind Yeomans.

'Should I be listening to this, sarge?'

Yeomans swung round.

Tim said, 'Sgt Yeomans, the charge is admonishing an NCO in the presence of a private soldier.'

The company commander was jubilant. He said he was sure Yeomans would not wish his unblemished record to be besmirched by a reprimand. The alternative was to accept a transfer back to the Educational Corps, which the CO granted with immediate effect. He was RTUed.

Yeomans methodically packed his things, took down the Queen's picture, and departed without a word.

The Case of the Missing Sergeant

The Education Centre, in reaction to the end of the Yeomans reign, became lax and libertarian. Durrant rewarded himself for his triumph by taking outrageous advantage of us. He held court, played cards with Tim Bradshaw, drank beer openly and regaled us with the details of his sex life. His wife was very young and he claimed to have trained her in various perversions he had learnt in the brothels of Cairo. He inflamed Atkins by promising to take him home one night and let him watch their antics.

It was oppressive to be permanently stationed in a training camp. It was a closed and heavily guarded place. Wild young animals were being brutally broken and tamed within; they must not be allowed to escape. Surrounded by high fences and barbed wire, all persons and vehicles were searched at the guard gate. It was a fortress. Despite the new freedoms within the Centre, Tim Bradshaw, in particular, found it stifling and claustrophobic.

A series of daring robberies occurred inside the camp. Thousands of cigarettes were stolen from the NAAFI; an officer's binoculars were lifted; a silver cup from the sergeants' mess was purloined; a large radio disappeared from the Education Centre. There was always a week between thefts, and as each was discovered, rigorous searches were made to no avail. The military police were called in. Nothing could get out, so the stolen goods had to be somewhere within the camp. The process of discovery would take most of a day. All kit had to be laid out, lockers emptied. It brought training to a standstill. Officers and NCOs also had to suffer the indignities of having their belongings rifled through. The conscripts were lined up on the parade ground with their kit bags emptied out on the ground.

The fragile balance that sustains military discipline and morale was crumbling. Conscripts who endured crass insults, who obeyed pointless orders, who painted coal white, who ironed creases into their blankets, became mutinous in the face of this investigation. We all felt accused, we all felt resentful. When my turn came to be questioned by the military police, I found myself blushing as I had as a schoolboy. Someone had used a key to gain access to the storeroom in the Centre where the missing radio was kept. We all knew where the key was hidden and suspicion fell on Durrant, given his history. He was grilled and threatened. He, who had evaded detection of so many crimes, was so indignant at being accused of a crime he had not committed that he would whimper and whine at the unfairness of it. Worse still, Durrant knew the identity of the real perpetrator, because Tim Bradshaw had boasted to him that he had worked out a way of smuggling stolen goods out of the camp.

Although in Durrant's twisted world you didn't split on a mate, Tim began to worry. The authorities needed a conviction and Durrant was the ideal victim, so he would be questioned closely. I noticed the two of them in tense, whispered conversations. One day, when we had had military police swarming over the Centre, Tim asked Capt. Adlam for a twenty-four-hour pass to go to a twenty-first birthday party in Birmingham. I agreed to cover his classes; he had done the same for me when I dashed up to London to do my radio show. The next day one of the investigators returned, wishing to continue his interviews, and was surprised to find Bradshaw absent. He became suspicious. He checked the railway station. It was a weekday and only one serviceman's reduced-price ticket had been sold. It was not to Birmingham, but to London where Tim lived. Military police arrived at his home and found him surrounded by the missing loot.

There was a post office in the camp and he had simply put the items into parcels and posted them to his London address. The post-office van, of course, passed freely in and out of the camp. He told me later that he got the idea from a Father Brown story.

We Education Sergeants now had a roster, taking our turns to guard Tim Bradshaw as he awaited court martial. Prankster that he was, he amused himself by devising plans for escape, and we never knew how serious he was. We suspected that this kidding around was a cover for his real intentions. For days and nights we sat with him in his quarters, which had become his prison cell. He told me his life story during those long hours – a mixture of fantasy and truth, I suspected, but it seemed that he had always felt the compulsion to put himself at risk. He was fascinated by crime and by the ultimate crime, murder. He weighed us up as potential victims, which kept us on edge. His incarceration and the prison-like atmosphere of the camp made us all yearn for escape. On Saturday nights we would go to Malvern or Worcester, get drunk and try to pick up girls. It always ended in miserable and messy failure. Our best hopes lay with the student nurses in Worcester. They were living, like us, in disciplined isolation, and had a similarly urgent need to break out. There is an entry in my journal describing a sergeants' mess dance when we invited a busload of girls from the Worcester Infirmary:

Amie is a slim tomboy. She wanted to see a barrack room. Risking dire consequences, I took her into a room of sleeping recruits. We turned on the lights. They watched blearily as she danced for them in her wispy dress then gave some of them a cruel glancing kiss and tucked them in, a parody of motherhood. I experienced that same tremor of fear I had felt as an eight-year-old when Wendy fiercely forced me to cover up her reckless escapades. There was an instant intimacy between us, a sibling ease, but she eluded me, slipped through my fingers.

I arranged to meet another nurse for tea one Sunday in Worcester. Betty was very pretty but quite different from Amie, passive and silent. We walked by the river and by the time we reached the tea room all possibilities of conversation had been exhausted. We sat sipping our tea. There was a fine view of the cathedral through the window and I shifted my chair so that she was framed by it. The sun was at a perfect angle and cross-lit the exquisite curve of her breast under a flowered cotton dress. I fell into a kind of trance, grateful for the silence she bestowed, willing her not to move, not to spoil the composition. It was an epiphany that transcended a soldier's lust.

This memory found its way into *Hope and Glory*. At the Christmas party I had the tipsy grandfather propose a toast to his past loves, turning their names reverently on his tongue, ending with '. . . I've seen half the wonders of the world, but I've never laid eyes on a finer sight than the curve of Betty Browning's breast.' The alliteration was to make it funny, but the drunken emotion of the wonderful Ian Bannen carried the heartfelt conviction that I intended. Strange that a visual memory should be converted into words in that most visual of forms, the movies.

I was deputed to be Tim Bradshaw's escort at his court martial. He and I cleaned our neglected boots, and buffed up our belt buckles and badges to the high standard required for such a solemn occasion. We were marched in at the double by the regimental sergeant-major: 'Prisoner and escort, HALT!' We hammered our boots in percussive unison on the polished wooden floor. Tim was defended in a perfunctory way by a Royal Engineers captain who simply pleaded clemency on the grounds of Tim's good record. We were obliged to stand at attention throughout the proceedings. My back began to ache, the pain spread to my legs. I willed the muscles not to go into spasm. I could feel the blood draining from my head and settling heavily in my legs. Dizziness. Knees trembling. I realised I was beginning to sway. Concentrating mind and body on remaining vertical, I lost all sense of the words that rattled around the room from the prosecution.

'Do you find it breezy in here, Sgt Boorman?' asked the court president, our beleaguered company commander.

'No, sir.'

'You seem to be swaying in some private wind.'

I responded gratefully to the command: 'Prisoner and escort, about turn. Quick march!'

The sentence was three months' detention in the military prison at Shepton Mallet.

Tim soon recovered his malicious humour. The grin was back on his face as he unfolded his plan to me. His mother must not know he was in prison: it would break her heart. He learned that he would be allowed to send only one letter a week, which had to be written on an army form whose printed heading was something approximating to 'AC 486, Army Detention Centre, Shepton Mallet, Somerset.' Shepton Mallet was greatly feared. It spoke of brutality and cruel incarceration. How else to threaten those already suffering under a harsh regime? Tim brushed it aside: 'It's just three months of jankers.' He left me stamped envelopes addressed to his mother. He would send me his weekly letter and I would then cut off the telltale top and post it on to his mother, which I gladly did. She never discovered that he had been in jail.

I was to escort him to prison. Before we left he gave me a gift, a paperweight, a piece of depleted uranium 235. Grey in colour, gnarled and twisted, it looked as though the terrible power had been tortured out of it. I picked it up. It was impossibly heavy, the densest substance on earth. I marvelled that anything so small could weigh so much. It made gravity palpable.

As we struggled on to the train at Malvern, the handcuffs inhibiting us, Tim's kitbag swung around and hit me heavily on the side of the head. I fell sideways and lost my footing. Tim grinned and hauled me up like a fish by the steel bond that bound us. I was sure he had done it on purpose, but he was all innocence.

We sat down in a compartment. An elderly man opposite eyed us distastefully.

'Which one of you is the criminal?'

Tim pointed at me, although by now he had been stripped of his rank while I still sported my stripes. Despite this, the man stared contemptuously at me. Tim begged me to take off the cuffs. I refused, remembering all his escape plans. There was a tradition that if a prisoner escaped from your charge on the way to an Army prison then you, the escort, would serve his sentence. The handcuffs were becoming irksome and Tim pointed out that the train was travelling at 60 m.p.h., too fast to jump. He gave me his solemn word, on his mother's life, that he would not attempt to escape. I got out the key and unlocked us. Tim leapt out of his seat and fled down the corridor. I raced after him in time to see him disappear into the next carriage, which was at the rear of the train. I checked all the compartments. No Tim. I doubled back, opening the toilets. Empty. I ran back to our compartment intending to pull the communication cord to stop the train. And there he was, sitting demurely in his seat wearing his insolent grin. 'I was dying for a piss,' he said. 'Nearly didn't make it.'

I was relieved to have in my hand a piece of paper, a chitty reading, 'Received from Sgt Boorman the live body of Private Bradshaw.' As he was led away and the gates closed on him, he looked back smiling and said, 'It's never really exhausted.'

He was obsessively fascinated with riddles, anagrams and puzzles. During the Yeomans era he would sometimes sneak into the mess during the morning and rapidly complete the *Telegraph* crossword puzzle. Part of Yeomans' daily routine was to do that crossword during the lunch hour: he took his break early in order to have first crack at the paper. He was enraged to find it solved. Underneath Tim would write 'Y so mean?' or more directly, 'Fuck you, Yeomans.'

1952: The Blonde and the Dark Lady

On the train back, Tim's riddle spun in my brain like a bad tune that won't go away. Tim's last prank: he still had a hold over me. 'It's never really exhausted.' As the train approached Malvern those improbable hills leapt out of a landscape that was prodigious with leaf and blossom. Spring had come and gone unnoticed. It was summer: the bleak winter of Yeomans and Bradshaw was past. I longed to hear music. After my privileged, cultured life in London, this was a parched existence. There was the Piers Plowman Club in Malvern where you could listen to recitals on gramophone records. It was there that I repaired each week. How quaint it seems now. Rows of people sitting on upright wooden chairs looking at a loudspeaker on a stage.

Beethoven's 'Pastoral' Symphony occupied the first half of one programme. As it followed its sublime path, seeming to rise like sap out of the earth of these very hills, I became aware of not one, but two girls sitting, one to my right, the other two rows ahead. The one in front was dark and slender. She could feel my eyes and half turned to reveal exactly the features I had divined from her back. I felt a shock of recognition. In some deep, dark place I knew that I knew her. I also felt a pull towards the blonde on my right. I assessed her in my peripheral vision. She was two seats away and I was well within range of her sexual aura. The passage of the music exquisitely suspended the need to make a choice between these alluring possibilities.

At the interval we were offered coffee and biscuits and there was the explosive chatter that follows enforced silence. Everybody smoked in those days. I edged towards the dark girl, an exploratory excursion. She smoked intently, wholly involved in the cigarette. She seemed fragile, hugging herself as though warding off the cold in that stifling room. She was both intensely familiar and deeply mysterious. She met my eyes for a moment, searchingly, as though I might have the answer to some urgent question. In that instant I saw a whole life spread out with her – passionate, musical, Mediterranean, melancholic, childless. Then she turned away as though warding off a blow. I felt the hand of fate on my shoulder, but whether it was impelling me forward into that imagined life or holding me back, I could not tell.

At that moment the sightline that joined us was fractured by the other girl as she stepped up with her friend to claim cups of coffee. It was a study in contrasts. Her blonde hair was swept up from one side into a roll. Her green eyes flashed the room, resting on me for a quick appraisal before skipping on to the next candidate. She laughed, open-mouthed, rat-a-tat. She wore a bright red woollen jacket over a white blouse tucked into a wide black elasticated belt. I took in the slender waist, the flared skirt not quite concealing the slightly heavy thighs. She said something in German to her friend, who stole a look at me. They asked me where I was from. They knew the camp. They were nurses at the TB Hospital, St Wulstan's. I glanced past them at the dark girl. She was watching us. When I looked back again she was gone. When we took our seats for the second half of the concert the dark girl's chair was vacant. I felt a sense of loss and desolation.

At the end of the concert, the blonde and her friend had to run to catch their bus. I asked if I could call her. She said the number of the nurses' hostel was pinned up in the officers' mess. I said I was not an officer. She suggested the phone book, but the look she gave me was not discouraging.

It was the summer solstice of 1952. We met in a pub. She came from a farm in the north of Germany, had answered an ad for TB nurses. No one wanted to do the job in Britain because the disease was so infectious. I told her something of myself, showed off about my broadcasting, but it meant little to her. Her name was Christel. She was twenty-six. I was nineteen. She had a vibrant vitality; her skin glowed with it, her eyes burned with it. She was like an electrical charge searching for an earth. She had a brittle, rather forced sense of humour, but her foreignness was arousingly exotic. I was captivated.

I walked back to the camp as the restless midsummer sun broke the horizon and my heart leapt up to meet it. I took a short cut across the cricket pitch I was to play on a few hours hence. It was silvered by a heavy dew. I lay down on it and watched the last of the stars fade from the sky.

The next day I was arrested, confined to quarters pending court-martial proceedings. I had been assigned the task of lecturing to soldiers who were to be posted to the theatre of war in Korea. There was a series of three talks. The first was a history and geography of the country; the second was concerned with the war itself, its origins and its progress; the third, something about the customs and everyday life of that remote land.

It was the second that got me into trouble. Having heard it, the son of left-wing Labour MP Ian Mikardo refused to be sent out or to have any part of the conflict, claiming that I had demonstrated it to be an immoral war. I was charged under section something-or-other of the Army Act with 'seducing a soldier from the course of his duty'. The boy's father demanded an inquiry and threatened to raise the issue in Parliament.

Two men from MI6 arrived. They were in dark pinstripe suits but their gravitas suffered when one of them opened his briefcase and a Littlewoods football pools coupon fell out on to the table. Did I have affiliations to the Communist party? No. Was I a member of CND? I was. They demanded my lecture notes. They were horrified. It was clearly seditious. How had I concocted this fabrication about the war? In fact, I had rather lazily cribbed the lectures from cuttings of reports in the London *Times*. Pre-Murdoch, *The Times* was the organ of the Establishment, a model of dry-bones accuracy. Hugh Cudlipp's biography of the paper describes a weekly competition amongst the subeditors as to who could write the dullest headline. One winner was 'Slight earthquake in Peru. Not many hurt'. But the paper's integrity was unquestioned.

I had described how the United Nations emissaries who had been despatched to investigate the dispute over the North/South border had been inept and corrupt. The escalation into war had been avoidable. The Americans were propping up an undemocratic regime in the South. All verbatim from *The Times*.

Was I disingenuous as to the effect those lectures were having? Yes. There was very little anti-war sentiment, but in researching for my talks I had became disgusted with the whole thing. In the name of resisting the spread of Communism, the United States seemed prepared to sacrifice the very principles of democracy that it claimed to defend.

Despite my unimpeachable sources, they were still suspicious. One of them picked up the severed top of a Shepton Mallet letter form, which I had carelessly left on my desk. I lied that Tim had written to me and I was keeping the address heading as a souvenir. In truth, I kept it there to verify to my friends the otherwise unbelievable story about Tim's crazy plan.

The other of the two agents picked up the paperweight, astonished by its weight. 'Uranium,' I said. 'Exhausted, of course.' Tim's riddle hit me like a metaphorical atom bomb. 'It's never exhausted.'

Would his twisted prankster brain go that far? Revenge by radiation? With an involuntary start, I jumped up from my desk and backed away, as though a few feet would make a difference.

They were both now eyeing me warily. How was a member of CND in possession of uranium? I explained how Tim, now in prison, had given it me as a paperweight. It sounded lame. How had he come by it? I explained that he had worked at the Atomic Research Centre at Aldermaston. Their questions became slanted towards my stability, mental and emotional.

However, in the face of the evidence they finally dropped the charges against me. Barrack-room lawyers urged me to demand a court martial to clear my record, which they said would be forever stained with the red or pink pigment of Communist sympathiser. In those paranoid days, such tendencies would exclude one from many possibilities. I decided one court martial was enough. I would take my chances.

I threw the uranium into the River Wye at Tewkesbury and for some years worried about the fish. Not only the fish. I fretted about all the uranium waiting in the tips of weapons, lurking in silos, cruising in submarines, a fearful shadow cast over our lives. Fear of the bomb.

Nuclear war was inevitable. It seemed futile to make plans. I had no thoughts of the future since it was unlikely there would be one. I had carried on seeing Christel. We became dependent on each other. We lived from hour to hour as I ticked off my army days. I suppose it was CND and the Aldermaston marches that kept the horror in mind, but suddenly, and I can put a date to it, at the end of 1959, we stopped worrying about the bomb. Just like that. Nothing had changed in the Cold War. In fact, it was to get worse with the Cuban Missile Crisis, but the cloud had lifted. We stopped worrying, and the sixties arrived and we decided to swing instead.

Return of the Soldier

It was 1953. I persuaded Christel to follow me to London and she took a job in a hospital in Tottenham. I was sucked along by her vitality. She had a strong peasant constitution. Life filled her and overflowed; it was her health I loved. She slept deeply but leapt out of bed as soon as she awoke. She had a boundless appetite for life. She tried to break up with me several times, but I hung on. It was our unborn children that held us together, demanding to be born.

I eked out a living with my writing and broadcasting. I was lost. I saw little chance of making films. Out of desperation, I went back into the dry-cleaning business, but hated it. Wendy and David were lovers. She had taken my place working with him, an arrangement that did not last long. Shortly afterwards, she took a new lover, a Cornish fisherman and boat builder whom she met on holiday in Mevagissey. He was fifteen years her junior. Forty years later they are still happily and devotedly married.

We made a trip to Christel's home in the far north of Germany near the Danish border. Her father farmed rich black loam that had been won from the North Sea by dyking. The motto of the harsh land, in the local dialect, *plat deutsch*, was '*War will net dyken mut wieken*' – 'Who will not dyke must go.' Her father's hectares had been in the family for hundreds of years, but he still paid the dyke tax so that Germany could push the sea back ever further towards England. Her father was a gentle, silent man who loved his land, who came alive weeding his huge white cabbages destined for sauerkraut. His son Janfriech worked with him. Her mother was a volatile, dominating woman who could reduce her two grown daughters to tears with the lash of her tongue, but she was loving and generous and a brilliant cook. She had numinous flashes of insight, which Christel inherited; the awkward banalities would suddenly be replaced by a shaft of intuitive wisdom. She had had a lover for thirty years, who still came to the house every afternoon whilst her husband was out in the fields.

Christel always judged the larger world by the yardstick of her small town. Everyone she met in England or America had their archetype in Wesselburen – thus she made sense of the world. I envied her roots. Three generations back and my family was lost in the murk of the industrial revolution. My father's grandfather was a carpenter. My mother's was a coachman. Beyond that, oblivion.

1955: Making News

I trawled film and television for a job, anything, a way in. Commercial television was starting up, and there were openings. I landed a low-key post at Independent Television News, checking the news film that came in and preparing it for viewing by the editors. We were on the eighth floor of the old Air Ministry roof in Kingsway, notorious as the place where London's official temperature was taken and published each day. I found myself plunged into a maelstrom of frenetic activity. We were not yet on the air, dummy bulletins were being prepared each day. It was daring and innovative. Until then there had been only a single BBC channel. The newscasters wore black tie and evening dress to read the news at 9 p.m. They solemnly presented a version of the radio bulletins – without a teleprompt – so we mostly watched the tops of their heads as they read from the papers on their desks. This was followed by a few minutes of semi-topical films, along the lines of the cinema newsreels of the day. All that was about to change.

ITN was led by the dashing Aidan Crawley. The day before transmissions began he called us all down to the newsroom on the ground floor and gave us an eve-of-Agincourt speech. We were about to make history, he said, to wrest power from the politicians and give it to the people. We were crusaders. He filled us with pride and inspiration. But the nerds were among us. The chief electronic engineer posed a technical question, bringing us down to earth with a bump: 'Mr Crawley, do you wish me to relinquish our signal as it leaves this building or retain control until it reaches the Post Office switching centre?' Crawley had absolutely no idea of the technical issues involved. A lesser man might have asked what the implications were. Instead, he made a rousing response: 'When it leaves this building, our job's done!' How we cheered.

The newscasters were the Olympic runner Chris Chatterway and Robin Day, who startled the nation with his spotted bow ties. Chatterway smoked and drank beer, and as far as I could see, the only training he did for the 1956 Melbourne Olympics was to run up the eight flights of stairs instead of taking the lift. He got a bronze medal just the same. They quickly became celebrities. The bulletins got sharper and better. They were hard-hitting and irreverent.

The first big news story to test ITN's resources was Russia's brutal crushing of the Hungarian uprising. Performing my humble task of organising all the incoming film and putting it up in the theatre for viewing, I saw over and over again shots of Hungarian youths throwing Molotov cocktails at Russian tanks. It was one of those iconic images that stirs the heart. I watched hours of rushes. There was so much more than could ever be shown. I was immersed in it each day. I felt I was living it.

Many years later, when I was making *Deliverance*, I hired the great Hungarian cameraman, Vilmos Zsigmond. He was a film student at the time of the uprising. He and a friend, Laszlo Kovacs, grabbed a camera, took it into the streets and filmed the battle of Budapest. With the film cans under their arms, with bullets flying around their heads, they struck out for the Austrian border. It was the first footage to come out of Hungary. It was they who brought out the images of youths confronting Russian tanks. Vilmos and Lazlo were besieged by the world's media. How much did they want for their film? All they wanted was to be allowed to go to America and become cameramen. Promises were made. And broken. They finally got lowly jobs in a film laboratory in New York. Vilmos told me that when they got across the border into Austria the first thing they wanted to do was drink Coca-Cola. They went into a café. One bottle was all they could afford. It was brought to their table. They stared at it with reverence. The Holy Grail. The very essence of America. Ceremoniously, they tasted it. Vilmos spat it out, disgusted. 'It tasted like medicine,' he told me with a wry grin, 'but when you live in America you learn to like it. Now I drink it all the time.'

How cowed were our leaders, how impotent we felt, how implacable Russian power appeared. Worse was to come. We surrendered the moral high ground with the absurd invasion of Suez. The Egyptians had taken control of their own canal. As a dying gesture of imperial Britain, Anthony Eden, the Prime Minister, a parody of the feeble Englishman, decided something should be done – but what? He hesitated, vacillated, changed his mind, and finally acted too late. The invasion was an inept disaster. Eden crumbled under pressure. They shipped him out to New Zealand, as far away as possible, where he could do no more harm. I remember his press conference. Only a fragment of it was transmitted but I watched the whole thing. He was politely deranged. As he left for the plane he said, 'God speed you all.' We were silenced by the line. After all, we were staying. He was the one going.

The ITN cameramen and editors had mostly come from the cinema newsreels which were going into terminal decline because of the immediacy of television. Brian Lewis, an exception, had been editing features. We were all intoxicated by the new opportunities. Reporters and cameramen were sent into the streets to question ordinary people about the issues of the day. It was Brian who devised the technique, which came to be known as 'vox pop'. He instructed the reporters to put the same question or questions to each person. The cameraman was told to frame matching close-ups, some looking camera left and others camera right, the size and position in the frame always the same. Brian then edited out the questions and cut the answers together, alternating left and right directions. This had a tremendous dynamic: it gave the illusion that people spoke directly to each other. The technique became widespread so quickly that it is difficult to convey the impact it had at the time. We had leapt over the stuffy newsreader, cut out the intervention of the reporter and found a new democracy of faces. People like us were on television, giving our views; the medium had broken free of the elite, the Establishment.

Oddly, the true origins of this breakthrough lay in radio. The advent of audio tape led to sophisticated editing. Denis Mitchell made a number of poetic radio essays where fragments of voices, sound effects and music were woven together to give an impressionistic account of a place, a community. He later transposed his methods to television. *Morning in the Streets* was his magnificent vision of Manchester. Ordinary people spoke out, but often their voices were there for atmosphere, for texture; they were not central to the message as they were in Brian's programmes. But Mitchell had an enormous influence on me and others, Brian included. I also revered the work of Humphrey Jennings. He had used ordinary people to convincing dramatic effect in his wartime films *Fires Were Started* and *Diary for Timothy*. I was drawn to this style of poetic documentary and would later practise it in my own work.

Apart from Brian's refinements we were witnessing a new primitivism as fragments of life were wrenched from the street and thrown on to our screens. The rawness was exhilarating, but there were diminishing returns. Brian's ideas became common currency, but without his technical control it all looked crude. At ITN there soon developed a conflict between the reporters and journalists on the one hand, and the cameraman and editors on the other. It was an unequal struggle and the word won out over the picture. The journalists wrested the power away from us. ITN's ratings soared, and in response, the BBC devised the *Tonight* programme, which played during the early evenings each weekday.

The editor was the quixotic Donald Baverstock, and the format was built around the personalities of the reporters and presenters – following the success of the ITN newscasters in becoming national figures, friends of the populace. The *Tonight* men went off across the world finding stories in every nook and cranny. It was fresh and witty, but firmly based on the cult of journalistic personalities. *Panorama*, *This Week* and *World in Action* also tackled subjects journalistically; there seemed no place for the more personal, impressionistic documentary, which required much more careful structuring and editing.

I could see that the cutting-edge work was being done by Brian Lewis. I campaigned to become his assistant. I had read Karel Reisz's book *Film Editing* and every other textbook I could find. But watching the way Brian could cut on movement to conceal cuts, juxtapose two streams of action – as D. W. Griffith had pioneered in *Intolerance* – and overlap speech and picture, was a revelation. My humble tasks were to wind up trims, keep the cutting room clean and join the shots together. I sat at the Bell and Howell joiner, scraping off the emulsion, painting on acetate cement and fusing them together with pressurised heat. I got happily high from the acetate fumes. But I was able to watch Brian at work. He was small, neat and compact, shy and inarticulate, but behind his thick rimless glasses his eyes were ferocious with intent. He saw himself as an artisan, an NCO, but I recognised an artist. I got him interested in film history and theory and made him aware of his place in it. I took him to the National Film Theatre. I drenched him in Bergman and Fellini and Kurosawa.

ITN started *Roving Report*, a weekly half-hour film in which a reporter and cameraman brought back impressions of some part of the world that was currently in the news. Brian was appointed the film editor. It was journalism tempered by a little of the more imaginative documentary style that we espoused. The attempt to marry topicality with technical sophistication meant that we had to work into the small hours on the three days before transmission. I would seldom get home before dawn. Brian devised a clever system that allowed us to make opticals electronically. Our rivals were stunned. Film that had been shot only two or three days before – even some of it on the day of transmission – was presented with mixed soundtracks, opticals and titles. No one could figure out how it was done.

Only Brian, and to a lesser extent I, knew how it all worked, which led to some jealousy from the other editors who wanted their turn on the prestigious documentaries, but could not master the system. Brian and I, having tasted this heady wine, could not contemplate going back to cutting news items for the bulletins. It was time to move on. Commercial television, which began in London, was spreading out into the regions. There were lots of jobs. Southern Television was starting up in Southampton; Brian took a job as a director/editor.

I had become obsessively absorbed in this learning and working, pleased to have film in my hands at last. I felt I was starting out on a journey. Christel found she was pregnant, and after a bit of soul-searching we decided to marry and have the child. A hurried ceremony was arranged. My mother's sisters and my sisters were the only guests. We signed up at the City of London Registrar's Office and ate cold-meat salad as a wedding breakfast at the Plough. Christel wore black. My sister Angela's Italian boyfriend lent us his car and our honeymoon was a Saturday night at the hotel on Eel Pie Island on the Thames. A pounding dance band beat incessantly on the floor of our bedroom, a metaphor for the sound and fury of the marriage to come.

We set up home in the attic of a pub, the Baptist's Head, near Smithfield market, with furniture fashioned from orange boxes. Our one indulgence was the purchase of a rubber Dunlopillo mattress. Our window looked down on to the cobbled street where hundreds of condemned men had been led to the nearby gallows for public execution.

On our first night in that place I had a nightmare, of a special variety that has always plagued me, one in which I dream that I wake up, making the subsequent events even more terrifying, because I believe myself to be awake. On this occasion I dreamt that I woke up with a feeling of intense anxiety, convinced there was some dread thing outside. I looked out of the window. Coiled on the wet cobbles below was a large python. It was moving towards the Baptist's Head. I ripped up the orange-box furniture and nailed the timbers to the window, so that the room was impregnable. Feeling completely secure I climbed back into bed and fell asleep. I awoke screaming with terror. The snake was in the bed. I clutched it with all my might. Christel cried out in pain. I was gripping her thigh.

In the mornings I would walk through Smithfield market on my way to work, past the bummarees carrying sides of beef on their backs, and marvelled at the mountain of animal flesh consumed each day by Londoners. During the night, Underground freight trains brought the animals in for slaughter, the daily Somme of the animal world. A month after our marriage Christel miscarried. Our haste proved unnecessary.

Commercial television had been bitterly opposed by those who saw it as part of the insidious Americanisation of Britain. The Act of Parliament called upon the companies that were awarded the licences to balance their entertainment shows with documentaries and cultural programmes. Commercials could only be shown in 'natural breaks'. The press, particularly the sections that had been excluded from franchises or were too morally lofty to apply, monitored it closely for aberrations. The *Manchester Guardian* appointed a scathing young writer, Bernard Levin, as its television critic. He lambasted the offerings mercilessly, particularly those of ATV and its flamboyant boss, Lew Grade. One of Levin's early pieces was headed 'Incessant Cataract of Drivel'. Lew's background was vaudeville and his main contribution to the new channel was a variety show, *Sunday Night at the London Palladium*, with a game show as its centrepiece. Stung by this virulent criticism, Lew decided to demonstrate his commitment to culture by putting on *Hamlet*. It was Peter Brook's production of Paul Scofield's Dane and was to be broadcast live, direct from the stage of the theatre, as an outside broadcast. This relieved Lew of the expense of mounting his own production. He wound up the publicity machine: a martyr to art, he was sacrificing a whole evening of peak viewing to this play. Did he identify with Hamlet in some way? Certainly not his indecision. Lew had never had a doubt in his life. I was watching at home. *Hamlet* was overrunning. The landlines that linked outside broadcasts to the network were controlled by the Post Office. Halfway through the duelling scene, an engineer in the switching centre, working by the clock, threw the switch that cued the commercials. Hamlet and Laertes were hard at it. 'A touch, a touch, I do confess' was followed by a shot of a frying pan full of sausages, accompanied by the rich voice of Alexander Gauge lauding 'Walls' sizzling sausages'.

Lew, watching at home, was enraged. His ploy had backfired in the worst possible way. This was what Levin and company had been waiting for with sharpened knives. Lew phoned ATV: 'Put me through to whoever's responsible for this outrage.' He was eventually connected to the humble Post Office engineer. 'This is Lew Grade here. What happened to *Hamlet*?' he demanded. 'Oh, he dies, sir,' was the reply.

I used to see Lew in the lift sometimes and breathed his cigar smoke.

Based on this minimal acquaintance, he later came to see me as his pro-
tégé and claimed some credit for my movie career. When he started
financing movies he approached me as a long-lost son with a script about
Dr Livingstone in Africa. It was intriguing, but needed a lot of work and
research before I could get to the point of knowing if it was makeable, or
whether I wanted to make it.

Lew would have none of my doubts and reservations. We were lunching
at his office suite together with the writer and a couple of Lew's executives.
'How much do you want to make it?' he said. 'A quarter of a million?'

'Lew, please,' I protested.

'All right, make it $350,000.'

'I don't know if it *can* be done, even if I did want to do it.' Lew bellowed out for his chequebook. He made out a cheque to me for half a
million dollars and signed it. He handed it to me. I refused to take it. He
got up from his chair and tried to stuff it into my jacket pocket. I fended
him off and we sparred for a moment, when with a deft movement he
stuffed it between my backside and the chair. I tried to ignore it, but I felt
at a distinct disadvantage from then on with half a million dollars of
Lew's money sticking up my arse.

He refused to talk about the project itself, the story, the script, the
casting – these were details for writers and directors to take care of.

'Let me tell you how I work, John. I don't want to read the script –
haven't the time. I don't see rushes. Don't show me a rough cut.' He
waved away such a trifle. 'You make it. You have final cut.'

I felt if I let him go on any longer, my silence would be construed as
agreement. I made a feeble attempt to interrupt. I reached out a protest-
ing hand. He thrust into it a cigar that looked like a cruise missile.

'I know what you're going to say, John. Other studios have given you
final cut, right?'

I nodded assent.

'But nobody has gone as far as I'll go.' He paused. We hung on his
words. How could he improve on final cut? 'I don't even want to see the
picture when it's finished!'

It all came to nothing, but he became a friend. He was irresistible. He
chain-smoked those huge cigars. He took no exercise. He ate nothing but
meat and potatoes. He was always in robust health and lived to a great
age.

Although I nursed secret dreams of directing movies, I was content to
be a film editor. I had acquired a skill. It was something I could do well.

Even when I took the leap into the freelance world to make my first movie as a director, I felt secure that if it didn't work out I could always go back to editing. It was already ambitious enough to aspire to the level Brian had reached. At the back of my mind was the fear that I was not worthy of such advancement.

The advent of ITV, besides jolting the BBC out of its worthy smugness, heralded the television era. The two competing channels became the daily cultural diet of the nation. Ordinary people felt more comfortable with ITV, its agenda was understood – to entertain and make money – and they liked the commercials which were funny and ingratiating and featured ordinary families like themselves, or like the people they aspired to be. The BBC was suspect, an instrument of the ruling class. They might be trying to educate us and improve us – eat up your greens – whereas ITV knew what we liked: straight to the treacle tart and ice cream.

Ironically, it was BBC programmes like *Tonight* that were constantly digging and probing at the Establishment. *That Was The Week That Was* would emerge out of the developing ethos of the Baverstock young lions, to scourge authority, and contribute to what we thought of as the revolutionary sixties.

1957: Southern Television

After only eighteen months as an assistant, I followed Brian to Southern Television. I, too, was elevated to the lofty status of director/editor. So Christel and I moved south and rented part of an old rambling Victorian house in Emery Down, buried deep in the beeches and oaks of the New Forest. There was a mulberry tree in the garden and we slung a hammock beneath it. The rich ripe fruit fell into it and scarred it like bullet holes in a body. One night we were woken by a nightingale singing outside our open window. I had never heard a nightingale's song, but like falling in love, you know it when you hear it. In the winter the New Forest ponies posed motionless, with snow on their backs.

It was here that our daughters were born within a year of each other. How early the die is cast! Telsche was full of grace, comic, reckless and athletic yet fragile, coming from a deep past, otherworldly. Katrine was a mimic, an entertainer, joyful and fearful. Through them I was able to reenter the magical garden of childhood and was licensed to be silly and frivolous.

In the lodge at the bottom of the garden lived a couple with a mentally handicapped son, Jimmy, he who was to point an accusatory finger at Father Maguire. He was eighteen, large and obese, and trapped for ever in his childhood. He played with cotton reels tied to lengths of string, which he swung in furious circles. Now and then he would release one and send it flying unerringly at an object or person or to entangle it around our telephone wires. He wandered where he wished and was tolerated. It was unnerving at first to look up and see him staring in at a window. Sometimes that accusing finger would pick out a particular person and he would let out an agonised cry. If it was me, I would flinch, half convinced that he had some special insight, that he could look into my heart and see the sin and corruption. I wanted to make a documentary about Jimmy, showing how he linked the people of the village, how he became a conscience, a warning, a reminder of our frailties, but Southern Television and later the BBC both recoiled at the idea.

I bought a red Heinkel bubble car and drove into Southampton each day. I was sent out to shoot short film sequences for studio programmes, sport, farming, current affairs. Brian did the more substantial pieces and I got the lighter, more frivolous items. We directed, then brought back the film and edited it ourselves.

My friend Barrie finally came to terms with his limited ability as a musician, and I got him a job as my assistant. I taught him all I had so recently learned from Brian. He astonished Brian by extrapolating a complete intellectual theory of film editing from his few weeks with us. He eventually went on to teach editing at the National Film School. Film schools have superseded the apprenticeship system, which had existed since film began. Cameramen and editors learned by assisting and working their way up. I like the notion that each cameraman stood in a direct line to Billy Bitzer, who shot D. W. Griffith's movies. Oddly, most film school graduates seem to reject the rules and grammar of film that we apprentices have cherished and preserved. They are more influenced by the anarchy of pop videos and commercials, perhaps reacting against the theorising of teachers like Barrie. Stanley Kubrick said to me once that film theory can be learned in three days, but in practice we grope blindly from mistake to mistake.

There was a religious epilogue each night before closedown, and I was sent from church to chapel, from presbytery to monastery to film priests of several denominations dispensing spiritual guidance to our viewers. Beautiful churches but scant belief, the priests were mostly versions of Sheppard Smith, dry and boring, strangers to God, going through empty rituals like sleepwalkers. There was but one who convinced, a strange young High Anglican, clearly homosexual. He spoke directly to fears and anxieties in a soft, intimate voice: 'I want to speak to those who fear the demons of the night, those who lie awake grieving for a lost loved one, who wait despairingly for the dawn . . .' The Anglicans were horrified by him. He was banished.

My short films, inventive and probably flashy, caught the eye of the bosses, Roy Rich and Berkeley Smith. I was always bombarding them with programme ideas, and one day they hauled me in and invited me to take over their ailing flagship programme, *Southern Affairs*. I countered by suggesting that I produce a daily programme. Why did I think I was qualified for such an ambitious enterprise, they wanted to know. I was only twenty-five years old. I pointed out that I had already been a journalist, broadcaster, soldier, businessman, film editor, film director, husband and father. I said Irving Thalberg had run MGM when he was even younger than me. They asked me for a proposal and a budget. I produced all that and they accepted. I called the programme *Day by Day*. It ran forty minutes a day, five days a week. I also took on the weekly half-hour programme: I was responsible for producing nearly four hours of television a week. I had fifty people working for me, including my mentor, Brian Lewis.

I had been almost killed by bombs, come close to drowning, lost everything to fire, but now, for the first time, I experienced real terror. Each day I faced yawning gaps that had to be filled. I worked night and day. I began to have anxiety attacks. I had to walk or run before going to bed, since I could only sleep when physically exhausted. I would wake up unable to breathe. Our nights were broken by the baby's screams. During the day I carried smelling salts to overcome fainting fits. Why had I wanted this? I hated the executive responsibilities. All I ever wanted to do was make films, write, and pursue my own vision, walk in the footsteps of Humphrey Jennings and Denis Mitchell.

It was, nevertheless, thrilling to be on this roller coaster. I wanted the programme to be something other than an animated newspaper. I devised a mix of impressionist films about places and people, satire, music, exploration of character. We transmitted each day between 6.15

and 7 p.m. The regions put out their local programmes early or late in the evenings, fulfilling their statutory obligations and leaving the peak viewing hours free to take the network diet of *Coronation Street*, quiz games, comedy shows and the occasional drama.

Day by Day became so popular that its ratings crept up to the level achieved in peak hours. The people who ran Southern Television and sold the advertising could not easily accept that a so-called 'balancing' programme could attract an audience comparable to an 'entertainment' programme, so they concluded that there must have been a demographic shift of viewing habits and that peak viewing had somehow shunted back an hour. They proposed to take off *Day by Day* and put on light entertainment in its place. Ray and Berkeley narrowly headed off that move. Lew Grade made a famous remark. When asked how he defined a programme suitable for peak-viewing hours, he said, 'A peak-viewing programme is any programme I put on during peak-viewing hours.' He was already gaining a reputation as a British Sam Goldwyn, although it was another ITV mogul who coined the phrase, 'Any TV franchise is a licence to print money.'

The show had its own momentum and my team and I were dragged along by it, or we dragged it along. Sometimes we flew, other times it was like walking in chains. One Friday, a hard-nosed reporter from Brighton called me with a story about an oil painting of the Virgin Mary which was shedding tears. He had witnessed it himself along with others. The picture had been discovered in a shed in a working-class district. It was pointless to film it. Everyone knew that the camera could lie. If it really was a miracle, it had to be broadcast live. In those days the outside-broadcast unit consisted of several large trucks and a crew of twenty. It was expensive to mobilise and arrange the transmission of the signals. I called my bosses for permission. They were all absent. I took it upon myself. The unit made the journey from Southampton to Brighton and got set up just in time for the programme. I had a camera fixed on the painting for the entire forty-five minutes. On the soundtrack we heard witnesses describing the weeping they had seen, but the camera never wavered from the painting. There were no tears of course, but the audience was mesmerised. Needless to say, thousands swore they saw the virgin weep. The audience rating was huge.

Shortly after, I was in dire need of a miracle myself. One Sunday in Emery Down when my darling Telsche was eleven months old and her sister-to-be was eight months in the womb, I heard a cry from the garden.

It was a deep animal howl, inhuman yet all too human. I ran outside. Christel held the lifeless wet form of Telsche in her arms. I felt for a pulse, a heartbeat. There was none. She was cold and white. Weed hung from her mouth. Christel had found her face down in the ornamental pond. With all the force of my will, with every fibre of my being, I cried out to the life-force, to the gods of my two lapsed religions, to my guardian angels, to the ones I loved who had died before me, to bring her back, to take me in her stead. A page of print flashed before my mind's eye. Dozens of stories and proposals crossed my desk each day. This one I had glanced at, but not read. It seemed worthy but unexciting. It occupied my eye for no more than twenty seconds. It was explaining a new method of resuscitation: mouth-to-mouth, hitherto unknown. Somehow I retrieved that page from my memory and was able to examine it as I had not done at the time. I absorbed the illustrated text in a microsecond. I blew into her mouth. And again. After five or six times, she spluttered back to life. The doctor arrived and examined her. She was fine. Subsequent checks showed no ill effects. Dr Darby, our GP, wrote up the case in the *Lancet*. It appears that babies have the ability to trap oxygen in the brain if the heart stops, a mechanism that can sustain life during birthing if the lungs do not immediately function.

F. Scott Fitzgerald describes in 'The Crack-Up' how a traumatic event breaks something in us, how a crack appears in our spirit meaning that we are never again quite whole. I was broken that day. Yet something else happened too. As Telsche got older, a bond grew between us. It was as if I had gutted myself and given her a part of me, perhaps the best of me. As a child, I too had come close to drowning. We had both escaped death by water. She was drawn to water ever after and both of us often experienced the temptation to swim out to sea and never turn back; both of us had the same sense of being temporary visitors to earth and air from watery places; and we shared a wisdom of the ways of oceans and the flow of rivers. For thirty-seven years she dispensed profligate love and light and laughter on all those, worthy or not, who came within her orbit, and when she died of ovarian cancer, the world darkened and diminished, and so did I. And sometimes still my little mermaid calls to me, but her voice is drowned out by the wintry waves that roar on the rocks, and my life founders too.

During Telsche's illness, I wrote a script, *Halfway House*, which is about memory. A man, whose wife commits suicide without apparent reason, has a recurring dream in which he visits a sort of clearing house

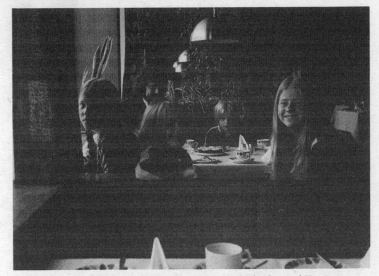

Telsche (on right) with the twins, Daisy and Charley, and Katrine

where people go when they die. They are given a videotape of their entire lives and before they can move on, they must edit it down to three hours of highlights. The result must be entertaining enough to absorb their fellow dead, who hang around waiting for the next good video to engage their jaded attention. I wrote it before and during Telsche's fatal illness. While it is concerned with memories and the past, it also proved prophetic. Somehow, either from the genes I gave her, or from the conduct of her life, or my life, or blind chance, her life was taken by ovarian cancer – an attack on the very source of life. All that is left of Telsche, all that I have of her, are memories. I make an effort each day to retrieve them, dust them off, shine them up, but she fades – the shadows claim you, my darling. Despite the story I wrote, which implies an afterlife, I cannot muster any such belief myself. Only when I address the past like this does it live, and the hosts of the forgotten rise up and walk fitfully on the page. Perhaps art is the only door into an afterlife – or is art the governance of memory, the afterlife itself? We cling to the notion of a heaven or even of reincarnation, because without it, the present surely holds cruel dominion, as each moment is snatched away from us and consigned to oblivion.

One treasured moment with Telsche: we went up to my tennis court to play. It was an autumn day, the leaves turning, but there was not a breath of wind to stir them. There is a lovely birch next to the court. It has a Japanese shape, twisted but harmonious. For some reason we were both drawn to gaze upon it, and at that very moment it suddenly shuddered in the embrace of a secret breeze, and a shower of leaves fell about it like confetti. The theologian, Martin Buber, suggests in *I and Thou* that God exists in the space between two people as they share a revealing moment.

1961: A Barbarian at the Gates

There were many defections from the BBC to commercial television. I was one of the very first to go the other way. BBC Bristol covered the South and West Country, and lost its comfortable monopoly to Southern Television. *Day by Day* stole away its viewers in droves. Desmond Hawkins, founder of the admirable Natural History Unit, and latterly programme controller, made discreet overtures. Would I take over their regional programmes? They had a gentle and bucolic weekly programme, *View*, fronted by a likeable Cornishman, Tom Salmon. I said I was interested in making film documentaries, that I had had enough of magazine programmes. Yes, you can do that, but first please take over our faltering show. I wanted to escape the treadmill of daily TV and the stress of the conflicting demands of work and family. I agreed.

Although I was assured it was a fix, I had to go through BBC procedure and attend an appointment board. I found I was one of several candidates. Desmond was among the six examiners. As they questioned me, not only about my production methods and ideas, but also about my ethics, my personal beliefs, my knowledge of the West Country, I detected distinct hostility from several members – not only from their questions, but also from facial expressions ranging from disdain to contempt. At that time, a BBC producer was like a university don. He did as much or as little work as he pleased. No one was fired. Everything was arranged in a gentlemanly way. I had expected to be greeted as a saviour, a white knight, come to rescue them from their antiquated ideas, but it was clear that they saw me as the barbarian at the gates. I was sitting across from them, separated by a highly polished table. I could see their upside-down heads in its surface. I leaned forward to make a point, placed my hot sweaty hands on the table and an arc of condensation radiated out from them. My judges watched aghast as this mist moved towards them, like a virus, obliterating their reflections. It came from the man who was to desecrate their sanctuary.

I arrived in Bristol on 1 January 1961. I was shown an office and assigned a production secretary and a production assistant, Michael Croucher. No one spoke to me. What films did they have in the works? What stories were being worked on? There was nothing. The cupboard was bare. I had to start from scratch. I struggled to get facilities, film units, budgets. I had exchanged the rough and tumble of ITV for a remote and snobbish BBC. I was a pariah. Their systems were arcane and bureaucratic. I fell foul of the administration. They dragged their feet when I sought facilities. At my first monthly programme board, where producers assessed each other's work, someone handed me a note in Greek. An assumption? Or a test? I commuted back to the New Forest at weekends. It was a miserable, lonely time as, once again, I had to crank up a programme. I got the existing show back on the air, following its old magazine format but with a little more bite. I eventually persuaded Desmond to allow me to transform the slot into single-subject films. With access to two production assistants and two film editors, I set out to make a thirty-minute film each week. We filmed a school, a department store, an orphanage, the factory making Concorde and many more. I became more and more interested in stories of ordinary people in their settings, and I was developing techniques to express the truth of their lives – following, of course, in Denis Mitchell's resounding footsteps.

I fell in love with the romantic symmetry of Bristol's Georgian terraces and crescents and yearned to live there, but they were well beyond my means, and eventually I settled for a newly built semi-detached house in Keynsham, an indeterminate town between Bristol and Bath. I took a mortgage, something I had sworn never to do, but I was a married man with two children living on a salary with no capital. I had sunk back into the semi-suburbs my mother so despised. It felt like a defeat: the suburban boy was back where he belonged. However, Christel's ability to create a home in her own image, to sweep away the conventions of suburban life, and her brilliant cooking, made it bearable. It made us feel like bohemian people passing through, rather than permanent residents.

BBC Bristol may have been a bastion of privilege and entrenched attitudes, but the country was in turmoil as the sixties began to swing. Change and novelty were the gods of the age. The BBC in London was painfully reassessing itself in the face of competition. Donald Baverstock of the *Tonight* programme had emerged as the head of television and was imposing his journalistic principles in the arena of documentary. The only refuge of imaginative film-making was Huw Wheldon's *Monitor*, where the work of Ken Russell, John Schlesinger and others, celebrating writers, composers and painters, seemed to elevate us: to suggest that we, mere TV hacks, could aspire to such heights. Particularly potent was the fusion of image and music that Russell achieved. If all art aspires to the condition of music, then we all began to hitch our pictures to crotchets in the hope of being artists. Huw's *Monitor* exuded both a reverence and an excitement for art. I wanted to be a part of it.

Tony Jay and Alastair Milne, alumni of *Tonight*, forged the theories of the Baverstock regime. They decided that production staff should be organised in groups of what they called mares and stallions. The stallion was the leader and instigator, and around him clustered a group of mares – directors and assistants who would execute the work. The implication was that the mares would love or fear the stallions and thus be motivated. As I built my team producing weekly half-hour films, Baverstock saw me as a potential stallion. My programmes were only transmitted regionally, but we felt we were breaking new ground. I was now being encouraged to submit ideas for the network. Was our tremendous excitement shared by the passive viewer, or was it the hubris of youth? I recall the let-down when I stepped into the street after a transmission of one of my films, to see all the people milling around who had not seen it, would never now see it (a single showing was the norm), and worst of all were carelessly indifferent.

Something to remember of those times. All our films were in black and white. Colour television was some way off, so we were luckily still trafficking in a contiguous monochrome world. It was familiar reality transposed into a parallel universe. It was *us* as *other*, and therefore more revealing. Colour takes us both closer to reality and further away from it. When people talk of realism in TV and film, they are talking nonsense. Reality is what we live, film is metaphor. I always tell young directors that they should hang over their desks a reproduction of Magritte's painting of a pipe under which he wrote 'this is not a pipe'. Although we were probing the lives of ordinary people, extending Brian Lewis's innovations, I tried to do it with style and imagination, with juxtapositions, so that it transcended the 'people to people' idea. I always probed the gap between what people said and what they did, or between what they said and the way they said it. I found that if you let the camera or tape recorder run after they finished their answer there would arise in them, in the potent silence, a Quaker-like compulsion to confess. It was as though the nation waited upon them and they felt obliged to own up, to tell all, in the promise of immortality.

What I was observing, at that time, was a significant shift in society, a revolutionary itch, and I wanted to explore it. The films we were making often challenged traditional views. I proposed to the network a series of filmed documentaries, which I called *Citizen 63*. Baverstock hated the idea. The lives that I proposed to study were of scant interest: why should ten million people spend half an hour watching a fifteen-year-old pupil in a secondary modern school. That is five million hours, sixteen lifetimes, he admonished. I began to feel ashamed as Donald worked himself up like a Welsh hellfire preacher, and launched into a diatribe that encompassed his theories of television. Potential documentaries should be judged on journalistic principles, on the importance of the story. Then, with a bewildering switch, he urged me to think about puppeteering. He saw it as a perfect TV form: 'Rod, string and glove,' he chanted. We thought he had lost his mind. Years later he was vindicated by the Muppets.

Finally, and reluctantly, he took my series. He was under pressure from the regions, and I had gained sufficient reputation that if he kept blocking my submissions, I would move on.

My first subject was a fifteen-year-old girl from a secondary modern school in Portsmouth, the very example I had pitched to Baverstock. I believed that the engine for change was the 1947 Education Act which set up the secondary modern schools. It broke the rigid pattern of the past, which divided children at the age of eleven into grammar or technical schools. The new schools taught music and art and the humanities and the first generation coming out of those schools was now engaging with society. The surge of pop music in the sixties was directly attributable to the teaching of music in secondary modern schools. I had already seen the force of this when one of my regional films had been bumped by teenage demand in favour of the first television appearance of a new group, The Beatles.

I scoured the schools, looking for a subject and for a school sympathetic to the idea. The headmistress in Portsmouth was a perceptive

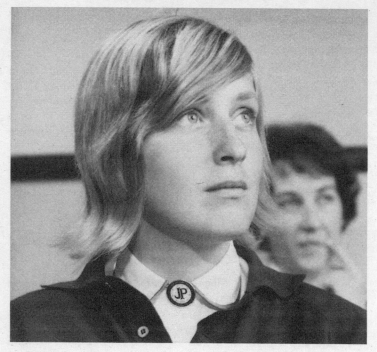

Marian Knight

woman. She suggested several girls, none of whom appealed to me. Just as I was leaving empty-handed, she hesitantly mentioned Marian Knight. She said this child was rebellious, had been adopted by an elderly couple, fervent members of the Salvation Army, but had qualities of leadership and grace. She thought the experience might help her self-esteem. I met her and she took me into her circle of friends. They thought of themselves as beatniks, a faint echo of the Beat Generation. Yet they were more interesting than the mods and rockers who were then emerging in all their decorative banality. Marian's group were bonded by their rejection of society: a normal, healthy reaction. These pushed the idea a little further – they held that by opting out of consumerism they could be free. A sleeping bag was all they needed. The emergence of the birth-control pill completed their liberation. Marijuana was the ritual, the religious surrogate. They played guitars and recorders. They made music all the time, but despised anything recorded.

It is hard to convey how shocking all this was to the nation. There was an outcry. Yet Marian was so honest and she argued her position so cogently that there was sympathy for her too. I felt at the time that we were on the verge of a social revolution, that people like Marian would finally overthrow our class-ridden, tradition-mired country and drag it into the modern world. I was not the first to underestimate the Establishment's capacity for disarming dissidents by embracing them, heaping spurious honours upon them, inviting them to their clubs and stately homes.

Two hundred years before, William Godwin had captivated radical opinion with his theory that man is essentially good and it is institutions that corrupt him. He understood that for change to be effective, the solutions needed to be radical and to start at the top. He proposed the dissolution of the monarchy and the aristocracy, the dismantling of organised religion and the end of that source of all servitude, marriage. The French Revolution erupted and gave impetus to his ideas. He and his allies came close to pulling it off until the Establishment closed ranks. They whipped up chauvinistic hatred of all things French. Godwin was reviled as a Froggie-lover, and the great moment was lost.

The 1947 Education Act, daring as it was, lacked real revolutionary conviction. The great tragedy of our time is that it did not go far enough, it did not abolish the public schools. If all children shared the same schooling, we might have achieved something, instead of what we have today, an antiquated society incapable of responding to changing conditions and still locked in a system of class and privileges. Ireland, for all its faults, is free of this.

I next tackled a Jewish businessman from Brighton, Barry Langford. He came from a family of silver dealers and dabbled in the pop-music scene as a promoter and manager. He was a gambler and a philanderer. He was also a show-off, and in his reckless need to exhibit his cleverness, he showed himself to be a shallow, predatory creature, exploiting others for his own ends. He was amusing and his frankness disarming. He was a harbinger of the consumer greed to come. Another subject was Dr Frank George, whose field was cybernetics. His predictions of artificial intelligence and a world run by computers were laughed at as fanciful. All these 'ordinary' people I had chosen seemed bizarre and outlandish to many of the audience. I was constantly asked how I found these people. 'He doesn't find them,' said Huw, 'he recognises them.'

Citizen 63 was widely praised in the press and internally admired within the BBC. It was often described as *cinéma-vérité*, but although I used some of the techniques associated with that genre – hidden cameras, etc. – most of my work was contrived with the collaboration of the subject. I would spend hours interviewing them on tape, selecting those fragments I felt were revealing. I would then film the life, the environment, the home, the workplace, and then, contrapuntally, set word against picture, pointing up contradictions and harmonies.

The series had a disproportionate impact, in part because the Baverstock current affairs and documentary regime had excluded this kind of impressionistic, sometimes poetic, approach. There was also shock when viewers discovered how much attitudes were changing.

Baverstock had become more dictatorial and ideological. He refused so many programme proposals that the BBC was running short of material. Huw Wheldon took over the documentary department and challenged Baverstock's ideas. He took me under his wing, asked me to take over *Monitor*, that jewel I had admired for so long. I was too intimidated. Wheldon was an inspirational figure and a brilliant raconteur. He fronted *Monitor* with great élan. He chatted as an equal with Henry Moore and Orson Welles. I always felt tongue-tied in front of Huw. I had a dream one night that he had (painlessly) extracted all my teeth and my gums were frozen.

Once again I was being offered an executive post, when all I wanted was to make my own films. I had an irrational fear of authority, which probably sprang from my insecurity. I felt I did not belong at the BBC – was made to feel that or imagined it so. It made me a snob, always trying to prove that I was better read and better bred than I was. Wheldon's approach to his director/producers was subtly different from Baverstock's. He said that most television programmes were repetitious and required steady hands. They were the daily bread and sustenance of the medium. But you also needed events. To make those, you needed stars. The star would have a free hand, more time and resources to experiment, to amaze from time to time, to make fireworks, to ring bells. I was duly anointed to this elite. Huw was wildly prejudiced. If he took against you, nothing you did would please him, but he nurtured his stars – Ken Russell, John Schlesinger, Humphrey Burton, David Jones. I was to join them.

I still had my weekly films to make for BBC Bristol, but Wheldon tried to lure me to London. Again, I resisted. I could manipulate and control a film, and by dint of working harder than those with more talent, I believed I could achieve good work. Working in a region, expectations were lower. I was afraid of rising higher, I felt undeserving. I believed my limitations would be exposed. Yet when it came to making a film, I was confident, in command, often reckless. Film was a refuge. It was home ground. With all the attention I was getting, I vacillated wildly between humility and hubris. Some years later, Fred Zinnemann told me that, although shy and uncertain in life, he was confident and commanding when making a movie.

BBC2 was due to open. It was to be daring and experimental. I was asked to do a documentary series for the inauguration of the new channel. I was already tiring of the character studies I had pioneered. They began to seem shallow. It was frustrating to be excluded from the intimate aspects of those lives. So much that was interesting occurred behind closed doors, where my camera was significantly absent. I wanted to open those doors.

I had become acquainted with a young couple, Alison and Anthony Smith, who lived in a tiny corner flat at the very top of a house in a Georgian crescent in Bristol, a kind of triangular eyrie that stood dizzily above the docks and city. He was a journalist, she had recently graduated from Bristol University. He was not unlike me: lower middle class, London suburbs, cricket-lover. I began to spend time with them, exploring their world, their attitudes and ideas. They were starting out in life. She was pregnant, which was why they had married so precipitously. I began to formulate an approach that would cut deeper and connect more to their social setting than my previous work. My idea was to make six half-hour films about them during the last three months of her pregnancy. Each film would be in a different style. I took Wheldon to meet them and he approved right away. His idea for a title was *Mr and Mrs Smith* – much better than mine: *The Newcomers* – but at the time I thought it too prosaic for the noble thing I was to make.

The first episode was an impressionistic account of their relationship with the city. He saw it as a journalist – West Indian quarter, the docks, the nightlife. She was more threatened, sensed the crime and violence that might lie in wait for her unborn child. She played the spinet: its delicate, tentative chords provided the music for the series, a John Dowland piece which expressed her own fragility. She was twenty-one. Anthony's best friend was a fellow journalist and aspiring writer, Tom Stoppard. He featured in the series, a Byronic presence. Even when he was destitute, he had an air that suggested that wealth and fame awaited him, and that he would greet them with grace and panache. Another film dealt with their fantasies: he playing cricket for England, she being a flamenco dancer. It was concerned with the things they loved – Sinatra, Hemingway, the icons of the day. Lyn Chadwick was a fashionable sculptor; his bronze figures – stalkers – were prominently displayed in the great museums of the world, though the one that loomed over the lobby of the Museum of Modern Art in New York disappeared as his reputation declined. Is there a museum of unfashionable art somewhere where curators send their mistakes? Anthony admired him, so we took the cameras to his home in Gloucestershire, near Stroud.

Chadwick lived in a decaying mansion. There were big empty rooms for his figures. There were several women in attendance and it gradually emerged that they were all ex-lovers, present lovers or potential lovers. An American woman doing the cooking told me how she had visited Chadwick with her husband. When she got back to New York she got a letter from Lyn which included a first-class ticket to England. Come whenever you feel like it, he said. Chadwick was interested in seducing women away from their men. His most famous coup was at the wedding of an artist friend, when he left the reception with the bride. The American woman told me how she was offended by the offer and stuffed the ticket into a drawer. One day after a row with her husband, she took it out and looked at it. It gradually became a secret escape hatch. If things got bad, she had an 'out'. One day in a fit of pique she jumped on a plane and threw herself into Chadwick's arms. Except that his arms were rather full at the time. She was stuck and yet obsessed with the artist. She could not bring herself to leave. She was doing the cooking.

Chadwick ignored Anthony and me and was soon deep in intimate conversation with the hugely pregnant Alison. Anthony did not seem to mind, but I felt an irrational jealousy. A couple of days later I recounted this adventure at a dinner party at the playwright Peter Nichols' house. Another playwright, Charles Wood, and his wife were there, as well as the Smiths. What is the secret of Chadwick's success with women, I asked rhetorically. Thelma Nichols, serving the meal, said she could enlighten us. She had been one of Chadwick's women. His method was simple. He would latch on to the physical characteristic that the woman was ashamed of – a too large nose, heavy thighs – in Thelma's case she had always hated her round stomach. Chadwick was entranced by her belly, wanted to sculpt it, to gaze upon it, stroke it. He would talk of nothing else. It rendered her helpless, utterly without resistance. Thelma said there was a lot of touching and talking, three or more in his sculpted bathtub and bed, very little lovemaking. Peter's face was twisted in pain as she told her story. 'Thelma's fucked half the men in Bristol,' he blurted out. 'My wife fucked the other half,' said Charles Wood.

The third film was taken up entirely by a party the Smiths gave for their friends, which included Nichols, Wood and Stoppard. The camera stayed until the last guest left. It recorded the drunken banalities, the flirtations, the way people drifted from one group to another, the obsessive repetitions, the shifting moods, the littered aftermath. Apart from some introductions by Anthony, there were no further interpretations. My intention was to make the viewer a member of the party.

At that time my films were transmitted without being seen by a superior. I had qualms, however, about this one – I asked Wheldon what the BBC's policy was about showing people rolling spliffs and smoking marijuana. Huw said, 'Let me explain how the BBC works. If you decide, for good reasons, to show these scenes, and they pass without comment, then the BBC will have formulated a policy. If, however, there is an outcry, then you will be chided, and the BBC will form the contrary policy. So do whatever you think fit.' I showed it. England was so innocent then. People thought they were rolling cigarettes.

The final film began as Alison left for the hospital with contractions and ended with the birth. In between I had a number of cameras out recording the events in the city of Bristol during those few hours – the births, the deaths, a man retiring from the aircraft factory after a lifetime, accidents, celebrations – a snapshot of a metropolis. I filmed the birth while Anthony paced their tiny flat, two steps back and two steps forth.

Alison and Anthony had married rather hurriedly, her pregnancy the spur. There was a curious distance between them. He treated her with a certain formality and she felt trapped by her pregnancy.

Wheldon hated the film dealing with their fantasies. The audience was confused by the switching styles. The Smiths seemed too self-aware and in some areas too guarded. He was a little glib and she reticent. But it was a pertinent study of their world, of people in the arts and journalism, the feeling of a provincial city. It lacked the emotional punch of *Citizen 63*, even though I shot and transmitted the films during Alison's third trimester and the audience was eager to learn about the baby or babies – twin girls, as it turned out.

I had entered their lives and unravelled them, yet Alison remained elusive. I was half in love with her from the beginning. She was uncannily like the dark girl in the Piers Plowman Club who had slipped away in the interval. Ever since that occasion, I had been always watching out for her, imagining glimpses of her in crowds, and here at last she had taken tangible form. Alison seemed to belong to the other side of things. She was at home in Southern Europe rather than the Nordic flatlands. Her language was French, not German. We shared a love of medieval music. As I write, I can see her long fingers touching the wooden keys of her spinet. I had her trust. She depended on me. When the series was transmitted she felt exposed, betrayed. She blamed Anthony rather than me. Ours had been that ultimate modern relationship – the probing tape recorder and camera. It was more intimate than her marriage. And, of course, it was abruptly truncated. I had experienced this syndrome before. Marian Knight became very dependent on Christel and me after her film. She and her friends would land on our doorstep. One of them arrived one night having walked from Portsmouth to Bristol, sustained only by periodic injections of heroin. I began to question the ethics of probing lives like this.

Alison and I had lunch once a week or so in the aftermath and danced around the flame. I convinced myself it was my responsibility to counsel and console her. We agreed that as long as we did not make love, we were not betraying our marriages. We held hands and wallowed in the exquisite agony of denial. We were at a party one night in a rambling Clifton house. It was late. I was drunk. Somehow she and I were sitting on a sofa together in a room, empty but for us. She and Anthony were leaving the next day for Dubrovnik. She offered me her mouth. We kissed. It was a joining and a parting. We belonged together and we could never be together. I looked up from the kiss. Anthony was standing in the doorway. He turned on his heel. The next day he left a note for me. It said, 'You are a shit.' He was right.

Years later I was invited back to Bristol by a producer who was making a programme about my work at the BBC. He used excerpts from my films and filmed me revisiting the places and people. Anthony had written a novel which drew heavily on our venture. Predictably, I came off badly in that. The twin girls were now twenty-one, the age Alison had been when we made the films. We all had dinner together. Alison and Anthony had been living separately for many years but were on friendly terms. They had had a further child, a son, a promising cricketer, to

Anthony's delight. I drove Alison home. We sat in the car and held hands, and it was as before. We felt as close as then. She had just gone to live with a man of seventy (she was forty-two) who had left his wife for her. She said she had Madame Bovary's disease. Was this all my fault? 'No,' she said, 'I had a roving eye before you came along.' Our ways had drawn us far apart. We exchanged life stories, but our passion had been preserved in denial. We indulged in the sweet melancholy of contemplating another life that we might have lived.

Christel was deeply intuitive. She understood my work was involving me with women in a way that she could not object to, yet was threatened by. She was ever alert and could recognise a woman I would find attractive often before I was aware of her myself.

When we locked a film, we would go to the BBC club and have a beer. John Merritt was my favoured editor, a morose horn player. One night the celebrations went on late. I arrived home in the early hours and when I woke up with a hangover, Christel was singing and dusting the house with a fur hat she had found in my car. It belonged to my secretary. I was innocent, but she rightly sensed a deeper guilt. My involvement with Alison had made me aware of other possibilities. Our combustible marriage was exhausting. We argued a lot in public, more than we did in private. When others were present we knew the rows could not go too far. We would bicker, but not go to the root of things. A friend described our marriage as a continuation of the Second World War by other means.

We moved into Bristol, a town house in Cotham. Telsche and Katrine were four and three. So close in age, they were devoted to each other. They started attending a Montessori school nearby, run by Christine Stair. Through her, I got to know her husband, Bill. Tall and gangling, a small bespectacled head perched on a collection of long uncoordinated limbs, he was a walking neurosis. An artist who taught art, he found the daily round unendurable. He reeled from imagined insults and slights. He was teaching at a comprehensive school. He became persuaded that the headmaster, his fellow teachers, his wife and his parents were all conspiring to have him committed to an asylum. He conceived a plan to thwart them. He took the bus to the mental hospital and presented himself at the door. He told them he was giving himself up, that he knew they were all trying to get him inside so here he was: 'Take me.' When they refused him entry, he was shattered. The imagined conspiracy had become the sustaining centre of his life, and without it to struggle against, he collapsed into a mental condition that *did* seem to warrant his family and colleagues committing him. When they attempted to do so, it reaffirmed his conspiracy theory and he quickly recovered his shaky equilibrium.

He had an original and brilliant mind that ran riot, a wild thing that he could not master. His stories were of his own ineptitude, his losing battle with inanimate objects that lay in wait for him, plotting his destruction. He had theories to explain the mysteries of the universe. Human life began, he speculated, when a spaceship carrying people intended for another planet made a forced landing on Earth. These people had been programmed for a place with less gravity and more oxygen, which is why we struggle with leaden limbs and get out of breath.

I tried to get him to perform these anecdotes on television. They were delirious flights of fantasy, untameable free associations, but we managed to hone several of them into a repeatable shape. When he was threatened or intimidated, Bill's mind froze. He was terrified of going in front of the camera. To assuage those fears I arranged to record them in a tiny one-camera studio with only myself and one cameraman present. I introduced Bill to the cameraman, who happened to be the son of Friese Greene, the inventor of the video camera. That was too much for Bill. He felt that he was on trial, that his performance had to justify the invention of this device to the son of the man who had made it. He seized up. We recorded one or two but they were stilted and strained.

I was never able to capture Bill's antic spirit, but I enlisted his help in my next film. As Wheldon moved inexorably up through the hierarchy of the BBC, his acolytes were sucked up in his wake. Humphrey Burton, a stalwart of *Monitor*, was now in charge of arts and music programmes. He invited me to make a film for his department.

I made *The Quarry*, the story of an imaginary sculptor. I decided to do it as a drama combined with some documentary elements. It was steeped in the Arthurian legend – I called the artist, with a nudge, Arthur King. The film opened with a block of stone being craned into the derelict ballroom of an old house (drawing on the Chadwick experience) and it chronicled Arthur's attempts to carve it, whilst struggling with his demons. I had made a documentary on the Isle of Portland and become fascinated with the textures and properties of limestone. I had explored Glastonbury and we had made a documentary about some of the people living there. Did they fall under the influence of its mystery? We discovered a Rabelaisian underbelly, little of which we could include in the documentary – wife-swapping and orgies. One prominent burgher showed me his snuffbox. In it he kept a pubic hair from each of his conquests. I asked him, wonderingly, how he managed to collect them. 'You usually get one stuck in your teeth,' he explained. I had also made a film in an art school and became friendly with an unscrupulous sculptor who taught there. I drew on all this material for *The Quarry*. I was already reaching out for the ultimate movie that would be about *everything*!

Arthur had a powerful wife and a compliant mistress. His struggles to find an image in the stone had him ruminating on the past. Bill Stair became my art expert. I had a scene where Arthur tells the story of art from cave paintings to Francis Bacon, illustrated by art-gallery postcards – the history of art in two minutes. Bill wrote that and it was the best thing in the film. There were brutal knock-down scenes between Arthur and his wife. They were the scenes Christel and I had not yet dared to play in life.

The ideas were undigested, and the film was under-dramatised and tried to do too much. I overreached myself. Arthur King's doubts were my own. Did I have something to say? The skill to express it? John Franklin Robyns played Arthur. Sheila Allen his wife. She got the picture at a glance and based her character on Christel.

The Grail legend hung over me, demanded my attention. *The Quarry* showed a modern wasteland, Arthur King's quest was for a Grail within the stone, an image of harmony that would reconcile the conflicting forces within his psyche. The fictional story was interlaced with the textures of contemporary Bristol society.

Despite its shortcomings the film was admired and I got a call from a producer, David Deutsch. He had just made a very hip movie with Clive Donner, *Nothing But the Best*. Did I have a subject I wanted to do for the cinema? I told David of my fascination with Glastonbury and the Grail legend. I suggested a contemporary version of John Cowper Powys's *A Glastonbury Romance*. There would be a pageant, and the film would slip back and forth between the myth and present reality. He was intrigued, and we made a trip to the location and climbed the tor where, legend has it, Joseph of Arimathea planted Christ's crown of thorns. Certainly there is a gnarled tree on the top of the hill which blooms every Christmas. A spray of blossoms is cut from it each year and placed on the Queen's breakfast plate on Christmas morning.

I began to write in earnest. I struggled to find an architecture for it. It became complex and hard to resolve. I could not control the characters. They would not come to life, yet they had enough reality to insist on going their own ways. I began to feel helpless among them. I was writing at night whilst still producing a thirty-minute film each week.

Of all the archetypes in the legend, the one that interested me most was Merlin; magician and trickster, he is the link between the pagan and Christian worlds, yet a deeply divided man, half-man, half-god, born of a Virgin and the devil. He is rather like a contemporary artist trying to make magic in a materialistic world. I had the Merlin figure arrive in Glastonbury to sell the idea of reviving an Easter Pageant that would draw tourists and make money for the town. The citizens were sucked in through vanity or greed or fear or desperation. This, of course, was long before the Glastonbury Festival was dreamed of. I was alarmed at the way the script sprawled. It was rather like the films Robert Altman would later make, with disparate characters connected by an event.

David Deutsch was tremendously encouraging, yet kept sending me gentle warning signals about the difficulties of getting such a film made. David conformed to the stereotype – Jewish, smoked Havana cigars – but in other respects he was the antithesis of a film producer: he was kind and thoughtful, an intelligent adviser, and a great supporter of his directors. How he spoilt me!

Curiously enough, his wife Claire had been married to Raymond Stross, whom I had met so disastrously during the making of *Tall Headlines*. David now worked for Anglo Amalgamated, which was Nat Cohen's film company. Nat was chronically inarticulate, particularly when he was angry or perplexed. He relied on David to supply the missing words. He had read our script. David and I awaited his response.

'It's too, it's too . . .'

'Yes, Nat, it is a little too long,' David offered hopefully.

'No. No. No. It's too . . .'

'Short?'

'No. Too . . . too . . .'

'Intelligent?'

'That's it. Not enough . . .'

'Sex?'

'That's it. And needs more . . .'

'Action?'

'Yes. And more . . .'

'Violence?'

'Now you're talking.'

I was impressed by David's ability to decipher what Nat wanted to say.

'It's not that difficult,' he said. 'Nat's fairly predictable.'

David's father, Oscar Deutsch, had founded the Odeon Circuit. His mother designed the extravagant art deco interiors. When David was at Oxford, Odeon architecture was a byword for bad taste and he kept very quiet about his mother. Later, of course, it became very fashionable, in a nostalgic camp way, and at last he was able to take pride in his family connection.

1965: *Catch Us If You Can*

The first Beatles film had come out and was a big success. Nat Cohen leapt on the bandwagon and sold Warner Brothers on doing a film with the Dave Clark Five. He got a price from Warners for the States that would more than cover the budget, and the rest of the world was his. Would I be interested in making it? David said that to have a feature under my belt would help me to get the Glastonbury film made. The real lure was that I would have carte blanche. As long as Dave and the band were in it, I could make whatever film I wanted. Since the film was already in profit, in a sense, Nat didn't care what the picture was like as long as it cost less than Warners were paying for it. But it had to be done right away, to be shot before the band's next American tour. David offered me a fee of £5,000. My BBC salary then was about £3,000 a year, so £5,000 for a few months' work seemed a fortune.

I asked Desmond Hawkins for leave of absence. He counselled me in his wise old owl manner. His voice was full of cracks and fissures, the words broken like someone speaking on a ship's radio. Apart from founding the Natural History Unit, he was an expert on Thomas Hardy and had had the shortest possible career as a novelist. His first and only novel, *Hawk Among the Sparrows*, was published at the beginning of the Second World War. Before it could be distributed, an incendiary bomb hit the printers and every copy was destroyed. It was never reprinted. He was a friend of T. S. Eliot and had recently been to visit him. He described how the poet was living happily with his second wife, Valerie, who had gradually colonised the flat with her taste, and how he and his books had retreated into a corner. It was as though he was slowly shrinking away to nothing.

Desmond was sceptical about David's offer. He knew that I was writing the Glastonbury script. He said it was a classic switch-sell. Desmond saw me as his successor, but he thought that if I could get this out of my system, encounter the horrors and hazards of the film business, I might be more amenable to settling down in Bristol.

I was still unsure. Could I devise a story that would fit? And of course, I had to meet Dave Clark and discover if we had common ground. I decided to enlist the help of a writer. Charles Wood was busy writing the second Beatles film. I went to another of our circle, Peter Nichols. Charles and Peter were playwrights, writing for television, but with ambitions in the theatre. They had both become full-time writers only recently. Charles had been an illustrator at an advertising house. As he drew all day he would compose scenes in his head, and at 5.30 p.m. when the office closed, he pulled out his typewriter and wrote furiously for an hour, the words pouring on to pages which he never had time to number. When he finally gave up his job he found the habit so ingrained that he would sit around the house all day, see a movie matinee, waiting for 5.30 p.m. when the words would once more jump on to the typewriter. Out of superstition, he continued his practice of not numbering his pages during the daily volcanic eruption of scenes. He wrote a play about the Indian mutiny, *H: Being Monologues in Front of Burning Cities*, for the National Theatre. It was impossibly long, but he received a telegram from Kenneth Tynan, who was the dramaturge, saying that although it was long, it was absolutely perfect. He insisted that not one single word be cut or altered: it would be mounted on the stage of the National exactly as he wrote it. This was thrilling for Charles, except that he subsequently discovered thirty pages that had slipped down behind the typewriter and lodged between table and wall. 'I'm in a dilemma,' he said to us, his friends. 'Tynan thinks it's perfect. If I send him the missing pages it makes him look an idiot. On the other hand, some of the best stuff is in here.'

In the event, he said nothing until a director was assigned, and then he quietly slipped him the extra pages. The director cut the play savagely. It still ran four hours and was a failure. I thought it was masterly. Tynan and I were almost alone in that view. At that time the Lord Chamberlain censored all scripts for the theatre. Charles was always clashing with him, his work being subversive, as all art must be. He wrote three one-act plays for the Royal Court. I travelled up on the train from Bristol to London one morning in his company. 'What do you call the plays?' I asked. 'I'm thinking of calling them *Piss*,' he said. 'Why?' 'Because it is one of the finest words in the language. Simple, onomatopoeic, insulting, essential.' The Lord Chamberlain refused it, as Charles expected. He was ready with the perfect euphemism: *Cockade*. He loved sticking it to the censors.

Peter Nichols was desperately short of money. He just about got by, writing plays for television. I proposed the Dave Clark idea to him. He would also get £5,000. Even so, he was gloomy about the prospect and reluctant to take it on. Nevertheless, he agreed to meet Mr Clark, and we went together to the large suburban house he had recently acquired in North London.

We were immediately depressed by his large, expressionless features and his flat, lugubrious voice. He played his new album for us at a skull-shattering sound level. There were speakers in every room. If you retreated from one, you would back into another. It became unendurable and I fled to the toilet where the door cut the decibels in half and I was able to enjoy a moment's respite. Suddenly, with a roar, the music crashed down on me with full force. I looked up. The whole ceiling of the lavatory was a loudspeaker.

When we arrived, we had some fragments of a story, but in conversation I began to improvise and surprised myself at how interesting it got. A trip across England, a roaming couple, encounters with, well, I wasn't sure yet, but the hypocrisies of the sixties ripped open, laid bare, the lies, the exploitation. Nonsense of that sort. Dave said, 'We want to be stunt-men.' He claimed to have done this work before his musical career took off, though in the event, he was too clumsy and slow to do anything of that nature in the film. I proposed that the band would not be seen play-ing their instruments, that their songs would be on the soundtrack only. They would play characters. Yes, OK, but could they be stuntmen?

Peter and I debated it afterwards. Peter is a cruelly accurate mimic and had Dave's North London accent off right away. By nature deeply pes-simistic, Peter felt it was a hopeless task, much as he needed the money. It was Peter's wife, Thelma, who settled it. She said, 'Peter, it will buy you the time to write your play.' They had had a severely retarded child and Peter wanted to write about it. It became *A Day in the Death of Joe Egg* – a great success, and it owed its existence to Dave Clark.

We sat in a room for three weeks and wrote the script. The Dave Clark Five were stuntmen making a commercial promoting meat. At the time there was an advertising campaign for milk featuring a sprightly girl,

Zoe Newton – 'Drinka pinta milka day' – and we invented a variation on that. 'Meat for Go' was our slogan. I set the commercial in Smithfield market where I had lived. The Meat Girl is manipulated by an Ad Executive (a Merlin surrogate) and she feels trapped. Dave Clark is disgusted with the situation and he and the model run away together. They are pursued across England by the advertising people and encounter a swathe of types from the burgeoning sixties, mostly drawn from my documentary experience. Marian Knight and her friends played beatniks squatting in an abandoned village on the Salisbury Plain that turns out to be an army training ground. (I had seen this place during my military service and stored it for future use.) They meet an elegantly depraved middle-aged couple in Bath (the Glastonbury experience).

They had in mind a haven, an island off the coast of Devon to which they flee. The final disillusionment comes at low tide when it ceases to be an island. Their dreams shattered, the girl goes back to the Ad Man and Dave drives off with the lads.

We drew a portrait of a shallow materialistic society, controlled and manipulated by advertising where youth was a commodity. It was a bleak picture, but expressed as comedy; Peter's pessimism was tempered by his comic gift.

When I arrived for work in Peter's room each morning he was either in deep despair or what I can only describe as manic hysteria. He would start each day by performing a scalding parody of the scene we had written the day before. Sometimes I found he had written a review of the finished film in the style of one of the critics of the day, C. A. Lejeune or Dilys Powell. 'This farrago of inconsequential banalities' was one that stuck in mind.

Thelma would ply us with coffee, tea, home-made biscuits and cakes. Peter's plays were usually about his family and Thelma was more often than not a leading character. He was savage about her, yet each evening he would read her what he had written. Her task was to praise the work, try to lift his gloom, laugh at the jokes which were often at her expense, and puff air into his deflated ego. Years later, Charles Wood, referring to his scripts for the Beatles film and *The Knack*, said, 'You and Peter and me, sitting in Bristol, miles from all those dolly birds, not even a sniff of pot, and there we were, inventing Swinging London.'

I included in the movie what were to become icons of the era: a white E-type Jaguar, the very first Mini-Moke (perfect symbol for the sixties, a toy jeep). Sally Jacobs did the costumes and invented several ideas that

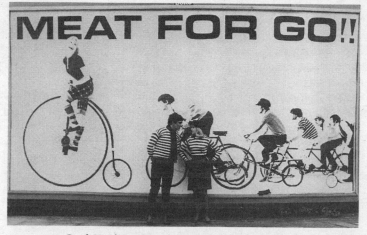

Catch Us If You Can: Dave Clark and Barbara Ferris

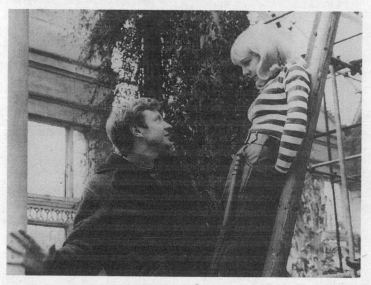

Me, directing Barbara Ferris

became fashionable. She put the girl in rugby jerseys, for instance. Three weeks to write it. Three weeks of pre-production. We called it *Catch Us If You Can*. I wanted Marianne Faithfull to play the girl. She was seventeen, the most exquisite creature imaginable, pale translucent skin, bruised mouth, long blonde hair. She turned me down. I could see why. How could you go from the Stones to the DC5? We cast Barbara Ferris, who had trained as a dancer. David Deutsch helped me put a crew together. It was Tony Woollard's first picture as a designer. David Tringham's first time as a first assistant director. Manny Wynn was an Israeli who had worked with Tony Richardson. It was his first outing as a Director of Photography. He was fat and prickly. He was scornful of my television background. He argued about my choices of camera set-ups. For long periods, he refused to cooperate. 'You work out what you want and when you're ready I'll give you the stop.' He was sure I would have to beg him for help. When I was ready, he would step in with his light meter.

It was the best thing that could have happened to me. The camera was my tool. I had lived with it, day in, day out, for years. I taught myself how to design feature scenes, to break down sequences into set-ups. The choices of where to put the camera are infinite, but I always knew exactly where to place it and how it should move, and if I didn't, I learned it was a sign that something was wrong with the scene itself. Solve the problem and the camera would find its proper place. Many years later, at a party in LA, I was talking with Marty Feldman. He was about to direct his first and only film, *The Last Remake of Beau Geste*. He pressed me into a corner and lectured me about film technique – the use of close-ups, the emotional function of camera movement, the role of pace and rhythm. He had studied the books but knew something essential was lacking. There was panic in one eye, fear in the other, as they took turns in looking at me. 'I've just this one problem. How do you know' – he asked in a whisper, for the young Spielberg and others were in earshot – 'how do you know where to put the camera?'

Inevitably, I was having problems getting a performance from Dave. I cut his dialogue to the bare minimum. I had to play him silent and taciturn. Often this came off as sullen. There was nothing light-hearted about him, nothing youthful, nothing graceful or rhythmical – and he a drummer. I used Barbara to get us through the scenes. This made him resentful. He thought I was favouring her at his expense. Barbara, in turn, was insecure about how she looked. With the right make-up and lighting and the correct angle, she could achieve moments of beauty that real life denied her, but her voice was thin and would not carry emotion. Her face and eyes were expressive of subtle feelings, but she lacked the effervescence, the exuberance that might have coaxed something from Dave. So I had to play her as somehow in thrall to the Ad Executive, and therefore unable to respond to Mr Clark's saturnine presence.

David Deutsch was hopeful and enthusiastic, always laughed in the rushes at the jokes, but my real ally, the one whose opinion I came to depend on for making changes to the script, was David's assistant, Alex Jacobs, husband of our costume designer, Sally Jacobs. He looked not unlike Marty Feldman, the same square Jewish face. He had been a pro cyclist, competed in the Tour de France, and had smashed one side of his face in a bad fall. It had been rebuilt and a glass eye fitted, so that he had a similar disconcerting way of looking yet not looking at you, as Marty had. He was steeped in film and became my passionate advocate and counsellor.

One day, shooting in the snow on the Quantock Hills in Somerset, Dave said something insulting to Alex's wife Sally, one of many jibes. He hated the clothes she made him wear. Alex flew into a rage. It was a terrifying sight. He frothed at the mouth. He smashed his fist into Dave's face. I was entranced by the blood on the snow. It seemed like the end, like a full stop. I stared at it. I felt rather as I had when our house burned down, a kind of relief, a lightness. It was all over.

David Deutsch's reaction was typically gallant. 'I hope Claire didn't see it happen.' I remember thinking, could his wife, Claire, really be this delicate and fastidious when she had been married to Raymond Stross?

For better or worse, after three days, Dave was ready to shoot again. I spent the intervening time filming the other four members of the band and the pursuing Ad Men. Poor Alex was banished. Sally retreated into the shadows, was kept out of the way and functioned through the wardrobe mistress. As neophytes we had been so intoxicated to be making a movie that we could overlook its shortcomings, but now a pall fell across the proceedings. Alex, who had been almost manic in his enthusiasm, was now Olympian in his detachment. 'Sow's ears never really make silk purses,' he said loftily. In a more sober vein we managed to finish the shoot.

Just before the film opened, I gave a press interview in which I said *Catch Us If You Can* was not a great film. The wrath of Wardour Street fell about my head. Nat Cohen was in paroxysms of word-groping rage.

David Deutsch said, 'Don't you know that every film is great before it opens? In fact, great is the very least you can say of it.' But I knew it was not. However brilliantly Peter and I had decorated the surfaces, it had a hollow centre.

A Warners executive appeared to view the film. He was exactly as I expected an American movie mogul to be – small, round, big cigar, loud voice, black silk suit – and for the first time I really felt I was in the movie business. His main mission concerned the European opening of *My Fair Lady*, but he found a couple of spare hours to see our picture. It turned out that the Warner viewing theatre was double-booked. David managed to find an alternative in a Dean Street basement. Halfway through the picture, the lights came up and the projectionist appeared, telling us that he had another booking. David apologised, said he would find another theatre. The Warners man waved this away. He turned to me. 'I get the drift. Just tell me the rest of the story.'

I stood in front of the screen. Foolishly I started to describe the film shot for shot. I pointed at the screen behind me. 'We track across the room. He says, "We have to leave," then she turns away. That's a close-up.' I stumbled on. He stopped me, the harsh voice cutting through the cigar smoke. 'Does he get the girl?' 'Well, not really.' 'What about the bad guy?' 'Er, she goes back to him.' 'The bad guy gets the girl?' The projectionist came in again. 'I've got people waiting.' We filed out into the Soho sunshine. How arrogant I was in the making, how chastened by the outcome.

Four months from the day Peter and I sat down to start writing, the picture opened. It was greeted with kindness by the critics. The only really bad reviews were the ones Peter had written before the picture was made. Although it was sucked along in the wake of the Beatles movie, the young audience was perplexed by its pessimism.

It opened shortly after in the States under the title *Having a Wild Weekend*. Pauline Kael praised it inordinately in *The New Yorker*, which gave it and me a degree of credibility in Hollywood.

I returned to the BBC and my family, remorseful and a little wiser. Not to be outdone by Alison, Christel became pregnant with twins. I joined the Music and Arts department of the BBC. We moved to London, bought a house in Putney, next door to Tony Woollard. How hip we became. We lunched at 235, the 'in' restaurant. We shopped at Bibas for the children's clothes. I gawked in wonder at the miniskirts on the Kings Road. London was swinging dizzily before my eyes.

Wheldon was now the boss of BBC television. He again made me an offer, this time to be controller of BBC2. I was tempted, but still intimidated. He then pressed me to do a series along the lines of *Citizen 63*. His idea was to apply the technique to other countries – France, Ireland and Italy. I said I knew someone who could do it – Brian Lewis. We met for lunch, the three of us. Brian shrunk into his shell, said nothing. Huw regaled us with stories. Never mentioned the project. I was furious with Brian. 'I set you up for this deal and you never said a word. It was embarrassing.' Huw sent for me. 'You're quite right,' he said. 'Excellent choice. He's a leader. Good organiser, insight and not unimaginative.' I was astonished. Once again I marvelled at Wheldon's unfailing instincts. Brian did several series, and they were a great success.

1965: Griffith, Isherwood, Elvis

I had two projects that I wanted to make: a study of D. W. Griffith and a film on Christopher Isherwood. These were not unrelated, because they were both to be meditations on the nature of cinema.

It was in Los Angeles, in a brief span of five years or so, while the First World War raged in Europe, that David Wark Griffith and his cameraman Billy Bitzer invented the entire grammar of the cinema, which remains fundamentally unchanged today, just as the camera invented by the Lumière brothers is essentially, mechanically, the same. It is easy to forget that film is a nineteenth-century technology.

Before Griffith, the camera was set up on a tripod and recorded a play acted out before it. It would then be placed at another location and a further scene performed. These were cut together so the audience became accustomed to these shifts of place, but the shock of the shift was softened by a written title card, so the experience was still close to that of live theatre. Imagine how startling it must have seemed when the camera first shifted its point of view, picking out a close-up of a character and then reversing itself to a close-up of another person. By having one look camera left and the other camera right, Griffith created the illusion that they are looking at each other. These conventions are artificial, but they were soon universally accepted. Even more daringly, Griffith began to move the camera – tracking, panning. The effect of a zoom could even be achieved by vignetting: Bitzer fixed a diaphragm in front of the lens which could close down to isolate one face in a crowd. The Babylon set in *Intolerance* is still the largest ever constructed, and to photograph its vastness they devised the equivalent of a helicopter shot. The camera was fixed to a helium balloon; using guide ropes, it tracked up and back until the whole edifice was revealed.

Since then the all-pervasive camera has probed into every nook and cranny of the globe. It has jumped into bed with beautiful women (and men), revealed the emotion in faces ten feet high, shown us torture and death, real and simulated, even penetrated the organs and fibres of our own bodies. There is nothing we can experience that we have not already seen on camera. Now the computer can manipulate reality, generate its own invented images. David Hockney said to me recently that the computer will kill the cinema, because hitherto we could believe that what we were watching had occurred at some time and place – no more. Now they are fooling us, taking us for a ride, a ride made up of noughts and ones.

When Griffith's *Birth of a Nation* opened in 1914, most films had been no more than twenty minutes long. This was three hours. Film was still thought of as a peep show. Griffith hired a legitimate theatre and a live orchestra, and had men backstage doing sound effects. The result was electrifying. Lillian Gish told me that people ran into the street afterwards and grabbed passers-by to relay the miraculous news of what they had seen. Griffith took his camera across the land. He said, 'I want to photograph the wind on the wheat.'

I decided not just to tell his story, but to extract a portrait of the America of his day from his films. There was only one man to go to for help, the film historian William K. Everson, who lived in New York. I spent days and nights in his Upper West Side apartment watching Griffith's entire extant oeuvre. The only furniture in Bill's living room was a couple of deckchairs and a projector. All other space was occupied by film cans. His two small children, Griffith and Bambi, played on the floor while Bill sat by the projector, adjusting focus and often, with worn copies, coaxing frayed sprocket holes through the gate. He had screened them over and over. He knew the history of every bit-part player. We gradually selected scenes that would eventually make up my documentary, *The Great Director*. Bill's books on the early cinema are some of the most penetrating and copious ever written. Probably only twenty per cent of silent films still exist. Bill saved and salvaged many that would otherwise be lost.

He spent his life with the blinds drawn against the day, only opening them at night. He had that special movie-buff pallor. Some time later he came to visit me in London. We went to the park. The sun was shining. In a reversal of the usual process, bright light made Bill drowsy. He fell asleep on a park bench. I noticed that his fingers were twitching and turning. I drew this to his wife's attention. 'He's projecting a movie,' she explained. 'He's adjusting the focus.' Many years later in 1993 on a memorable cross-desert journey to the Telluride Film Festival led by Tom Luddy, I was delighted to meet up with Bill once more. He had cancer but he bravely ventured out. We stopped in Monument Valley and Bill and I and others saddled up and rode out into John Ford country. How often Bill must have travelled that landscape in the confines of his room. And here at last was the reality, the hard bright light, and Bill did not flinch. It was one of the things he was determined to do before he died. He was a dear and generous man.

After my work with Everson, I went on to LA to meet Christopher Isherwood. I rented a car at the airport and drove down the length of Sunset Boulevard until I came to the Pacific. And there was the promised sunset in the promised land, sitting in its smog-enhanced glory on the flat oily ocean. I stared at it in lonely wonder. No one to tell. LA caught me unawares: the flimsy facades, the absence of architecture, its shape defined only by neon signs and vast hoardings, tangles of power cables looping across the sky – it all looked so insubstantial and temporary. I could find no purchase, no point of reference. I stayed at the Bow and Arrow Motel in Santa Monica. In the Robin Hood Bar I drank beer and listened to the pianist playing 'Blue Moon' and 'Autumn Leaves'. Across the street was a restaurant called The Broken Drum; underneath was inscribed 'You Can't Beat It.'

I went to meet Isherwood at his house perched high up on the Santa Monica Canyon. I met his young lover, Don Bachardy. Although born and raised in the San Fernando Valley, Don had assimilated so completely that he spoke with the same clipped middle-class English accent as Christopher, the same hesitant, constricted vowels. On the phone it was impossible to tell them apart. Of all the couples I met when I first went to LA, theirs was the only marriage that endured. Don was eighteen and Chris fifty when they met. They lived together for thirty years. They were devoted. Don drew or painted portraits during those years and accumulated a vast gallery of writers and movie stars.

On that first encounter, Isherwood took me to dinner on Santa Monica pier and described his life in LA. I could understand his need to escape the prejudice and narrowness of England, exacerbated by his homosexuality. He had followed Aldous Huxley to LA; Huxley, in turn, was seeking enlightenment through peyote and by sitting at the feet of a renowned guru. Isherwood's adventures with his own master are described in *My Guru and His Disciple*. Although the main attraction was that LA was a homosexual haven, Chris loved the lack of structure and the absence of boundaries, even the blandness. He described the comforting Californian habit of amelioration. He had just visited a friend in hospital. The nurse said, 'I'm afraid your friend is not doing too well.' Isherwood asked if he had had a relapse. 'It's a little worse than that. He passed away.'

He and Don became our friends and we saw them on every trip. On one occasion we were invited to a party where the attraction was Tiny Tim, all the rage at the time. 'Tiptoe Through the Tulips' was a huge but unlikely hit. It was the kind of camp that Chris and Don adored. It confirmed their belief that the human condition is essentially foolish. Shelley Winters arrived with her teenage daughter. Shelley had been born into vaudeville, travelling the circuit with her parents and appearing on stage from the age of three. Tiny Tim had all the old songs from the twenties and thirties written out in childish script in school exercise books. Shelley knew the words and they did wonderful duets. When Chris arrived Shelley begged him to convince her daughter that she had met Dylan Thomas. 'Then she'd give me some respect.'

Chris was persuaded to tell the story. He'd got a call from Dylan. He was at LA airport and Chris was the only person he knew in town. Chris drove down and picked him up. Dylan had been invited by UCLA but had arrived several days late. He had been drinking solidly on the plane and refused to go home until he met a female movie star. Chris toured the hotel bars and restaurants until finally he caught sight of Shelley Winters sitting on a bar stool. Dylan was so excited that he lurched towards her and knocked her off her stool, falling heavily on top of her. He was a great bear of a man. The barman leapt over the bar and said, 'Is this man bothering you?' Isherwood said that to her credit she replied, 'Not at all.' 'I didn't know who he was,' said Shelley. 'He sent me poems and, can you believe, I never kept them.'

I regret that I never made the Isherwood film because I felt that his writing had a special connection to the movies. 'I am a camera,' he wrote in *Goodbye to Berlin*, an admission that has consigned him to minor status. For was he not simply recording actual events and characters? Can he really be described as a novelist? After all, he appears in them as a character under his own name. Like a crackle of electricity he seems to jump the terminals, short-circuit the mysterious process by which a great writer subsumes his raw material, passes it through the murky acids and leaden depths of the unconscious before it flows out again at an even voltage on to the page.

When Isherwood said 'I am a camera' I believe he meant that it was impossible for a writer to reflect life in the old way once he and his readers had experienced the cinema. The movies were an overwhelming presence, a refracting glass slid between conscious and unconscious. The reader's view of experience had been fractured, altered out of mind. Isherwood addressed us as fellow moviegoers, fellow fans.

His ironically onanistic writing presaged the cult of celebrity. The Andy Warhol invented by Andy Warhol is based on Isherwood's technique of recreating yourself as a work of art. Stephen Spender said that the young Stephen Spender as depicted in Isherwood's novel, *The Memorial,* is much more like the young Stephen Spender than he ever was himself, just as Hockney's portrait of Chris and Don looks so much more like them than they did themselves. Isherwood seems to have used himself up so completely in his books that I often felt there was nothing left of him in life, that the creature who remained was a fraud, an imposter. 'I am a camera' was the cry of a prophet, the shutter of doom.

Isherwood's first encounter with the film-making process is described in *Prater Violet*, easily the best novel ever written about the subject. It tells of a distinguished director, Friedrich Bergmann, an Austrian Jew, a fugitive from Nazi Germany, who is hired by a British film studio to make a kind of Ruritanian operetta of surpassing banality. They look for a German-speaking English writer to help Bergmann with the script. (It was the girl who inspired Sally Bowles, now returned from Berlin and working as a secretary at the studio, who suggested the impecunious Isherwood. She apparently felt responsible for the author who had reinvented her.)

Isherwood describes how he and Bergmann talk about everything except the matter in hand. Writers and directors know this syndrome well. You can't jump into bed without getting to know each other, so you talk of art and politics and tell each other stories, all of which, you convince yourselves, have a subtle bearing on the script you intend to write.

Somehow it becomes more and more difficult, then impossible, to suggest the bedroom. Starting to write is so intimate, so wrenching. Bergmann finally says, 'And now, the horrible but unavoidable moment has come when we have to talk about this crime we are about to commit; this public outrage, this enormous nuisance, this scandal, this blasphemy . . .' He goes on to teach Isherwood about the process. 'Do you know what film is? The film is an infernal machine. Once it is ignited and set in motion, it revolves with enormous dynamism. It cannot pause. It cannot apologise. It cannot retract anything. It cannot wait for you to understand it. It cannot explain itself. It simply ripens to its inevitable explosion. This explosion we have to prepare, like anarchists, with the utmost ingenuity and malice . . .'

Isherwood realises that what Bergmann needed was not a collaborator, 'but stimulation and sympathy . . . He needed an audience.' Try as they will, they cannot breathe life into their corpse. Bergmann confides to his young helper, 'You know what my wife tells me when I have these difficulties? "Friedrich," she says, "go and write your poems. When I have cooked dinner, I will invent this idiotic story for you. After all, prostitution is women's business."'

In contrast to Bergmann's wisdom and brilliance, Isherwood presents himself in his customary way as silly and venal, but his relationship with Bergmann deepens in the white heat of making the film. He starts out as a pupil, becomes a fellow conspirator, a comrade, and finally a friend. They end up with a profound understanding, yet are conscious of being actors in a drama of their own making. After the end-of-shooting party, they walk home in silence. In a brilliant internal monologue, Isherwood speculates about identity. The whole experience coalesces for him, the movies as metaphor, the possibility of acting versions of himself. Perhaps I might have turned to Bergmann and asked, Who are you? Who am I? What are we doing here? But actors cannot ask such questions during the performance. We had written each other's parts, Christopher's Friedrich, Friedrich's Christopher, and we had to go on playing them as long as we were together . . . the mother's boy, the comic foreigner with the funny accent.

One of the last occasions that we met was at dinner with Don and my daughter Katrine, who is a flamboyant dresser. She wore a hat, a feature of which was a white dove. A springy wire attached it to her hat and gave the impression it was hovering over her head. Chris was spellbound. He gazed at her and it all through dinner, his eyes sparkling, a grin fixed on his face. It perfectly expressed for him how wonderfully ludicrous life was. It was a movie hat that had somehow escaped into real life.

Bachardy drew Isherwood constantly throughout their relationship. During the last months of Chris's life Don painted him every day. Not long after his death, Don showed the paintings to me. It was overwhelming, watching him die day by day. They were unsentimental, brutally frank, yet done with such love that the ugliness of decay achieved a transcendent beauty. It was as though he was trying to restore the reality that had been squandered in those books, trying to fix him, definitively, to prevent him from slipping away. If somehow he could make the perfect drawing, then Isherwood would live for ever. I was moved and haunted by them. Years later, Don is still grieving. Each day he wears some item of Chris's clothing.

I had met Bob Chartoff and Irwin Winkler in Nat Cohen's office in London, and they invited me to look them up at MGM when I was in LA. They were young New York agents handling comedians. As a sideline, they bought English films and sold them to US distributors. They had done business with Nat and their big coup was to sell John Schlesinger's film *Darling* to MGM. This coincided with a witch-hunt in the US press. The major distributors were buying up semi-pornographic films and putting them out on some minor label, thus concealing their involvement. This caused MGM to get panicky about *Darling*, in which Julie Christie had a discreet nude scene. MGM said that if Bob and Irwin could get them out of this deal, they would make them producers at the studio. They happily resold *Darling* to Joe Levine and found themselves in Culver City with an office in the Irving Thalberg building.

But what would they produce? The studio gave them the next Elvis Presley picture. It was being directed by the veteran, Norman Taurog; Elvis's manager, 'Colonel' Tom Parker, controlled everything and was effectively the producer, so Bob and Irwin just got to sit and watch and learn.

They met up with a press agent, Judd Bernard, who also wanted to be a producer. They had a deal but no projects. Judd had scripts coming out of his ears, but no deal. They formed a partnership. The problem that emerged was that Judd's scripts – which he had acquired as free options or with promises to desperate writers – were mostly dross.

I went to visit them. I was in awe, walking into that greatest of all studios. Mack Sennett, Garbo, Gable, Astaire, Louis B. Mayer, Thalberg, had passed through those gates – so had Bob and Irwin and Judd. I was a long way from Rosehill Avenue.

They took me to the set and introduced me to Elvis. His handshake was so limp that his hand felt boneless. We talked movies. He'd seen mine and, of course, the Beatles film, and he said how much he would like to do movies like these. He was shy, embarrassed. He behaved as if I had surprised him in the nude, or had come to confront him about some shameful act. He showed me his touring bus. He was very proud of that. He was quite isolated and subservient to the Colonel, who rode around the stage in a golf cart.

I sat down with the triumvirate and they asked if I had a project. I mentioned the Glastonbury story, but their eyes glazed over. I said I also would like to do a modern noir thriller. They perked up.

I saw more Griffith material, then returned to London where I started on the editing.

1966: *Point Blank*

Judd turned up in London. He had a script called *Very Special People*, a love story set amongst the rich and beautiful. MGM would do it if he could get Julie Christie who – after *Darling*, ironically – was the new hot thing. Judd took a suite at the Hilton at the studio's expense. He was a passionate shopper and he looted Carnaby Street and the Kings Road, usually managing to have the clothes sent to the Hilton and charged to his suite. He felt that MGM would want its producer to be properly attired while he stalked the actress and her agent. He sent me a script based on a Richard Stark (Donald Westlake) pulp novel. It was appalling. He also gave it to Lee Marvin, who was in London shooting *The Dirty Dozen*, and arranged for us to meet. I suggested a modest Italian restaurant in Soho. I was intimidated by Marvin's presence: his height, the huge head, the deep resonant voice. Everything around him seemed diminished – the tables and chairs were too small, the waiters dwarfed. I felt like a miniature creature from another, tinier, planet. He had just won the Academy Award for *Cat Ballou*.

Lee had no interest in small talk. 'What do you think of this piece?' I said it was a collection of clichés. Judd was kicking me under the table.

Lee said, 'I agree. It's a piece of shit. So why are we here?'

'The character, Parker, is interesting,' I said, 'and I like the idea of a man betrayed by his wife and best friend and the futility of his quest for revenge.' I stumbled on, not saying much more than that, and realising as I spoke about it that, once again, it reflected the story of my father and mother and Herbert. Perhaps there was some kind of emotional resonance in my voice that Marvin picked up. He said very little. The conversation turned to *The Dirty Dozen*. Judd did all the talking. He talked about stars, quoted their credits, ridiculed their performances, then cast them in imaginary movies. In wilder and crazier flights of fantasy he costumed them, humiliated them, married them off to unlikely mates. 'If Lee Marvin married Lee Remick her name would be Lee Marvin.' On and on he went: 'the longer they listen to you, the greater the obligation,' he claimed afterwards – although I often felt that Judd dug verbal holes for himself and fell into them.

Lee left as soon as he had eaten. Judd was furious with me. Never demean your material. All you had to do was tell him how great the rewrite would be. I get you in a room with a major star and you blow it.

He made me promise to call Lee and try to retrieve the situation. It took me several days to gather the courage to do so. In the interval I worked on the story. I showed it to Bill Stair. Bill knew everything about comic books and pulp fiction. We explored the character. Bill did some drawings. When I finally called Lee, he invited me for a drink at the flat he was renting. I talked about the character. I suggested that he had been emotionally and physically wounded to a point where he was no longer human. This made him frightening, but also pure, in a certain sense. He was beyond vanity and desire. His only connection with life was through violence, yet he lacked the conviction or cruelty or passion to take pleasure from it, or satisfaction from vengeance. I realised I was painting a bleak picture. Yet Lee was intrigued.

We met several times subsequently. Lee was alone. His marriage was on the rocks. He was involved with Michele Triola, the woman who would later drag him through the courts in the infamous palimony case. She was back in California.

One warm autumn night we talked till the small hours. We drank a lot. Lee began to speak of his war as a Marine fighting the Japanese through the islands of the Pacific. He had killed, been wounded, knew fear, had committed terrible acts. He was afraid that he had lost some essential element of his humanity in that brutal experience. The story, as

I described it to him, touched on something that he dreaded to confront in his own life, yet was drawn to.

At the end of that evening, Lee looked at me in the eye and said, 'I'll do this flick with you, on one condition.'

'What's that?'

He tossed the script out of the open window. It floated down two storeys, opening out, the pages fluttering like wings, until it came to rest in the gutter, a dying bird. It was a defining gesture. His acting was a continuous search for the cinematic metaphor, and this one was so perfect that both he and I were in its thrall. How could we not follow an enterprise so beautifully begun?

Many years later Mel Gibson did a remake of *Point Blank*, called *Payback*. I was asked at a press conference what I thought of it. I replied that although I had not seen it, I had read the script and that it bore a remarkable resemblance to the one Lee had thrown out of the window. I could only surmise that a very young Mel had been passing and picked it up from the gutter.

I called Judd in LA and told him Lee had agreed to do the picture on the condition that I totally rewrite the script. Was he drunk or sober, Judd wanted to know. 'He meant it,' I hedged. Judd spoke to Meyer Mishkin, Lee's pompous little agent, who said, 'When Lee's drunk he'll do anybody's picture.' I was terribly disappointed because it had seemed to me a profoundly serious covenant. A week or two later Lee's work on *The Dirty Dozen* concluded and he returned to LA.

Another call from an incredulous Judd. Lee had told his agent that his next picture would be with me. 'You'd better get over here right away before he changes his mind. But before you get on the plane, go to a shop in Oxford Street. It's called C & A. Talk to Mr Jenkins in the men's department. He has a grey herringbone suit, forty regular, thirty-two-inch waist. Tell him it's for me. I'll pay you back when you get over here.' Judd's vanity betrayed him. It had been many years since his waist was thirty-two inches. He would buy clothes in his manic phase, then try to sell them off to me in the depression that followed. He was a compelling salesman and I almost always succumbed. I would take these suits home and never wear them.

On the strength of Lee's promise, I was innocent enough to resign from the BBC. I had finished my Griffith film, a salute to the father of film, but had yet to start on the Isherwood. I had kept up with Alex Jacobs and we had strong – that is to say, arrogant – views about films and film theory. I asked him to come to LA to write the script with me. It was November 1966.

So I arrived with a stocky ex-cyclist with one eye and a broken nose, the gangling paranoid, Bill Stair, a wife, and four children, including the six-week-old twins. We checked in to the Bel Air Motel where the San Diego Freeway meets Sunset Boulevard, and the children rejoiced in the pool while Bill, Alex and I toiled on the script. We got a draft out in about three weeks. It had problems, many of which never got solved until well into shooting.

Although we were conscious of making a genre picture, we were heavily influenced by Renoir in the fractured structure, and by Pinter in our laconic and oblique dialogue. The script was originally all set in San Francisco. I met Edward G. Robinson in a restaurant the night before I went up there to take a look. He said, 'You'll love it. It looks like it was built by a drugged-out art director.'

I was appalled. The gentle hills, the clapboard Victorian villas in pastel colours – it was all utterly wrong for the bleak, cold picture I had in mind. The colours were particularly problematic. This was the first time I would be shooting in colour, and the story cried out for black and white. I decided to design each scene in a single colour. I would start out in the cold colours, greys and blues, then move through the spectrum as the character warmed up, ending in a sombre red.

San Francisco did not fit this scheme. I decided to shift the body of the action to LA and utilise its empty arid spaces. I gave Bill the task of policing this scheme, coordinating design, costumes and props.

The head of the MGM art department sent a memo to the head of the studio denouncing my plan. He said, 'There is a scene in a green office with green furniture where seven men are present, all wearing green suits, green shirts and green ties. It will be laughed off the screen, if it is releasable at all.'

I argued that each of these greens would respond in different ways to the film emulsion, some veering towards yellow, others to brown. I was anxious to avoid blocks of colour jumping across the screen on cuts. A cut can be disorienting, can jerk the audience out of the movie, if the action does not match or if there is a change in the intensity of light. These are the conventional definitions of the jump-cut, but with the advent of colour, a new kind of jump occurs which is hardly acknowledged. On a reverse cut a red blouse will jump from the left of the screen to the right. The woman wearing it is in the correct position but her red-ness is distracting to the eye. Some colours take longer to decay from the retina than others, so the eye carries those colours across the cut into the following scene. By working with a single colour, this was avoided. It was as close as I could get to monochrome. In the event, I don't think a single critic picked up on it, and there were certainly no complaints – on that score at least.

It was only possible for me to defy the might of the studio because of another remarkable gesture from Lee Marvin. He understood much bet-ter than me how much opposition I would encounter with the film I wanted to make. He called a meeting with the producers, his agent, and the head of the studio. He said, 'My contract gives me script approval, cast approval, and approval of key crew?' They all assured him that was indeed so. He said, 'I defer these approvals to John.'

He stood up, turned on his heel and strode out, allowing no discus-sion. The eyes followed him to the door then turned on me with looks of such resentful hostility that I can see them still. With one stroke he had disarmed my enemies, but also my friends, collaborators and colleagues who might seek to modify, dilute, accrete, compromise, ameliorate my intentions. It was his signal to me to be bold, to stick to my guns. Except, of course, the studio still had the option of not making the movie, and that threat was suddenly upon us.

My script was duly submitted. There was an ominous silence for some days, then I was summoned to the office of the studio head, Bob O'Brien. Bob Chartoff warned me that the MGM executives were bewildered and dismayed by the script. I sat out in the waiting room of destiny; the dilat-ing nostrils of secretaries signalled that they could smell my bitter odour of failure and fear. Men with urgent intent came and went. MGM was engaged in a proxy fight, various interests were vying for control of the Hollywood giant. O'Brien was immersed in all this and had little time to spend supervising productions.

I was summoned at last. I sent urgent messages to my legs to raise me from my seat. As I made the long walk from the door to his desk, my legs forgot the rules of walking. A memory: Orson Welles's comment to Micheál MacLiammóir when making *Othello* – 'You don't know how to walk. You just *act* walking.' I made it without falling over, but the effort left me exhausted. I slumped into a seat.

O'Brien's desk was polished and clear, except for my script, which he lifted and held in both hands as though weighing its merits. 'We want to make a Lee Marvin picture, but what is this? You'd better explain it. It sure as hell makes no sense to me.' He started slapping the script now, corporal punishment. I concentrated all my efforts on getting my mouth to work. 'When he's shot, think of it as though everything that follows is what he imagines in the moment of dying: his unlived life flashes before his eyes.' A mistake.

O'Brien's face reddened. He put the script back on the desk and pummelled it with his fist. Don't hit a script when it's down, I thought. The phone rang. He picked it up. 'I said no calls.' Then a pause. He sat up to attention. 'Put him through . . . David! The dailies are great! Sensational. Hey, it's kind of late for you in Spain. Midnight? Go to bed. Get some rest . . . How many more days do you need? That's with the big crowd, right? How many? Five thousand? . . . Sure, David. Of course, David. If you need it, David, I guess you need it.'

He hung up. He looked off into the distant reaches of his office. Was he mentally calculating the momentous sums he had authorised? Or perhaps dreaming of crowds lining up to see *Dr Zhivago* – a hit that would subsequently save the studio. I sat in respectful silence sensing that I was witnessing a profound and private moment. He looked across at me at last, startled to find a stranger sitting in his office. He had clearly forgotten why I was there and who I was. He stood up as a way of dismissing me. 'Make a good one,' he said.

When *Point Blank* came out David Lean wrote me a generous note praising it. Later I was able to tell him how the picture might not have been made, but for his accidental intervention. I owed him my career.

We rented a house in the Malibu Colony and lived on the beach and put the children in school. They played in the sand with the swarms of kids who lived there then. I submerged myself in the ocean every morning, summer and winter. I swam far out. I left my land life behind. I lost myself in water. I had no weight, no thoughts, no feeling, no self. Some days the waves were huge. The house shook as they pounded the beach. You have to dive under and through them to get beyond the break line. I always felt an emotional cocktail of fear and exhilaration as the waves towered over me. The lure of the water, the need to immerse myself in it, has always been stronger than the fear of drowning, the fear of wishing to drown, the sweet memory of drowning.

When it came, it caught me off guard in a silly lapse, a careless moment. On the beach was a dinghy with a glass-bottomed dome for observing fish. I took the boat out one day and as I was surfing it back in on a monstrous wave, it flipped over and the force of the wave buried it in sand. I arched my back against it, but could not free it. There was a bubble of air caught in the glass dome. I got my face up to it and sucked in a breath. The dome was like a fish-eye lens and I could see the whole beach with my children playing happily just yards away. For all my profound experiences with water, this seemed an ironic way to go – yet curiously appropriate, fool that I was. People were walking past, talking, laughing, lounging, as though they were immortal, careless of life. I used up the last of the air as a large wave crashed on to the boat and broke it free. I took a deep grateful breath of the smoggy air.

We had a start date on Lee, and not enough time, so the writing, designing and casting had to go on simultaneously. The design of a set and the choice of location, for me, have a profound effect on the scenes. I often remake or restructure a scene to fit a location. Sometimes a location seems so right for the movie that I will write a new scene in order to include it.

The production manager was a tough old pro, well into his seventies, Eddie Wohler. He had spent his whole life at MGM and I plagued him with questions about the past. His responses were always made from the perspective of a production manager. He had worked with Mack Sennet. What was he like? He always stood at the gate in the morning to see who was late. Greta Garbo? Very good. She was always on time. The only problem with her was that she had a clause in her contract stating that she did not have to shoot when she was menstruating, and she was quite irregular – made it difficult to schedule her pictures.

Eddie said, 'You tell me what locations you need. The locations department will show you photos and you can choose from them.' I said I didn't know what locations I wanted until I saw them. I'd drive around and look. 'You can't do that. You have to go with the location scout.' I said I wanted to go on my own. A compromise was reached. I would drive my car. The locations group would follow in theirs. Judd wanted to be involved. So he followed in yet another car with a studio driver.

I would stop, get out, look. Then Judd's face would thrust into mine, obscuring the view, giving *his* view. By running a couple of reds, I managed to lose them. They gave up after that.

At the end of the day I would drop in on Lee, find him squinting out at the sunset on the terrace of his one-bed beach house in Malibu. We talked about the scenes I had written that day with Alex. I described how when Walker bursts into the bedroom of his faithless wife, expecting to find her in the arms of his friend, Reese, the bed is empty, unmade, the sheets twisted. I told him I wanted him to shoot the bed. I was nervous of his response. Would it get a bad laugh? It was intended to show his frustration, the emptiness of revenge.

Lee loved the idea. His mind was already searching for the right gesture. He chose to use a Smith and Wesson 45 Magnum, the largest of all handguns, later appropriated by Clint Eastwood for *Dirty Harry*. He decided to exaggerate its recoil so that his arm would be thrust back, as though the gun was kicking back at him, his revenge was turning on him. He had found his metaphor.

Lee's responses were always allusive, oblique. He leapt from metaphor to metaphor, and when he was drinking, the leaps got wider. I would follow him as far as I could, and there was always wisdom there, deep dark thoughts that touched on our enterprise – but beyond a certain level of vodka, he sailed out on his own into deeper waters where no mortal could follow.

The crafty Michele Triola was on hand. She handled him. He needed a keeper. As the binge progressed he would crash from these great spirited heights and land in the gutter, a crude, base creature full of self-contempt who deserved no better than Michele. Lee would warble the Beatles song, changing the words to 'Michelle, you're hell.'

She called me every day. Lee doesn't like this or that actor. Why don't you cast so and so (a friend of hers). Lee's unhappy about that scene. I'll try and talk him round. Lee was both Prospero and Caliban. The ground was always shifting under my feet and here was this cunning woman whispering confusion in my ear.

We went to dinner at Jack's on the Beach – Lee and Michele, Christel and I. Lee was on his best behaviour, then he snapped. It was something I said about the movie, something out of key, an error. It started him on the martinis. He must have had doubts about me, why wouldn't he? He was risking his reputation on this untried Englishman's ability to make a quintessential American movie. It was 2 a.m. before we could prise him out. The restaurant was at the end of the pier. We had arrived together in Lee's Chrysler station wagon. He was staggering, drunk. I begged him to let me drive. 'Fuck you.' He drew back a fist. He had a whole repertoire of violent gestures, many of them cribbed from his hero, Toshiro Mifune. I tried to grab the keys, but he slashed me with his imaginary samurai sword. These were movie blows. They stopped an inch short of your neck or chin.

I snatched the keys and got into the driver's seat, the women in the back. 'Get in, Lee.' Another battle of wills. How could he meekly submit, this warrior, this conqueror? We pleaded with him. He stalked and staggered around the car, raining blows on it. Finally he found a way of saving face. He climbed up and crouched on the roof rack. Despite our entreaties, he would not come down. I decided to drive slowly down the length of the pier, hoping that the cool ocean air might sober him up. I stopped as we got to the public road. I got out. He snarled at me, would not get down. I was at my wits' end. The streets were deserted. I drove slowly down the Pacific Coast Highway towards Malibu. Flashing lights in my rear-view mirror – sirens. I pulled over. The patrolman approached the car, warily loosening his revolver holster. He looked up, then at me. 'Do you know you have Lee Marvin on your roof?'

During the three-day post-binge hangovers, Lee was scornful, spiteful, consumed with self-contempt. The next phase was sobriety. He fell into quietude and stillness. He saw people for what they were, his intelligence and hypersensitivity gave him no respite. He registered all the hypocrisy and common pettiness and pain around him until it became an unbearable burden, and he would start to drink again. The first three drunken days were glorious. He was loose and funny and full of love and he embraced the world and the world hugged him back.

One Saturday morning after a night's drinking in what Lee called a gin-mill, he was carefully driving home down Sunset, concentrating all his residual faculties, and was relieved to turn into the driveway of his house intact. He went to the front door, fumbled for his keys, which he could not find, rang the bell. A woman opened the door. She was a stranger to him. 'What are you doing in my house?' he demanded. 'You sold it to me three months ago,' she replied.

He drove back down Sunset unable to recall his new location. To his great relief he saw someone selling maps of the stars' homes. He stopped and bought one. He searched in vain for his name. He fell asleep for an hour and when he woke up his memory returned.

He paced his drinking on the shoot, confining it to weekends. One Friday, he finished his last shot of the week just before lunch. He was free to hit the juice. He bunkered down in the prop truck with a couple of grips and a stuntman. He could let himself go, knew he would be looked after by the full support system of a film unit. He'd be in the company of regular guys, not producers or actors or journalists – like being back with the Marines in a dug-out.

We were shooting in a house in the Hollywood hills. I had some shots to do with other actors. In the late afternoon, LA was lit by a strange light. Clouds banked up and the city was spread below us, hyper-real, sharply defined, the clarity emphasising the improbability of this place. I said, get Lee. I set up the shot looking out at LA and lined up the composition with a stand-in. Lee had drunk hard and fast as he sometimes did after a long abstinence, vodka straight from the bottle, a fast wipe-out. They came back and told me he was out of it. I coaxed him. 'It's just a reaction shot.' 'No way, baby.' 'Lee, get up!' I yelled it. An order. I got two grips to lift him to his feet and frogmarched him out into the garden. They pulled on his jacket. The grips knelt one each side of him and supported him at the hips. We adjusted the shot so that they were just out of picture, then I stood by the camera so that I was in his correct eye line. 'Lee, look at me. Lee! Can you see me? See me!'

When I printed the shot there were four or five seconds during which his eyes were focused. Those are in the movie.

Towards the end of the picture we flew up to San Francisco to shoot the scenes in Alcatraz. We arrived late at night and had to shoot early the next morning. I was exhausted. When Phil Lathrop, the cameraman, asked me where I wanted the camera, I blanked out. It was like an anxiety dream I used to have during filming, in which I cannot decide what the shot should be, or the camera is jammed and will not pan and follow the actors. I was in that nightmare. Suddenly, Lee was at my elbow. 'You in trouble?' My denial was not very convincing. He walked back to the wardrobe truck and started roaring. I looked across, as did the whole crew. He emerged staggering and fell headlong on the concrete floor. He rolled around hollering and singing.

Eddie Wohler came over to me. 'You can't shoot him in that state.' They poured black coffee into him. With the pressure off, it took me only ten minutes to figure out the shots and break down the scene. I went over and told Lee I was ready. He made an immediate and total recovery and we made the scene and the day.

In one sense *Point Blank* was a study of Marvin, and I saw it as an extension of my documentary work, the studies I had made of individuals. The young Marvin, wounded and wounding, brave and fearful, was always with him. The guilt at surviving the ambush that wiped out his

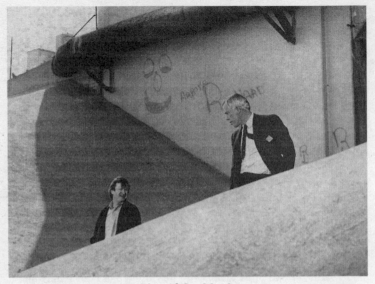

Me, with Lee Marvin

platoon hung to him all his days. He was fascinated by war and violence, yet the revulsion he felt for it was intense, physical, unendurable.

His power derived from this. He should have died, had died, in combat. He held life, particularly his own life, in contempt. Yet he was in possession of a great force that demanded expression. So *Point Blank* starts with a man shot. Lee knew how to play a man back from the dead. Superficially seeking revenge, but more profoundly trying to reconnect with life.

He is the executioner, as he strides through the deserted airport corridor on his way to his errant wife. I intercut this with shots of his wife, Lynne, in the beauty parlour, being metaphorically anointed and embalmed for her death. His suits (a different colour for each scene) were severely tailored to allow no wrinkle or ruck – they were armour. Lee took meticulous pains over costumes. The polished brogues beat a knell on the concrete floor, the rhythm of the reaper. When Lee died, his widow Pam invited me to choose a memento. I took those shoes.

Walker is contained, watchful, the spring is wound. The beat of his stride continues as he waits outside her apartment. He bursts through

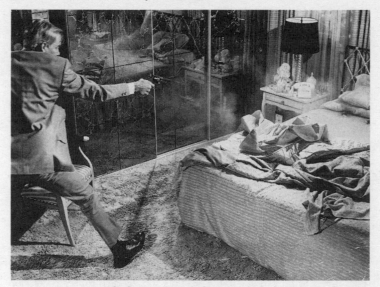

Point Blank: Marvin exploding into the bedroom

the door, grabs her, hand over her mouth, gun in the other, sinks to his knees, drops her to the floor and heads for the bedroom. Lee paced it out. We rehearsed it by numbers. It would be explosive and physically punishing. We wanted to make it work in one take. His grace and power were mesmerising, but he also had a bunch of tricks that he used over and over in his movies. In this case, he enhanced the dynamic by looking left and moving right. The camera operator's cue was exactly that. As Lee snapped his head to the left, he should be ready to pan the opposite way. In the violent speed of the action the operator panned the wrong way. We did it again. Again he missed it. Lee's look left was so intense, it fooled the operator again. Phil Lathrop took over. Phil had been one of the great operators, noted for his work on *Touch of Evil*. He lit his pipe, and made a perfect pan.

This whole sequence is the most ambitious in the movie and exemplifies my collaboration with Lee. On the face of it, it was a standard genre scene. Walker returns, expecting to find Reese, his friend, in his wife's bed. He is not there. Shooting the empty bed is a measure of the hollowness of Walker's revenge. He then questions his wife about how to find Reese.

When we came to rehearse this interrogation, Lee was supposed to ask a number of questions. 'Where's Reese?' 'Who brings the money every month?' etc. After shooting out the bed, with its obvious sexual connotations, we played the following scene with Walker spent, post-coital. He tips out the empty cartridges and the gun flops down. The penis parallel is rather overt, but mitigated by graceful slow motion.

As we rehearsed, the actress, Sharon Acker, getting no questions from Lee, waited, then simply went through her lines. Lee was signalling to me that it was impossible for Walker to start questioning her in his depleted state. We were about to shoot. The set was lit. I quickly rewrote her responses so as to include the questions: 'Reese? I haven't see him. The money? A guy brings it. First of every month.' Lee sat impassively as she answered his unasked questions.

We were driving the story deeper into the mind of this fractured man. Next morning, he finds her dead. The body disappears. The apartment empties of furniture. Later, in the empty room, as he awaits the messenger who will take him to Reese, the lighting echoes that of the cell where Walker was shot. I improvised these scenes and Lee was always ready to take things as far as I wanted. The shots show a disturbing progression into madness.

I was sent for by Bob O'Brien. He had watched these scenes which did not appear in the script. Could I explain them? A man sat in the corner of the room, listening, a psychiatrist. My sanity was in question. How could I possibly say what I really felt – that I made those shots working at the edge, functioning beyond my limits, open to the instant, in unspoken harmony with the actors, in a state of grace, somewhere between terror and ecstasy.

Phil Lathrop had recently shot another movie at MGM – *The Cincinnati Kid*. Sam Peckinpah was the director, but had fallen out with the producers over casting. He wanted to get off the picture, but did not want to resign because he desperately needed the money. If he could get himself fired, they would have to pay up. Sam instructed Phil that as Steve McQueen began the dialogue he should pan down to his feet, or that as Edward G. Robinson dealt the cards, Phil should tilt up to the chandelier. It took several days before they caught on to what he was doing. Norman Jewison took over and it launched his career, while Sam followed his own stony uncompromising path.

If I was heading the same way, into perversity or insanity, they wanted to act quickly. Lee backed me again. He let it be known that he understood exactly what I was doing. They did what they always do: they deferred to the star.

The studio brass announced their intention of visiting the set the next day. I was using the little unblimped Arriflex camera to get the kind of flexible movement that was hard to achieve with the big cumbersome Mitchell. Phil Lathrop gave me good advice. He said I should use the Mitchell for the studio visit. 'If they see all that money disappearing into this tiny camera they are going to get very nervous.' The Mitchell may have reassured them somewhat but they were mystified about the scenes it was recording. I could sense them staring at me and muttering to each other, but the proxy fight weighed heavily on them and they melted away, back to the offices that could be snatched away from them at any moment.

Meanwhile, my relationship with Judd was deteriorating. He interfered, arguing hysterically. Our relationship had become strained by an incident during pre-production. One day I was hauled up before the studio executive in charge of personnel affairs, Frank Davis. An actress had complained to the Screen Actors' Guild that when she came for an audition I had made a pass at her. Since I had spent the previous afternoon in the art department with several witnesses, I was able to assert my innocence. But the girl persisted with her claim that she had come to my office and I had groped her. They brought her in to confront me. She looked me over and said, 'That's not John Boorman.' A little further investigation revealed that it was Judd who had been posing as me. I learned two lessons that day: never trust a producer, and always have someone else present when conducting auditions.

Judd had good qualities. He had a feeling for casting and story, and he had sophisticated taste in cinema, but he thought I was taking the movie down an uncommercial route and he was probably right. He needed this picture to launch his own career. Bob Chartoff, on the other hand, was sympathetic to my vision and was very supportive, as well as diplomatically tempering my excesses.

Judd would remonstrate with me. Why does it have to be so bleak? You need more extras. Why are all the streets deserted? I tried to explain. You're not making an art movie, he screamed. He would finally resort to selling me some items of clothing, or making me promise to read one of his scripts. To sell a pair of pants gave him as much satisfaction as selling a movie to a studio. At the climax of these arguments, Judd would threaten to take over the editing once the picture was shot. 'And remember there is such a thing as a reshoot.'

One of MGM's complaints about the script was that it was too short. The timing department said it came out at seventy-five minutes. The timing department turned out to be a little old lady in a broom cupboard. I went through it with her, giving my timing for the scenes. 'You mean,' she said when I finished, 'there's going to be a lot of leerin' and peerin'.'

It is surprising how many directors go into production without timing their script, or without facing up to the reality of its length. If the first cut is three or four hours, as is often the case, and has to be reduced to two, it means that a third or more of your time and resources have been wasted, and could have been spent more diligently on the scenes that remain. It is much easier to cut and reshape a script than to repair the film in the editing room. Of course, it is good to have some slack. There are always scenes that don't work as well as you hoped, which need to be trimmed or truncated, but in the case of *Point Blank* I was so nervous of how it might be traduced by others that I would stop the camera on a word where I wanted a cut to be. I shot less stock than almost any film in the history of MGM.

As I edited, Judd hovered, demanding to see what I was doing. I kept him at bay by adding to my wardrobe. Meanwhile, he made a deal at Paramount for a Western called *Blue*. Judd's office at MGM was lavishly furnished. He had good, if flamboyant, taste. He had thrown out the institutional MGM standard issue and put in his own things – a fake Louis XIV desk, convincing art deco lamps, pseudo-Persian carpets, good copies of cubist and expressionist paintings. He no longer required the office and offered to sell the contents to MGM for a very reasonable sum. It was impressive, and they agreed to buy it in order to keep it intact for the next important producer. Later they discovered that Judd had furnished it entirely from the MGM prop department.

While he was always amusing, and I enjoyed his wild ravings, I was getting tired of his bullying. I put up with him because I was in his debt for putting me together with Lee Marvin. But finally, I kicked him out of the cutting room and told him to stop plaguing me with his lousy scripts. I finished my cut and was summoned to screen it for the legendary Margaret Booth. She was Louis B. Mayer's editor and had a fierce reputation for savagely re-editing films that she found inadequate. She had her own screening room. I sat down next to her. She was toasting her slippered feet before a small electric fire.

After the screening she made one or two minor, but very good, suggestions. I made these changes and she then showed it to the MGM executives. When the lights went up they were clearly baffled and began mumbling about changes and reshoots. Margaret Booth growled from the back of the room. 'You change one frame of this movie over my dead body.'

I pointed out to Ms Booth that Judd's intention was to do just that. The scandal over his office was discovered at the same time and he was banned from the studio.

I continued the post-production with more peace of mind. It was a relief to be free of Judd, but I missed him too. One day I was walking to the commissary when a car pulled up next to me. A hat pulled low over his face, dark glasses, Judd lowered the window and called me over in a theatrical whisper. 'Give me twenty dollars,' he said. 'What for? Why?' 'Just give me twenty dollars. You won't regret it. Trust me.' 'I don't trust you, Judd. That's the problem.' He held up a grey bundle. 'The best pair of pants you'll ever own. Your size. Give me twenty dollars.' I gave him twenty dollars. He thrust the pants into my hands and roared off out of the guarded gates. It was like being served a writ. There was a script wrapped inside the pants.

The picture opened and did well but it was not a blockbuster. *Time* magazine called it 'a fog of a film', and other reviewers were irritated by the fractured style, but many critics saw it as a kind of breakthrough for Hollywood. The French hailed it as a masterpiece. Michel Ciment of *Positif* magazine and Pierre Rissient championed it, and this reputation reached back to America. It began to get on lists of the ten best thrillers of all time. It launched my career, and I have Lee to thank for that – not just for trusting me, but for all I learnt from him. And I owe thanks to Judd, who put us together. Judd's Western, *Blue*, failed in a fairly spectacular way. He made other movies but he never quite recovered from that debacle. He wore a gold bracelet on which was engraved his allergies: 'No penicillin. No onions.'

I got back to London in time to buy *Sergeant Pepper's Lonely Hearts Club Band* on the day of its release. I listened to it with Tony Woollard, the designer. It defined an era. We sat staring at the cover, identifying the heroes. We felt on the brink of a brave new world. British films had freshness and vigour, and above all confidence. It was the place to be. The Hollywood studios competed for the talent. American producers took up residence. *Tom Jones* had won the Best Picture Oscar. Ken Russell was in full flight. Jack Clayton made the *Pumpkin Eater*. Karel

Reisz made *Saturday Night and Sunday Morning*. Dick Lester did *The Bed Sitting Room*.

While London was jumping, I had been in the LA backwater. It was very provincial in those days. I had scandalised the town by putting Angie Dickinson into a miniskirt. The newspapers scarcely acknowledged the existence of New York, let alone the rest of the world. Ford, Sirk, Hitchcock, Hathaway, Wilder were ageing and slowing down. It was somnambulant. Other than diners, there were few places to eat well. There was the Brown Derby, Scandia, Musso and Frank's and a couple of delis. The food had the neutral aftertaste of the deep-freeze. People drank highballs before the meal and water with it. Wine was hard to find. Now LA has some of the best restaurants in the world. Over the years I watched the fashion change as movie people went from bourbon to martinis, from martinis to scotch and from scotch to red wine, then from red wine to white wine, from white wine to Perrier and finally from Perrier to Evian.

1968: *Hell in the Pacific*

Before I returned to London, Lee had spoken to me about another project. He had been approached by a producer, Reuben Berkovitch, with a one-page outline of a story about an American airman and a Japanese naval officer who are washed up on a tiny island during the Pacific war. Having fought in this war, Lee was attracted to the idea, but what really sucked him in was the possibility of working with Toshiro Mifune, whose Samurai cries and sword thrusts he appropriated when drunk.

I was not entranced by the story, but how could I refuse Lee? And so it was that I returned to LA, leaving swinging London behind. I was to miss all the revolutionary excitements of '68, and would be, once more, in the wrong place.

We set sail on the *Queen Mary*. She was in terminal decline and creaked and groaned across the Atlantic. By chance, Tom Stoppard was a fellow passenger. My four children and his two marauded the swimming pool and cinema while he and I sat in our deckchairs playing chess, rugs tucked around us by attentive stewards, who plied us with hot toddies. He was flushed from the recent London success of *Rosencrantz and*

Guildenstern are Dead, I from *Point Blank*. He was heading to New York to open the play on Broadway, where it would also enjoy extraordinary success.

I had followed the genesis of his play from our Bristol days, when he had first mooted the notion of viewing *Hamlet* from the point of view of these minor characters. There was an occasion when he speculated on another mutation of the Hamlet story. We were playing cricket against the Royal Shakespeare Company at Stratford. David Warner was rehearsing for Peter Hall's production of what came to be known as the Hippy *Hamlet*, it being the sixties and all that. David had recently starred in *Morgan, A Suitable Case for Treatment*, and he was a bit of a heart-throb. There were girls squealing on the boundary. Deep in his role, he appalled us by coming in to bat wearing jeans and sunglasses. I was bowling, and to express our disapproval I attempted a bouncer. It kicked up feebly, just enough to strike him on the hand. He dropped the bat and his gangling limbs writhed and contorted as he wrestled with the pain. He retired, mortified, to the pavilion. Tom, who was keeping wicket, said, 'You realise that's his duelling hand. This could be the first time in the history of *Hamlet* that Laertes wins.'

There we were, the Czech immigrant and the boy from the Blitz, sailing into the future on one of the last symbols of imperial wealth and privilege. There was a bad storm. The chess pieces slid off the board. We ate in the empty mirrored dining room. Waiters staggered towards us as though essaying some complex dance-step; those insulting, servile waiters who could make 'sir' sound like an insult. They may have felt contempt for us jumped-up Johnny-come-latelys, but they still felt privileged to be treated badly by the sprinkling of real aristocrats who could still afford to travel on the *Queen Mary*.

The *Mary* listed slowly over to port and sat there interminably. Tom and I exchanged fearful glances. I was sure it would never come right. Then it would heave its way up and sink wearily down to starboard with the sea washing the decks. The waiters gave up trying to serve food. The dining room was eerily empty. Were we really going to die on this old tub just when we were enjoying a bit of success?

My daughter, Telsche, had stuck it out while her siblings and Tom's children had been taken out, one by one, to heave up their food. As we finally left the dining room, lurching and weaving, Telsche caught a glimpse of her reflection in one of the mirrored pillars. When she saw how green her face was, she projectile-vomited on to the mirror, and the sight of this yellow sick sliding down the ornate bevelled glass finally had Tom and me heaving up lunch too.

We rented Rod Steiger's house in the Malibu Colony. It was a rambling wooden shack with verandas sprawling on to the beach and a small pool in the back garden. It was so much like those Shepperton bungalows of my childhood, but more generous and careless, and with the pounding ocean rather than the gentle Thames. It was mostly families, kids and dogs in those days. Now those beach lots are so expensive only the very rich can afford to own them. They tear down the wooden bungalows and build concrete fortresses, angular, blinding white. They visit these homes for the odd weekend and a couple of weeks in the summer. For the rest, the Colony is sadly deserted, occupied only by Japanese gardeners, Mexican maids and Filipino house couples walking the pampered dogs. Don't look to buy in the Colony if you don't have ten million dollars to spare. If you are lucky you can rent one of them for the month of August for forty thousand.

I wanted to keep my team together, so I brought Bill Stair and Alex Jacobs back with me to work on what was to become *Hell in the Pacific*. The notion of being shipwrecked filled Bill with dread. Just thinking about solitude made him ill. So I had him work on two other ideas: a project with Tom Wolfe, and a script about the history of music which we called *I Hear America*. While Bill loved and feared LA, Alex had found his spiritual home in Hollywood. He was a movie buff. He could pitch ideas. There was no one better at meetings. He was, as they say in Hollywood, 'great in a room'.

He eventually became a rewrite man, a script doctor. When they had a project with intractable problems they would send for Alex. He would demolish the script, reduce it to rubble, then when everyone was in despair, he would rebuild it into a potential masterpiece. I used to marvel at his profligacy. 'There's the germ of a great idea here,' he would say, slapping the script or twisting it in his hands, as though squeezing out that little pip of importance from the hundred or so pages of dross. Or, 'The audience is way ahead of you. This script is just the first third of the movie.' He bamboozled. He bludgeoned. He knew how to cut through to the quick, to what was essential, as he did on *Point Blank*. Sitting down and writing it, justifying what he had improvised at the meeting was another matter. He was at his best pacing a room. A typewriter did not inspire him. He had the temperament of a producer rather than a writer.

But *Hell in the Pacific* silenced him. We pondered it, we pushed and pulled at it, but got nowhere. We had come to the end of each other. Alex's face was heavily scarred from the accident he suffered on the Tour de France, but he was so animated that his personality overwhelmed those old wounds. Now, he suddenly contracted Bell's palsy, which made one side of his face, the good side, go slack and lifeless. It would take many months before those facial nerves would repair. The dead side of his face felt like a metaphor for our script. It was as blank as the paper before us. Alex got angry and tetchy. One night after a dinner he said, 'I don't want to see you any more.' I was preparing to go on a trip through the South Pacific with Lee, to look for locations and revisit some of Lee's battlefields. Perhaps Alex felt he should have been included in the trip. I told Lee the next day that Alex had quit. Lee said, 'Your horse died. Get another horse.' Alex made a living as a rewrite man for many years and remained in LA. He wrote a very good script about the Tour de France, *The Yellow Jersey*, but it was never made.

Lee was getting very excited about our trip, drinking a lot and doing his Mifune impersonations. He was attempting to break free of Michele Triola, but it was proving difficult. I called in on him one night at his house on Carbon beach. He was alone and drinking, but very subdued, morose. I sat with him and we talked. He was getting to the stage of free association. He was linking and looping, making penetrating insights about life, death, men, women. There was no sign of Michele, although she was on his mind. From his oblique comments, I got the impression that he had finally thrown her out.

It was a tiny place, a living room and a bedroom side by side, both facing out to the beach. I had to go through the bedroom to get to the only bathroom, and I was surprised to see Michele asleep on the bed, fully clothed. There was something about the way she was lying that disturbed me. A wave of drunken déjà vu engulfed me. I had already shot this scene – the empty box of sleeping pills, Lee slumped in the next room. I was back in *Point Blank*, where Walker goes into the bedroom and finds his wife dead from an overdose.

I went back into Lee. I said, 'I think Michele . . .' 'Fuck her,' he said. I went back into the bedroom and felt a faint pulse. I said, 'Lee, we've got to get her to the hospital.' We lifted her between us and staggered out to the car. Although she was quite small and plump, we just could not seem to stuff her into the back seat. Limbs tumbled out and Lee fell on his knees. Her legs and arms flopped in all directions. She seemed boneless.

I got inside and pulled while he pushed. I was alarmed and sobering fast. She felt like dead meat. We drove to UCLA. It was 2 a.m. I told Lee to stay out of sight and I got her admitted. She was in a coma for three days. Each time she came around, the drug would metabolise in her liver and she would sink back into unconsciousness.

He took her back out of guilt. It clamped her closer to him than ever. He was going to call her bluff. I did what she expected *him* to do. I never spoke of it to a living soul. Years later I was to testify in his famous palimony case. Preparing his brief, Lee's lawyer questioned me in detail about my dealings with Michele. Lee suddenly said, as if to pre-empt what I might say about that night, 'If John hadn't dropped by my house one night there wouldn't be a case at all.' The lawyer looked from Lee to me. 'Never keep anything from your lawyer, right?' said Lee, giving me permission to confess. I could only see it as damaging to his case. I said nothing. 'Is there anything more you want to tell me?' said the lawyer. 'It's up to John,' said Lee. 'No,' I said.

We set out for the South Pacific, Lee, our production manager, Lloyd Anderson, and I. Lee knew Hawaii well; he had shot *Donovan's Reef* there with John Ford and developed his passion for big-game fishing in those waters. He loved showing it to me. Could we shoot the picture there? I recoiled from its lushness and indulgence. It was like a beautiful, easy-going woman who had been fucked too many times by too many men. I was seeing it through the eyes of the movie. Just as I had preferred LA to San Francisco, for this movie I needed something starker, bleaker, as a setting for these two men to fight out the Second World War in miniature. So I could not allow myself to wallow in the pleasures of this glorious place.

We rented a single-engine Cessna to view the volcano on Maui. Lloyd hated flying. Even on a commercial flight he sat with all muscles tensed. He was in the back with Lee, I sat next to the pilot. We climbed up over the black lava beds and soared over the crater. Magnificent. Alarmingly, the pilot then flew down into the crater, which was a mile or so in diameter. In a steep banked turn we circled this primeval place. The crater walls reared up around us. I smelt the sulphur fumes. The volcano rumbled below, throwing up hot currents of air, tossing the little plane like a dinghy on a stormy sea. The pilot was determined to impress Lee. OK, tough guy, what do you make of this? I was terrified but exhilarated. It was like a flashback to the beginning of time. The majesty of it was such that it finally drove out fear. As we climbed back over the lip of the volcano, the engine spluttered and failed. We lost height. The jagged lava beds came rushing up to claim us. I pressed my feet down on the floor to keep us airborne. The pilot screamed, 'Fly, you bastard! Fly!' I turned to look at Lee. He wore an expression of the utmost tranquillity, with just the hint of an ironic smile. It was a relief, a release. I saw the peace he found in impending death, and realised in that moment what a burden his guilt and shame imposed on his life. How appropriate for Lee Marvin to die on a volcano. Then again, he was an actor. Was that face of exquisite calm assumed for the benefit of the pilot who had wanted to test his courage? The pilot coaxed the plane back to life and the engine screamed as we skimmed that brutal surface and climbed away.

Lee drank a lot of Mai Tais that night. So perhaps he had had the inner shakes. Then again, he was always on the lookout for an excuse to drink.

He had a severe hangover as we waited in the VIP lounge for the flight to Guam. A five-star general and his aide de camp were waiting with us. I got talking to him. He was in charge of all the installations involved in the Vietnam war – airfields, ports, army camps. He told me with some pride that he had spent more money than any other individual in the history of the world. Lee took no part in the conversation but sat with his head in his hands. I questioned the general closely about the war. This was 1967, and the protest movement was gathering momentum. He defended the war with patriotic zeal, glancing from time to time at the ex-Marine hero at his side. Finally he said, 'What do you think about the war, Mr Marvin?' Lee looked up blearily and said, 'I think it's very rude.' Then the general's hat, which he was nursing on his lap, caught Lee's eye. 'What's more,' said Lee, 'I'm going to eat your hat.' He took it and bit into the 'scrambled egg' insignia. He tried to tear it off with his teeth. When that didn't work he put the hat on his head. The general was appalled, dumbstruck.

At that moment the flight was called. We got up and walked across the tarmac to the 707, Lee wearing the general's hat. I looked back. His badge of office, his dignity, his very identity challenged, the general was gesticulating angrily to his aide de camp. Finally, he hurried out, his hand covering his shameful, hatless baldness. Lee sat down in the plane, pulled the hat down over his eyes and fell asleep. After a while, the general sent his nervous aide de camp to retrieve it. He crept up to Lee and stealthily removed it, terrified that Lee would wake up and bite him, or worse.

It was a typical Marvin gesture, to find a perfect metaphor to express his disdain for the war. 'Those two guys have never seen combat,' he said when he woke up. 'You can always tell.'

I had been poring over maps and pictures of the islands of the South Pacific in my search for *the* perfect location. Micronesia beckoned. The island of Guam was an aircraft carrier for the Vietnam war. It was shocking to see the vast number of planes flying in and out of there. There were huge stockpiles of napalm, bombs and munitions. It revealed the scale of the war.

We made a detour to Saipan where Lee's platoon had been ambushed and almost wiped out. Lee was one of two or three survivors. The platoon had hung together and fought through the islands. Lee wrote a moving and cinematic account of the event which appears in Pam Marvin's wonderful book about her husband, *Lee* (Faber and Faber, 1997):

Saipan, Mariana Islands, June 1944

At the signal we moved out. Mike Cairns and I were the 'point' of the assault platoon. Moving at a slow walk, we bore to the left and forward. All was quiet. We had just passed an abandoned thatched hut when suddenly there was a shot and a loud slap to the immediate left of me. It was Mike and he was down. He said a quiet 'Oh', and then, 'Corpsman', just as quietly. There was blood on his dungaree blouse. I went down to him and tore open his jacket, and there, just one inch below his left nipple, was a small dark hole. The blood was pink and bubbly, a lung shot. I tried to put my finger in the hole, but it would not fit. His eyes were closed and he said 'Corpsman' twice more in a whisper and was dead.

High-sounding Jap machine-gun and rifle fire, then I heard Mac's voice, our platoon leader, shouting for all BAR men to stand and fire magazine. Mike's BAR was next to me. I picked it up and put twenty rounds into the brush at the base of some palm trees, but didn't see anything. Mac was shouting for me to pull over to the right and join the rest of the platoon. There was no way that I could get Mike's ammunition belt off him as it had shoulder straps, so I pulled the trigger group off his BAR and threw it away and, grabbing my M1, headed off low and fast where I thought the rest of the platoon were. All was chaotic, shouting voices, the heavy sound of our weapons and the high, shrill, fast sound of theirs. I still could not see the Japs!

They were close, for I could feel the blast of their weapons. Then I could see the 1st Platoon, they were all down, some firing forward, some on their backs and sides. 'Oh my God! They got us!' As I was running, the twigs and small branches were flying through the air as their machine guns were cutting everything down. I figured I had better get down too. And just in time. All the brush around me knee-high just disappeared. I looked forward and my leg flew to one side. I couldn't feel anything. 'This is getting bad.' Looking down my side, I saw that the heel of my boot had been shot off. Looking up again to see where it had come from, there was another crack and my face was numb and eyes full of dirt. It had a set-up of rhythm I knew. Burying my face in the ground and gritting my teeth in anticipation, SLAPP!!! The impact caused a reflex that lifted me off the ground. I lay still for a long time. I shouted, 'I'm hit!' and a voice nearby said, very calmly, 'Shut up – we're all hit.' I was slowly tensing my various muscles. By the process of elimination, I figured it was somewhere below the chest. By then Schidt and Pedagrew crawled up and told me I was hit in the ass and proceeded to dump some sulpha in the wound and said they would try to get me out of there and to follow them. I disassembled my M1; my cartridge belt had already been cut off, so we began to crawl to the right. I could not believe the number of dead marines. I would recognise certain personal touches of equipment my friends had and there they were, lifeless. We got over to the 2nd Platoon area and they were as badly off as us. We started back towards our line. Now most of the fire was Jap. Where were our mortars and tanks? All at once we were stopped by an opening, completely with no cover, a fire lane about twenty feet wide. There was no way to get through there crawling. Schidt said, 'If we can get you up, can you run?' They did get me up and shoved me out in the cover on the other side, then crawled to a large-trunked tree. Rose was sitting there with his back to the fire. He asked me if I wanted a cigarette and gave me one; he also offered me water. On returning the canteen to him, he leaned out a bit to put it away in its cover on his cartridge belt. He was hit immediately and fell over on me and died without a word. I could not get him off me. Then somebody stepped on my wound. I shouted. Fortunately, they were stretcher-bearers. Then Callelo was brought in; he had been hit in the head and was screaming that he could not see. They loaded him on the stretcher at the same time they got hit again, killing one of the bearers. Callelo was out of his head now. They got him out of there fast. I shouted, 'What about me?' They said I was next.

What frightened me now was that I would be lying face down on the stretcher about a foot and a half above the ground. Just the height their machine guns usually were set at. There was nothing I could do. I had to get out. The bearers were running as fast as they could, the fire was all around, then one of the front bearers went down, only a stumble, they got me back to Battalion aid, still under heavy fire. At Battalion, a guy, stripped to the waist with two nambu pistols stuck in his belt, asked me if I needed plasma but I didn't know. He gave me a surrette of morphine and had me put behind a long stock of 81 mm mortar high-explosive shells. They were still in their clover leaves and I could hear the strays hitting them. All at once I noticed Schidt squatting by me and he was asking me for my .45 automatic, which I had in my shoulder holster. I had to give it to him, he had gotten me out of there. I told him it was my father's pistol and not to lose it. He thanked me and took off.

Just then somebody in the distance started shouting, 'Counter-attack, counter-attack,' and the panic of trying to get the wounded out of there began. By now my leg was totally useless. Then a terrific explosion, a big ammo dump about a hundred yards away had gone up and I could see people floating through the air. A lot of confusion and I found myself in a stretcher jeep, two of us and two ambulatory, but we were going the wrong way, back to the fire fight. I shouted at the driver a number of times and finally he swung around and headed for the beach. I don't remember too much of that trip. When the haze cleared, a corpsman was filling out a tag and attaching it to me with its wire. Then he took a red crayon and made a mark on my forehead saying that he had given me morphine. There was a lot of heavy stuff going off around us. I was under a torn canvas fly on the beach: equipment was stacked everywhere and it was getting dark. I asked him if there was any chance of getting off tonight and he said, 'No!' My heart sank. The Japs had the beach zeroed in and were pounding it. We would never make it through the night. Above all the noise, a voice from the water shouted, 'Anybody going out?' The corpsman hollered, 'How much room you got?' The next time I awoke, I was face down on a stretcher and was aware of much light, then a pair of shiny black shoes with white trousers. A lot of shouting, then I was in a bright companionway painted yellow with Glenn Miller's 'Moonlight Serenade' playing from somewhere. The hospital ship. A nurse in white was reading my tag and asking if I wanted some ice water or ice cream. I didn't know what to say. Some man's voice said, 'GU' and they took me away. Still on the stretcher, I was next to a low bunk with a thick mattress and white sheets on it. A voice asked if I could climb on to the bed. I said I'd get the sheets dirty, and the voice said, 'That's OK, we got more.' They cut the dog tag off my shoe and put it in my hand. I asked them not to take my helmet, and please turn off the lights. 'Don't worry.' In and out of focus for a while, then I heard it: from the islands, the fire-fight was still going on. My company, what was left of it, was still there and I was safe on a hospital ship. Ice cream, water, clean sheets, Glenn Miller, nurses. I was a coward! And I cried.

Lee wanted to revisit the place where his friends had died, but the island was covered with a layer of pampas grass six feet high. We ploughed through it in a jeep, but everything had been submerged by it. It was impossible to identify the place where he had been shot. It was as though the battle, the past, the memory had been obliterated. The grass covered it like shame. In another part of the island we did find Japanese bones and skulls in caves. It was a matter of deep resentment and anguish that the Americans had still not allowed them to return to bury their dead.

We moved on, island hopping. I was entranced by the Palauan archipelago, hundreds of islands, some only six feet across and all of them undercut, eroded at sea level so that they looked like mushrooms. A disease had killed off most of the palm trees. Waving palms on a beach signal ease and plenty. The audience had to believe that these men were suffering deprivation. Palau looked threatening, a sombre beauty, it had the remoteness of an alien planet, the architecture of dream. I felt a thrill of excitement as I looked down from the plane. For the first time I could see the movie in my head. Only three of the islands were occupied, Koror, Babaldub and Peleliu, where a bloody battle had been fought in the Second World War. Palau had been a German colony, then Japanese and was now a US protectorate. In the midst of the jungle I came across a black marble headstone recording the death of a twenty-one-year-old woman, presumably the wife of a member of the German colonial service. Apart from the name and dates of birth and death, there was only one word carved on the stone in large letters: *Warum?* (Why?)

Enter the Japanese

To get to Palau you climbed into an old Dakota in Guam, and five hours later you landed on a red dirt strip in Koror. It would be a week before the next plane came to get you. How were we to make a movie in this remote location? No hotels. No infrastructure. I must have been unhinged.

We found a way. We chartered a ship from Taiwan, which the crew would live on, sailed it to Japan, loaded it with film equipment and food supplies and sent it to Palau. I recruited a mainly Japanese crew so that Toshiro Mifune would be comfortable. A Chinese ship, Japanese crew, American producers, British director – it was an explosive brew, and explode it did. But more of that later.

From Palau, we travelled on to Japan to meet Mifune. Lee did his Mifune impersonation and Mifune roared back at him. They were in love. Next day at a tea house, Lee, Mifune and I made many toasts in saki and agreed to make the picture together. Mifune was acutely aware that he was shouldering the honour of the Japanese military.

So I had a ship, an island, two actors and a crew – but not a script. I met and hired a Japanese first assistant director and I discussed the film with him and told him of the difficulties I was encountering. He had worked for Kurosawa and was due to see him. We were particularly stuck on finding an ending. I said, tell the great man the story and see if he can come up with an idea. The problem was presented to Kurosawa. He thought long and hard. My man waited for the words of wisdom. Finally the master spoke. 'They meet a girl.' There were moments when I wished I had followed his advice.

Mifune took us to his top-flight geisha house. It was frequented by cabinet ministers and bankers as well as movie stars. It was disappointingly sedate. I was asked what my hobbies were. Chess. A geisha presented herself. She spoke good English, very charming. She beat me two games out of three. I had imagined she would have been trained to let me win. Maybe if I had been Japanese it would have been different.

Because it was essential that Mifune's behaviour on the island should be authentic, I had the notion of employing two writers, one American and one Japanese. I met with Shinobu Hashimoto, one of Kurosawa's men, who had written *Rashomon*, amongst other films. Back in LA, Reuben Berkovitch, a pallid, frail man who lived in fear of disease, waited. He had provided the story and in return he got to be the producer. All he needed to do was hang in there. He did, however, recommend a writer to take Alex's place, a near namesake, Eric Bercovici.

So we set up offices in Goldwyn Studios in Hollywood: three connecting rooms, Hashimoto in one, Bercovici in another and me in the middle. I would sketch out a scene and they would each then write it from the point of view of their characters. Hashimoto pointed out that Kurosawa often worked in this way, sometimes with several writers. They would all go off separately and write the same scene. He would choose the best or put elements of several together. Kurosawa was a purist. He insisted that nothing should be written that could not be shown. Hashimoto once wrote, 'The crow flies wearily home to its nest.' Kurosawa chided him. 'We see a crow flying. How do we know it is flying to its nest? How do we know it is weary? This is prose writing, not film writing.'

We translated the Japanese into English and the English into Japanese, made revisions and translated them back again. It was slow and tedious work. The back-story was a battle at sea. Mifune was a naval officer whose ship was sunk; Marvin, an airman who had been shot down. They are both washed ashore on this uninhabited, hostile island.

Back and forth we went, and slowly and painfully we constructed the movie. There was almost no dialogue, just the two men. Most of the conventional dramatic devices were absent. My documentary about D. W. Griffith and all the great silent films I had seen at the National Film Theatre – Eisenstein, Gance, Von Stroheim, the German Expressionists – stood me in good stead. I attempted to apply those early visual techniques. We had dragged ourselves through a couple of drafts and had achieved a rickety structure, but it had still not come to life. We were weary, and weary of each other. Hashimoto, who was an addicted gambler, asked me if he could go off for a couple of weeks to do a draft on his own. He ached to see Las Vegas. I agreed.

I had taken on Tony Pratt, a young storyboard artist from England, a nephew of Boris Karloff. I had found a beach in Palau with a cave at one end, a sheer cliff at the other; hemmed in by dense jungle, it would force the men into confrontations and competition for its meagre resources. I photographed it thoroughly and Tony worked from my pictures. It proved easier to progress in pictures than words, and we made great headway while Hashimoto was away.

I managed to persuade one of the greatest of cameramen to photograph the picture, Conrad Hall. While waiting for Hashimoto, I took

Hall and Pratt to scout Palau. We stayed overnight in Guam. We woke up to find a hurricane approaching. At the airport our old DC4 had a magneto problem. All aircraft had to be evacuated or risk destruction by a wind that was already bending the palm trees half way to the ground. It was like watching the history of aviation in reverse. First the modern bombers and fighters engaged in the Vietnam War flew out, then the Second World War relics, and finally a few old biplanes left over from the Great War. Meanwhile, they were still working on our Dakota as we three nervous guys watched from the rattling windows of the passenger building. Soon ours was the last plane left on Guam. In desperation they ran it up and down the runway, hoping that the three good engines would help start the bad one. Finally it spluttered and the fourth propeller turned.

They herded us urgently to the plane. The wind was now over a hundred miles an hour and completely steady. You could lean into it at forty-five degrees and it would support you. However, the gale was carrying a lot of debris and some of it was rattling against the plane. 'Should we get on this crate?' I said to Conrad and Tony. 'It's going to be wrecked if it stays here. Don't you think that might cloud their judgement about its airworthiness?' I was saying this as we got to the steps of the plane. 'You want to stay here?' said Conrad. I looked back at the impending disaster. A small wooden hut was cartwheeling across the runway. The plane door closed against any possibility of deliverance. The engines screamed and we took off into the full force of the storm. The wind speed was greater than the take-off speed, so we rose vertically; in fact, we were moving slightly backwards. The plane rattled and shook. This was 1968. The last DC4 had been made in 1947. This one had gone through the war and had endured thirty years of tropical humidity and salt corrosion. The sky was slate-grey and dark. A very tense pilot came on the PA. 'We have to go back. My instruments are showing that the wheels are not retracting. They won't go up and they won't go down. They may be stuck halfway. Or it could just be the instrument at fault.' We went through the procedures for an emergency landing. Heads between legs, etc. He banked the plane and we juddered around and made our vertical landing into that maelstrom. As soon as the wheels touched and were firm, he knew it was an instrument fault, and went straight back up. In five minutes we had flown out of the hurricane into placid blue skies. It was hard to believe we had gone through it so easily, like waking from a nightmare. The DC4 had a chemical toilet at the back of the plane. I went back and as I opened the door, the handle broke off in my hand. I had held myself together up to that point, a stiffened upper lip. I raised the handle up for Conrad and Tony to see. What condition was the rest of the plane in? They joined me in a bout of hysterical laughter. What were we getting into?

Conrad Hall's father co-wrote the book of *Mutiny on the Bounty*, which was made into the classic film with Clark Gable and Charles Laughton. Conrad lived in Tahiti with his family and was able to get a job on the Brando remake of the old film, making a start in the movie business. He knew the South Pacific well. When he saw my remote beach it was his turn to start up the hysterical laughter. 'You're out of your mind, Boorman,' he said. 'I love it.' He and Tony got on famously, the tough wily American and the very polite, apologetic Englishman. We stood at a rickety quayside in Koror watching the children diving for fish with sharpened sticks. The girls wore cotton dresses and would jump in holding their skirts out wide to trap the air and float like flowers.

A beautiful girl of about eighteen emerged from the water with a harpoon in her hand and a fish in her mouth. She looked at the three of us with her big saucer eyes. She took her time, considering each of us in turn, then she knelt before Tony and put the fish at his feet. Tony flushed with embarrassment. Conrad and I enjoyed his discomfort. 'Thank you very much. Awfully kind,' he said. She spoke no word of English, of course, but her intentions were clear. She took him by the hand and led him away. Tony turned back to us. 'Sorry, terribly sorry.' 'Tony, you forgot your fish!' said Conrad.

Tony blushed. He was a tangle of inhibitions. Palauan women, on the other hand, were sexually uninhibited and totally unapologetic. Palau was a matriarchal society. Only women could own land. Children took the mothers' names. The men's possessions were limited to their canoes and the nets, harpoons and accoutrements of their craft.

The next day Tony described how the girl had led him in pitch darkness to an *abai*, a large thatched hut on stilts with open sides, and there they had made love. The dawn light revealed thirty or so other people, men, women and children all sleeping in close proximity. Tony retreated, muttering apologies and consumed with excruciating embarrassment. However, the girl became his companion throughout the movie and did wonders for his inhibitions.

When the US army took charge after the war, they found that despite the abundance of fish and fruit, no Palauan would sell them produce.

This was not a political stance, but simply that the Palauan would fish until he had enough for his family, then go home and take his ease. The Americans solved this problem by giving out free cigarettes. Once the Palauans were hooked, they needed money to buy more, so they kept fishing all day and entered the market economy. The Palauan coral reef is considered the most profuse, varied and most beautiful in the world. It abounds with fish and lobster, and the fishermen had an intricate knowledge of its currents and seasons and the behaviour of its fauna. For instance, some fish are poisonous at certain times of the year. The Palauans had lived in harmonious symbiosis with the reef since time immemorial. But cigarettes made them capitalists, and they had taken to dynamiting the reef to stun the fish and increase their per-man-hour output – a practice now happily outlawed.

Despite this innovation, life in Palau proceeded much as it always had. It was my first encounter with an undeveloped society and it taught me more about our world than about theirs. It brought into sharp focus the stresses we live under and they are spared. The rules and laws that constrain us, the disciplines of education and the workplace, the need to earn money, pay mortgages, meet tax demands, save for retirement – all blissfully absent. Because there is an hour of heavy rain most days, they had no water storage. Because there are no seasons, there was no necessity to store for the winter. They lived in their ease.

Back at the Goldwyn Studios, Hashimoto had delivered his new draft and a translation was awaiting me. There were no new scenes. The structure was intact. But he had radically altered the tone. It was now a comedy. Mifune was a buffoon and Marvin a clumsy oaf. There was a lot of eye-rolling and pratfalls. I told Hashimoto that he was way off beam. He accepted that with a shrug and we went back to the familiar method.

I was getting on so well with Tony that I decided to appoint him art director, to work in harmony with the Japanese art director I had hired. There was an irony here. Tony's family was living in Singapore when the Japanese attacked. He and his mother were evacuated, leaving his father behind. He was never heard of again; he must either have been killed, or captured and put to work as slave labour.

Lee, of course, had served in the Marines in the Pacific theatre. Mifune, less auspiciously, had been a quartermaster. The closest he got to combat was issuing saki to kamikaze pilots before their missions.

Ship of Fools

The ship duly arrived and the crew took up residence on board. Apart from Tony, an American film editor and Conrad's camera crew, a prop man and Art Brooker, the key grip and his best boy, the rest were Japanese. The ship's dining room was divided in two, one side serving Japanese food, the other American. We had a tank landing craft to take us to work each day. The front was lowered down and we waded on to our beach.

Before shooting began, Mifune proposed that he and Lee should lay wreaths together in Peleliu, where so many on both sides had lost their lives – an act of reconciliation. Lee agreed, but was uneasy about it. He was edging his way into character, casting himself back into the war, into the fear and hatred of the Japanese. He admired Mifune, but he had to think of him as the enemy. It was psychologically disturbing for him to make that gesture. For Mifune it was a profound ritual, to help atone for his unburied fellow countrymen. As always with Lee, his response was to get drunk that evening. He felt he had betrayed his fallen comrades by this act. He came roaring into the dining room and stood over the Japanese crew. They looked up, the clicking chopsticks fell silent. 'Which one of you jokers put that Jap skull in my bed?' Happily only Mifune's interpreter understood, and he pretended not to.

Mifune had learned the script and ostentatiously did not carry a copy with him on to the set. His interpreter was an obsequious Japanese-American from LA, Aki, and all my communications had to pass through him. We had a little light rehearsal on board ship, and I quickly became suspicious that Aki was editing out any hint of criticism in my directions to Mifune.

Conrad's camera operator, Jordon Cronenworth, was finishing another picture and Conrad was planning to operate himself for the first two weeks. However, when the first day of the shoot arrived, Conrad was in bed with bronchitis. For the first three days I operated the camera myself and the gaffer did the lighting and had charge of the exposure meter. The early scenes went off without incident. They were simple enough: Mifune sitting in his cave, Marvin clambering out of his rubber boat. On the fourth day, the first of many disasters struck. As we stepped out in the landing craft, it began to rain. A tropical storm closed in. We crawled under tarpaulins to wait it out. It didn't let up. The locals advised us that it would go on all day, but I kept the crew on the beach until four o'clock before abandoning the day.

The next day, the pattern was the same. An air of gloom descended upon us. After the first week we were well behind schedule. We began the second week with the first meeting between the two characters.

Mifune was ready. We rehearsed. He played the scene like his character in *The Seven Samurai*, a boastful clown. I was horrified. I took him to one side and told him how I wanted it: serious, fearful, dignified. He nodded. We did a take. He played it exactly the same. I told him again. He listened imperviously. Aki was getting nervous. In the next take he made no adjustment, no concession to my directions. I asked Aki, 'Are you telling him what I said?' Aki said he couldn't translate exactly because Mifune would lose face in front of the Japanese crew if he was corrected by me. 'Tell him precisely what I said.' He did so with many apologies and much bowing of his head. Mifune's response was to shout abuse at Aki, who fell abjectly to his knees. I called for another take. Mifune did not alter his performance one iota.

Lee retreated from the confrontation. He wandered down to the other end of the beach and cracked open a beer. I watched this out of the corner of my eye with some alarm. I sat down with Mifune and talked about the scene, the character, his thoughts and feelings at this point, what he had been through, etc. He listened impassively to the translation. I tried another take. He would not budge. I called a wrap and we went back to the ship and tried to work it out. Lee had had a few beers by now and was at his free-associating stage. Using sound effects instead of words, he played the scene first as his own character then as Mifune. Mifune was amused, at least. I rebuilt the scene for Mifune step by step, inch by inch, and by the end of the day he was finally in accord.

However, he did not appear for dinner. A lot of shouting was heard from his cabin. Aki was prostrate outside his door.

As we were finishing our meal, Mifune suddenly burst into the salon. He was brandishing a .22 rifle. He was very drunk and very angry. He shouted what sounded unmistakably like dire threats. Meanwhile, he was attempting to load a clip in the chamber. He looked so violent and dangerous that everyone ducked under the tables, except for Lee. I was sitting next to him. He said, 'Relax. Look what he's trying to load the rifle with.' It was a packet of Wrigley's chewing gum.

The next day we shot the scene. It was fine. However, when we started rehearsing the next scene, he was the clown again. I took him aside, explained. He shouted at Aki. We did a take. Exactly the same. Stopped shooting. Back to the ship. Endless discussions. Same palaver.

A ghastly thought struck me. I asked Aki to translate, quickly and roughly, the scene in Mifune's script that was in contention. I listened with mounting horror. Hashimoto had given Mifune his comic version of the script – whether by mistake or maliciously, I shall never know.

Despite explaining this to Mifune, he would not give up his interpretation. Each new scene was a monumental struggle. At one point, rather than be corrected by me, Mifune told me to rehearse with his stand-in and when it was how I wished it to be, he would step in and shoot it. Kurosawa had found a Mifune lookalike and trained him to simulate Mifune's characteristics. He was a stunt double who also acted as stand-in.

He did my bidding and was so good that he looked more like Mifune than Mifune. He was too good, in fact. Mifune found that when he came to shoot the scene he sometimes could not do it as well as his double. He put a stop to that experiment.

We slipped further behind. Reuben Berkovitch stayed on the ship, drinking hot distilled water and saying nothing. He spent his time trying to get through to Hollywood on the ship's radio through the high seas operator. Morale had sunk to a disastrous level. Even the ship's crew was miserable. It was a hotel, not a ship. They were waiters, not sailors. Reuben constantly complained to the captain of the inadequacies of the ship's services.

Christel found a hut in the village and we lived there with Telsche and Katrine. The twins, eight months old, were left behind in LA in the care of a gothic American couple, Mr and Mrs Miller.

Lee's girlfriend Michele only lasted two weeks then flew back to LA. On the beach next day, Lee looked at his watch and called out in a booming voice, 'Michele has landed in LA.' One hour later he announced at the top of his voice, 'Michele is getting laid.'

At the palimony trial Michele claimed that she acted as a de facto wife during this period, that Lee was such a drunk that without her help he could not have functioned as an actor. I testified that she had left after two weeks and that Lee had managed on his own. It came out at the trial that she had, indeed, had sexual encounters while Lee was off in Palau. Lee knew what he knew.

Reuben deferred to Hank Sapperstein, the executive producer, who was in charge of the finances and made all the deals. Unlike Reuben he was impatient and obnoxious. He was enraged by our delays and contemptuous of my inability to control Mifune. Most painful of all, I knew

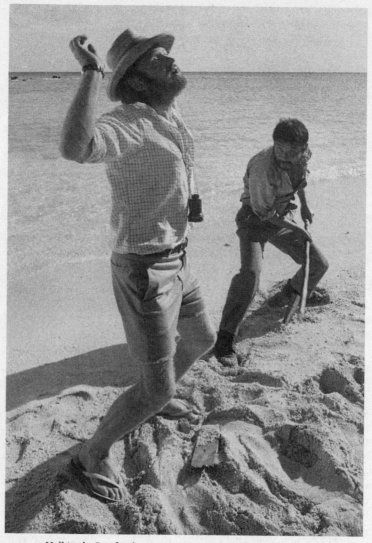

Hell in the Pacific: demonstrating a scene with Toshiro Mifune

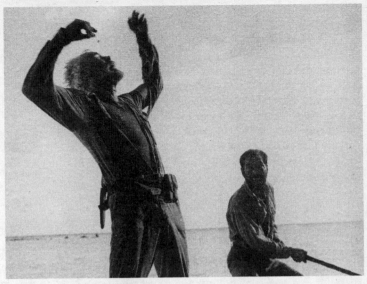

The completed scene with Marvin and Mifune

Lee was disappointed in me, and although he didn't say so, he also felt I should be handling Mifune better.

I pressed on. We built a rostrum and anchored it to the reef at low tide, and Conrad and I manned it for a shot we needed. A huge freak wave crashed against us and toppled the rostrum, dashing the camera and us into the spiteful coral reef. I gashed my knee. Coral, of course, is animal, and coral poisoning occurs when the live coral gets into the flesh. The knee quickly festered and swelled alarmingly. I was running a high fever.

We had brought a doctor with us, Hampton Fancher. Hampton had been dying of angina when a colleague he had studied with called him up and told him he was experimenting with bypass surgery. He had tried it on two patients and they had both died. Hampton was going to die anyway. So he went under the knife, and it worked. Hampton celebrated his reprieve every single day, mostly at the Boom Boom Room, the only bar on the island. Lee usually helped him drink to his stolen days. Hampton had been a boxer, as his flattened nose testified. He had one eye, one lung and one testicle – the right side of his body had somehow failed.

Hampton gave me antibiotics but the knee got worse. Each of the islands throughout the South Pacific had a 'medical officer'. They took the brightest kid from each place and sent him for a year's medical training in Fiji. Ours, Domi, had already impressed us. A Chinese crew member from the ship had ruptured his spleen in a fall. Domi removed the spleen in his tin hut. There was massive blood loss. He had a chain of people with the right blood group taking turns to give blood directly by a connecting tube from the donor to the patient.

Domi examined my leg. He knew about coral poisoning. He told Dr Fancher that he had to cut out the coral right away or I would lose my leg. He handled the anaesthetic himself. Fancher stood next to him. He had been drinking. The last thing I remember was Fancher slurring out the words, 'Don't worry about a thing.'

I woke up in the Nissen hut. There were tubes draining my leg. There were four Palauans in the other beds. When it came to dinner time, the wives of the four other patients arrived, lit fires at the end of the beds and cooked supper.

We had stopped shooting. Hank Sapperstein arrived to deal with the crisis. He saw this as an opportunity to get rid of me. After all, I had dragged everybody to this impossible location, I was hopelessly behind schedule and over budget, and I couldn't handle Mifune.

He and Reuben put the case to Lee. Boorman is sick, who knows if he will be able to work, we have to replace him. Reluctantly, Lee acquiesced. He was tired and kicking his heels. Maybe someone else would make a fresh start with Mifune. I was hurt that his support, which had been so strong and decisive on *Point Blank*, was ebbing away.

Their next call was to Mifune's cabin. 'You'll be glad to hear that we are replacing Boorman,' they told him. Aki translated and listened attentively to Mifune's reply.

Aki recounted this meeting to me later in the 'hospital'. Mifune said he could not agree to this. 'But you hate Boorman. You don't get on with him.' Mifune said that was true, but he had agreed to make the picture with me. We had toasted this arrangement with the best saki in a tea house in Tokyo. It was a matter of honour.

Aki said with glee that the astonishment on the faces of Sapperstein and Berkovitch was something to behold.

'We're making a movie here,' said Sapperstein. 'What has honour got to do with it?'

Mifune was baffled by the question.

The production was stopped for three days. I resumed directing on a litter carried by four Palauans. I still had a drain in my knee. Mifune had saved me. Surely now our problems would be over?

On the contrary, the struggle resumed. In fact, it got worse. We clashed badly on the very first scene on resumption. Unbelievably, Mifune was back with the Hashimoto version. I exploded. 'Is he deliberately making problems?' Aki said, 'Please don't make me say that.' 'Translate it, just like that.' Making his body language as obsequious as possible, he did it. Mifune was terrifying. He screamed abuse at Aki, while turning to me from time to time with a reassuring smile, as though I had nothing to do with it.

It got worse that evening. I went through the scene, step by step, explaining what I wanted him to do. He would not yield, his face impassive. Then he repeated his understanding of what I had said. Incredibly, it was still the Hashimoto version. I was weak and in pain. There was no end in sight. I thought I would die before I finished the picture. 'Are you stupid or just malicious?' I said. 'I can't say that to him,' said Aki. 'You're not saying it, I am saying it.' 'He'll kill me.' 'Translate, or you're fired.' With head bowed, he mumbled the words. Mifune hit him with a clenched fist. Aki fell to the floor and stayed there prostrate at Mifune's feet.

Many years later, a collection of British directors gave a dinner for Kurosawa when he was in London promoting *Ran* – his film inspired by *King Lear*. I was deputed to give the eulogy. It was hard to be fluent when I had to pause for each sentence to be translated. It reminded me of that ghastly experience with Mifune, the frustrating waits and the fact that thirty seconds of English could take two minutes to render in Japanese. Kurosawa had been very still and silent throughout the dinner. Attempts to engage him in dialogue had failed. He seemed determined to remain silent. David Lean was sitting next to me. I asked a question. 'Is it true Kurosawa-san, that you only do one set-up per day?' Kurosawa thought about it deeply before he answered, then he said, 'How many set-ups does Mr Lean do each day?' 'No, no. He asked you first,' said David. More translation. A long wait. Finally, the answer came. 'As many as necessary.' His face was still expressionless. There was no hint of humour or irony.

So as I made my broken speech, waiting between sentences, the Mifune story came to mind. Impulsively, I decided to tell it. When I came to the point where Mifune punches Aki, Kurosawa's face reddened. He started heaving, and guttural sounds came up from his belly. We were alarmed. Was he having a heart attack, a seizure? His body was shaking. It was as though he was trying to hold back some internal volcanic eruption. Finally, he let it go and began to laugh uncontrollably. 'Mifune!' He kept repeating the name. Eventually he recovered his aplomb, but as he was leaving he whispered in my ear in rather good English, 'Very funny. Very, very funny.' He went out chuckling into the night.

Wounded and weary, I persevered. Conrad Hall's enthusiasm and drive kept me going. He loved his camera. Often when he had finished lighting, he would look in the viewfinder and let out orgasmic cries, so impressed was he by the beauty of what he had created. Designing the shots and making compositions is something that I do alone. When I had set up a shot, Conrad would move the camera six inches to the left or push it in a foot closer. He had this need to make the shot his own. I learnt a great deal from him about lighting. He always had a paint can at hand to spray out hot spots or dull down obtrusive bright objects. Most of our scenes were exterior, but he would paint leaves and rocks, moisten dull surfaces, punch light across foliage to highlight it. He also taught me how to use time, to make the most of every moment, to have an alternative standing by if a shot was delayed. 'Cut. Print. Next shot.' Then I call for the viewfinder and the lens. '75 mm lens.' No celebrations. No post mortems.

After *Hell in the Pacific* Conrad was going to photograph *Butch Cassidy and the Sundance Kid*. There was a plan to shoot a sequence over-exposed. He devised a clever way of testing this. On the head of each shot we film the slate – the clapperboard that records the scene and take number. He over-exposed each slate by one or two stops, so that he could judge the effect in many different lighting conditions – day, night, backlit, the effect of over-exposure. He went on to win the Academy Award for that picture. More than thirty years on he got another one for *American Beauty*, and then a posthumous one for *Road to Perdition*.

Tony Pratt was having the same kind of problems with the Japanese art director as I was having with Mifune. We would discuss the set to be built. The Japanese art director would produce designs which were incorrect or needed adjusting. Tony and I would explain what we wanted. The set would go up without the changes. It would all have to be redone. The Japanese floor crew, on the other hand, was exceptional. They didn't talk or eat on the set. They kept still until required. The prop men were very skilful. They could make anything.

I had an American key grip, Art Brooker, who had worked with Conrad Hall on many pictures. He was six foot four inches tall, a Gulliver surrounded by a squad of Japanese grips half his size. One day they carried a rostrum into the sea; Art was in front with three Japanese grips holding up the back. As Art got chest-deep in water, they were totally submerged. Art was facing out to sea and could not see them. Rather than give up, so dedicated were they, they took turns coming up for air and kept going underwater.

I had a gay Japanese set dresser. When I asked him to fetch something he would shuffle off slowly, taking tiny little steps, a kind of ritual running. When he brought me the object he would say 'Excuse me,' except it came out sounding like 'kiss me'. Then he would pant three times to indicate that he was ritually breathless from his ritual running.

Our slow progress, the heat and humidity, the isolation from the world, were taking their toll. The Chinese sailors were clashing with the Japanese. Our big tough Americans started whining like babies when we ran out of peanut butter. The Japanese crew were all convinced that the Americans had dropped the atom bomb on them and not on the Germans because the Germans were the same race as them. Deep resentments surfaced across all the divides.

Reuben Berkovitch's endless complaints to the Chinese captain were finally too much for him. He accused Reuben of being 'a Jewish running dog' – whatever that was. One night Captain Chan got drunk, picked up a billiard cue and challenged Reuben to a duel. Reuben insisted that since he was paying for the ship, he was the ultimate authority. Captain Chan's answer was quick in coming. When the crew awoke next morning they found they were on the high seas. The Captain had upped anchors and was on his way back to Taiwan.

Lloyd Anderson, our patient production manager, was sent up to the bridge by Reuben to negotiate a return. We still had a month's shooting to complete. Messages were sent back and forth. The Captain wanted apologies, a new charter defining his authority. Reuben was to be banned from speaking to the Captain. Reuben capitulated. Another shooting day lost.

Free Love

Despite the racial tensions between the outsiders, the Palauans, on the other hand, simply loved all of us: the women's sexual generosity was touching, although it inspired fear in some of the crew. Something so freely given must be suspect. Where's the catch? What are they after? One member of the crew, Charles, had fled with his family from the Nazis in 1939. He found himself in England speaking only German. He was eleven. Although he was a Jew, to his fellow schoolboys he was a German. They could see no distinction. In order to escape their retribution he acquired a flawless English accent in record time. He remained in England only for the duration of the war. His family moved to America where he had spent the past twenty years. His English accent had so branded his brain, so seared his soul, that not a trace of American pronunciation had been able to get a footing. He was a pedantic, rigid fellow. He was horrified by the loose ways of the Palauans and felt particularly threatened by their promiscuity. He seldom ventured from the ship.

Towards the end of the shoot, the Palauans proposed to give us a party. In his voyages, Captain Cook would drop off a pig and a sow on islands that he visited to provide meat for subsequent voyages. Their descendants lived on these beaches eating papaya and wallowing in the warm waves. Occasionally one of Palau's sea-going crocodiles would snatch one. A large pit was dug in the sand and lined with rocks. A fire was set to heat the stones. A pig was dropped in and covered with sand. It simmered for three days, steam bubbled up and the odour of roast pork wafted across the island, an olfactory invitation to the party. The pig was duly disinterred. The slow cooking and the diet of papaya made the flesh tender if slightly bland. The dancing on the beach, the food and wine loosened even Charles's rigid morals. Dragged into the bushes by one of the girls, he finally succumbed.

The next day he reported to Dr Hampton Fancher with a case of the clap. Hampton's one good but myopic eye examined Charles's penis at close range but could find no evidence. The problem obsessed Charles for the remaining days on the island. He consulted Domi, who had saved my leg, but he could find no visible symptoms either. Charles was in despair. He dreaded facing his wife. 'What if she should become amorous?' he said. On the way home he stopped off in Hawaii and found a urologist who also failed to find evidence of venereal disease. Charles insisted that he felt a vague pain around his genitals. He was in a knot of guilt. He felt his suffering was deserved. In LA, he checked in to the UCLA hospital. They said that to investigate further, they would need to insert a rod into the penis with a lens attached, to examine the bladder. He was given an epidural. Nothing was found. However, the epidural injection left him with an excruciating back pain. He had to walk with a stick. But he was content. At last a punishment had been inflicted that matched his sin.

Not with a Whimper but a Bang

We dragged ourselves through to the end. We shot pretty much in sequence. The pattern of the story began with the men discovering each other, being consumed with fear. Mifune was there first and had established a water supply and found food. Lee terrorises him, trying to steal his equipment. He conducts guerrilla warfare. Mifune captures Marvin but finds he cannot kill him, cannot destroy the only other human life on the island, perhaps the only human contact he will ever have. Lee is trussed up but his eyes follow Mifune everywhere. Mifune cannot bear it. He blindfolds Lee. Lee escapes and turns the tables on Mifune, but finds being the master more difficult than being the slave. Out of exhaustion and despair they collaborate on building a raft in an attempt to escape. After great suffering they succeed in reaching a larger island and discover a deserted, ruined army camp that has been held by the Americans and the Japanese at different times. They shave their beards and find uniforms. Once they are defined by their insignia, it is impossible for them to remain together. Neither can they kill each other. A kind of bond had been forged between them. Mifune salutes and walks away.

That was my ending, at least. The picture did not do well commercially. Mr Sapperstein, without consulting me, found a stock shot of an explosion and blew them up before their parting. So it ended not with a whimper but a bang. The effect was deeply and cruelly pessimistic. They had made this huge effort only to be crushed by a stray bomb. My statement was that enemies forced into such intimacy would at least not kill each other, even if their cultural and nationalistic divide would not allow them to become friends. Some kind of similar bond existed between Mifune and me. We shook hands at the end. If there was little affection, there was some respect. We had come through it. Lee and I were never to work together again, although we made several attempts. Our bond was strong. We remained close friends until his death.

1968: Back to LA

I got back to LA and went out to dinner with my lawyer, Ed Gross. I was exhausted, my nerves in tatters. I told him the story of the shoot – the bitter struggle with Mifune, Lee's loss of faith in me. I started to weep. I couldn't stop. I never wanted to make another movie. I wanted to flee America. But I had sold my house in London, and I had months of post-production ahead of me at Goldwyn Studios.

William Faulkner said of LA, 'You go there to write a picture. You stay on to do one more. One perfect day follows another. Then, one day, up in one of the canyons, a leaf falls from a tree and suddenly you are old.'

Back in Malibu in the LA summer limbo. The kids on the beach, the surfers waiting for a wave. The morning mist bleaches out at noon into blistering heat. The hot sky, the white ocean, the dazzling sand conspire to numb the sense of time. In my fragile state it felt an ominous place with no purchase, no seasons, no substance. A bland metropolis threatened by fires, quakes, floods, slides. A place that might, at any moment, slip off the face of the earth.

The people seemed sapped of instinct. They walked and talked just like people, but something essential was missing. They had to learn how it was done, nothing was bred in the bone. California worked for those, like Isherwood, who deliberately wished to free themselves of an abhorrent culture, who had the inner resources to reinvent themselves, but most were lost, without bearings, with no sense of themselves. They bought books on how to be human. I recall a woman lying on the beach reading a book on how to bond with your baby. Thirty yards away the nanny played with her baby.

While I was in Palau, Bill Stair had stayed on in LA to work on the Tom Wolfe idea and *I Hear America*. He toiled fitfully under the protection of Chartoff and Winkler, who, following the success of *Point Blank*, were hot. They tried to repeat the trick by making another of the Parker stories of Donald Westlake. It didn't click. I found Bill had become surprisingly at ease in LA. He met other paranoids and his mental condition did not seem at all unusual in that place. A fellow sufferer recommended a psychiatrist. Bill hated being tall and gangling. Inside, he felt he was a short and stocky person. As he walked into the consulting room for the first time, he was devastated to discover that his therapist was a dwarf with a hunchback. Bill's first paranoid thought was that the paranoid friend had maliciously sent him there, knowing how troubled he was about his height. How could he possibly complain about being too tall to someone four feet high? As it was, Bill had plenty of other problems to discuss, and went twice a week. Each time he promised himself he would get around to the height issue, but never could.

Tentatively, Bill and I started working on the two projects. I looked over the work that Bill had done. I had lost my nerve and Bill sensed it. My ability to make decisions, to be in control, was comforting to Bill. He flourished in a secure environment. Now, confronted by my doubts and uncertainty, he clamped up. He became stiff and tight. We blamed LA. Bob Chartoff showed us a short story by George Tabori, a friend of his; it was called 'The Prince' and was about a European aristocrat set down in a black ghetto. Bill and I fell upon it. It could be set in London. I thought of Notting Hill, the Caribbean quarter I knew through my sister Wendy. It offered a way of escaping America, whereas the other ideas would have clamped me to it. After the narrow meanness of England, I had found America exhilarating, but these two pictures had been too much for me. America, like Lee Marvin, was big, violent, generous and dangerous. It was an exciting love affair but I didn't want to get married. I wanted to go home.

1969: *Leo the Last*

Back in London we quickly outgrew the Tabori story but revelled in the script it inspired. We called it *Leo the Last*. A European aristocratic ornithologist inherits a mansion in the midst of a slum and watches his neighbours through a telescope. The Notting Hill district of London is comprised of large middle-class family houses. Many of the owners fled when the war started and the exiled Polish community moved in. After the war, the Poles mostly drifted away and the houses became tenements for the immigrant West Indians. They were disgracefully exploited by landlords (many of them Polish), a situation that came to light with the Rachman scandal, revealing conditions in which thirty people were packed into a single room. The word 'Rachmanism' was coined to describe the behaviour of these ruthless landlords. We appropriated the situation for our story.

We gave Leo some of Bill's paranoia. Leo could connect with the vivid life of the street through his eyepiece, but his grasping friends – lawyer, doctor, Polish patriot, predatory woman – were grotesquely distorted, seen through his mental anguish. Bill gave him a line which reflected Bill's own inability to connect: 'The closer I get, the further away I feel.' Leo eventually discovers that his leisured life has been supported by rents from the slum that surrounds him. He is mortified and attempts to give his house and money to the people of the street, with predictably disastrous results. We wanted to imply that we are all Leos, living off the poor of the world.

As our story grew in ambition, my anguish diminished and hubris took its place. In the air at that time was the belief that we were on the verge of a breakthrough, that film could evolve into something transcendent. The silent era rapidly produced a system of visual conventions that allowed the expression of complex emotions and ideas, films like *Greed* and *Intolerance*. With the coming of sound, the word became dominant and the cumbersome sound camera meant that the movies could hardly move, let alone fly. It was a setback, but now there were intimations that a great new surge forward was imminent. The French New Wave had swept all before it. Directors in England and the US were seizing the day. The Hollywood studios had been defeated by television and no longer knew what to make. They abdicated in favour of directors. Maybe experiment and originality could work.

In *The Newcomers*, and to some extent in *Catch Us If You Can*, I had tried mixing styles. Dangerously, I pressed the idea much further with *Leo the Last*. Besides the contrast between the gritty reality seen through Leo's telescope and the highly stylised scenes in the mansion, I built a complex soundtrack comprising songs that spoke the thoughts of the characters and a mélange of voices, including my own, which commented on the action. In the first scene, as we see Leo's face in a car driving into the slum street, the words of the song are:

> Who's that man coming down our street
> In a great big motor car
> I've seen that face before
> He's a movie star.
> It was pre-post modern!

We were heavily influenced by Luciano Berio's musical collage of voices. Fred Myrow, who wrote the music and songs for the film, got the Swingle Singers to use their marvellous range of vocal sounds to weave the various textures together. I wanted the audience to be aware that they were watching a movie and that the movie-makers were playfully commenting on their own work. I conceived it as a series of layers. This, of course, flies in the face of what movies do best, which is to suck you in, manipulate your emotions and hold you in the grip of an illusion. During the making and editing of the film, I often felt it slipping out of control; 'things fly apart, the centre will not hold,' was one of many poetic quotes on the soundtrack. To harmonise and draw these elements together I again considered the colour question. I decided to exclude all colour from the sets, the street and mansion – flesh tones being the exception. We painted the street black and eliminated all colour from props, clothes, furniture. I wanted to give the impression that the audience had entered a parallel world where the rules and behaviour were slightly skewed.

Marcello Mastroianni

As we were writing the script, we kept thinking about Marcello Mastroianni, and soon we could imagine no one else in the role. I went to Venice to persuade him to do the movie. I found him sitting with Faye Dunaway on the terrace of the Gritti Palace Hotel. It was not long since *Bonnie and Clyde* and Faye was the hottest thing in Hollywood. Tourists on gondolas and water-buses glided past, heads turned in awed unison at the sight of the Latin legend and the American goddess. Marcello wore the bemused but resigned air that we all know so well from his movies,

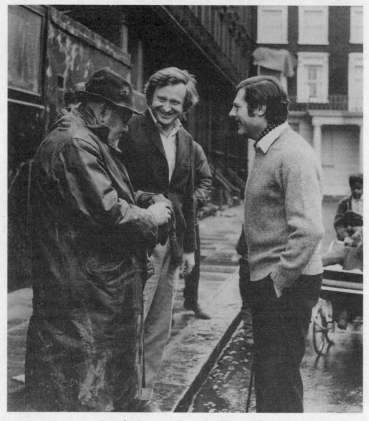

Leo the Last: on the set with Marcello

the one that says, 'I have no idea why people think I am a movie star, or why beautiful women want me to make love to them, but since it is so, it would be churlish of me not to respond.' I came to realise that he was that rare creature, an actor without vanity, self-deprecating, yet completely at ease with himself – which was the source of the enormous, effortless charm that included and beguiled all who came into his presence.

He came to London and we made the movie. He brought Faye with him and hid her away in an apartment that he decorated in shades of black. She was on the run from the pressures of new-found stardom and was content for a while to play the role of Italian housewife, having Marcello's pasta ready for him when he got back from the set. Whatever his current liaison, he would phone his wife, Flora, every day, without fail. He had an almost religious respect for women, which is perhaps why his affairs never seemed to end in bitterness. Somehow, he always contrived that the women left him. They broke his heart and they left on tiptoe.

One morning, Marcello arrived on set and I could see from his face that some tragedy had befallen him, the death of a loved one perhaps. I enquired delicately, consolingly. I was, after all, his director, his confidant, his confessor. He said, 'It's finished. My life is over.'

'Marcello, tell me. I'll help you.'

'You cannot help. I have just heard that they have legalised divorce in Italy.'

Some time later I visited him in Paris when he was living with Catherine Deneuve. The apartment was very modern, chrome, with white furniture, like a negative photo of his London flat except that the blonde was still blonde. Catherine went to the kitchen to make coffee. Marcello turned to me and whispered, 'John, you have no idea what my life is here. She is . . .' he gestured at the cool décor, 'so cold.' Catherine came back in. He smiled sweetly at her. I found myself feeling sorry for him because he had to live with the divine Deneuve. Everybody was always sorry for Marcello. Everyone wanted to help him. Women were alarmed at his helplessness and threw their arms around him to protect him, and that was where he was at home and at ease – not exactly in the bosom of his family, but in his extended family of bosoms.

He said to me once, 'Why do Americans find acting so difficult? For me acting is like making love. While I'm doing it, I enjoy it, and when it is over I hope I can do it again tomorrow.'

He would arrive in the morning, no more conscious than a side of beef. His dresser, Fred, would administer a cup of the severest espresso, which he drank while putting on his costume. With the clothes he also put on the character, Leo. It was a total transformation. He stayed that way throughout the day. I could have filmed him in his lunch break. At six, he put on his own clothes, shed the character he was playing and never gave it another thought till the espresso hit him the following morning. He was like a skilled artisan, working contentedly but always glad to hear the whistle.

He could make any scene work and live. A lift of an eye, a gesture could render lines of dialogue redundant. Technically, he could manoeuvre himself through the most awkward moves to make a camera position work. I would show him a complicated series of marks that he had to hit. He would shrug. No problem: 'Sophia Loren would only be photographed on one profile, so I was always dancing around her to get on the good side. This is nothing.'

Marcello understood that film actors spent most of their time waiting. And most of them hate it. They tense up. They send out vibrations of resentment. Kubrick kept his actors waiting more than most. During the making of *Barry Lyndon* I ran into Patrick Magee in the Hibernian Hotel in Dublin. He had been on call for three months and had yet to shoot a scene. 'Indolence is the sepulchre of the intelligence,' he bellowed alcoholically. Marcello, on the other hand, waited profoundly. He waited in the hotel lobby where Fellini was preparing *8½* and trying to cast an American star. Marcello did not insist, he did not protest, he did not plead, he was simply present. Either Fellini couldn't find an American he wanted, or the one he wanted didn't want him. As the options narrowed, the patient Marcello was still there.

I never felt the need to apologise to Marcello for keeping him waiting. I had a scene where he was asleep in bed. While we were lighting and lining up, he simply fell asleep in the bed. I had to wake him up, so that he could act being asleep.

I had dinner with him in Paris, not long before he died. A girl of twelve came over for his autograph. He said, 'When I started out the young girls would come and they would say, "It's for my sister," then I got older and they would say, "It is for my mother."' He signed for the little girl, saying, 'I suppose this is for your grandmother.'

I always came back early from the lunch break so that I could walk the empty set and arrange my thoughts. One day towards the end of the shoot, I found Leo's house on fire.

I carry the film in my head, shot by shot. Each night before I go to sleep, I run it through, connecting the shots we have made to the ones yet to be filmed. This helps me to control the rhythm and pace. Confronted with the fire, the movie flashed through my mind's eye at ultra-high speed. There were several shots in the house yet to be done. In a microsecond I calculated which ones could be done with alternative props or on a substitute set. There was only one essential shot that could not be replicated: Mastroianni, clutching a vase of white lilies, goes to a window and looks out. It was a direct cut from a shot we had done of Marcello climbing the stairs. The lilies had to match. I raced up the stairs

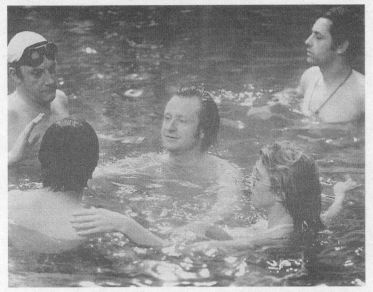

Leo the Last: directing Graham Crowden (far left)
and Billie Whitelaw (far right)

through the heat and dense smoke and retrieved the lilies and the vase. The London *Times* carried the story with the headline: 'Film director risks life for plastic lilies.' They were real lilies, in fact, but plastic made a better story. *The Times* was already in decline from the high standards of those Korean War days.

Ironically, we were planning to incinerate the house as the finale of the movie. So we restored the exterior, then set it alight, this time with several cameras recording the event. It was a beautiful ending. I wanted it to match the wonder of burning houses I had witnessed in the Blitz.

When my friend David had tried for a job as a clapper-loader we both thought of such a humble job not as a starting-off point, but as a sublime fulfilment, a vocation. David did eventually snag a job and got his ticket. He would get occasional gigs, and dropped everything to do them. He neglected the dry-cleaning business and finally it ran down and he sold out. We lost touch, but when I was shooting this final scene we brought in extra cameras and crews and David was among them, still a clapper-loader. By now he had broken up with my sister Wendy.

We were delighted to see each other. We fell into an orgy of silly voices and wracking laughter. We swore to keep in touch, but I was seldom in the country. When I did look him up, I was shocked to discover he had died.

One Saturday night at the end of a week's shoot we went to dinner at Mr Chow's with Tony Woollard and his wife Joan, who was designing the costumes for the film. It was stuffy and crowded. I was exhausted and wishing I was at home in bed. Christel was disrupting every attempt at conversation, and interrupted particularly whenever I spoke. It was her way of objecting to my lack of attention. She was right. In the white heat of making the movie I had neglected her. Nevertheless, I felt an irrational rage rising. I stood up and said, 'We're leaving.' She refused to move. I took her hand and tried to pull her to her feet. She resisted. I gave another tug just as she decided to get up after all. She went flying past me. We were at a table next to a narrow spiral staircase. She spun down it, half falling. I rushed after her, pulled her to her feet and hustled her out into the street. A taxi had stopped outside in the convenient way that usually only happens in the movies. I bundled her in. We sat in silence. I thought this must finally be the end of our rocky marriage. She said, 'As I was falling, I saw all these women's eyes and I could see that they all wished they had a man who cared about them enough to throw them down the stairs.' She had got my attention. We both started laughing.

Unknown to me, the legendary agent Bobby Littman was dining at Mr Chow's that night. So entranced was he by the drama that he stepped up and paid our bill and sent Christel flowers, congratulating her on a wonderful performance. He became a friend, though never my agent. We usually met up when I was in LA. One night at dinner he boasted of a deal he had done that day for Ken Russell to make a movie of Oscar Wilde's *Salome*. 'Is that the version with Lindsay Kemp?' I asked. Bobby paled. He said, 'You have to swear to me not to mention this to anyone until the deal is signed. You are the only man in town who knows Lindsay Kemp is a man.' He had told Columbia that Lindsay Kemp would be playing Salome, but not that he was a fifty-year-old queen. They must have found out eventually, for the film was never made.

Ireland

We did the post-production for *Leo* at Ardmore Studios in Ireland. We rented a castellated Victorian house on the beach in Killiney and explored the Wicklow Mountains. The soft, feminine folds of the hills, the bleak bogs, the ancient oak woods, the black lakes, the urgent streams somehow corresponded to an inner landscape. It was harmonious. It fitted. It felt like a setting for the Arthurian legend.

I liked the ease of the people, the teasing banter and the way that music and theatre were a part of life and not something separate. Although hag-ridden by priests and oppressed by the Church, I felt Catholicism was only skin deep, that underneath it was a pagan place. For all its sorrows and suffering, Ireland had at least escaped the brutalising effect of the Industrial Revolution which, in England, had sucked people from the land to the misery of city slums. In Ireland in 1969 most people were only a generation or two away from the land, from the farm. They had a robust sense of identity, which the people I came from had lost. Of course there was the flip side of the coin. For a subject people, the rebel tradition had left an admiration for the law-breaker and a tolerance of corruption. The banter could quickly become spite; the ease, fecklessness; the charm could mask hypocrisy.

The deep connection I felt was tempered by being an outsider, embraced but at arm's length, which suited me well. I discovered the poetry of John Montague and Seamus Heaney. They defined the authentic Irish experience. I met Garech Browne and he introduced me to Irish music. My Irish grandmother's blood stirred my heart. We thought how fine it would be to have a little holiday cottage in the hills. Christel and I searched in a half-hearted way. We still had not decided whether to go back to the States or return to London. We were drifting along in limbo.

One Sunday we were directed to Annamoe to a Church of Ireland rectory that was for sale. It stood in a lovely wooded valley and a river ran through it. It was a plain late-Georgian house. I discovered it was being auctioned the very next day. There was no time to have it surveyed. These old houses in rainy Ireland are full of wet rot. Besides which, it was hardly a cottage, much too big. I put it out of mind. Next day, I happened to be in Dublin and I found myself passing the auctioneers. I dropped in out of curiosity. The bidding began. There were two parties vying for the property. In a kind of out-of-body experience, I watched the two contenders. One of them appeared to be me. I was being congratulated. My unconscious had settled the matter. I sank all my savings into the place. It became our home by default. I have lived in that same house ever since.

I became entranced by the fast-flowing river that emptied the mountain bogs and curves at the foot of the house. Further downstream, still on my land, is a hidden swimming hole, shrouded in overhanging trees. There I swim naked and alone in the black water. This was formerly a glacial valley and the water has a profound coldness, a glacial memory. To swim against that flow is to make its force palpable. It washed away the last traces of the suburban boy. I belonged at last.

The Lord of the Rings

United Artists financed *Leo the Last*, and before it came out, while I was still in good odour, they asked me what I would like to do next. I gave them a treatment I had written about Merlin, inspired by my new home. David Picker, the head of the company, did not respond to it, but asked me to make a film of *The Lord of the Rings*, to which they owned the film rights.

I had nurtured the notion of making a movie about the Grail legend from the very beginning. My script of *A Glastonbury Romance* still lay in my drawer. This myth had guided me since childhood. Tolkien's trilogy draws on that legend, as well as various Celtic and Norse sagas. Frodo is the classic young innocent, entrusted with a momentous and terrifying quest. He is helped by the wizard Gandalf. For Frodo read Arthur, for Gandalf – Merlin. To compress the three volumes into a three-hour movie was a hugely ambitious undertaking, but I was grateful to have the chance to try. I was interested in the central metaphor, that the One Ring is of such power that it corrupts whoever possesses it. Gandalf entrusts its safekeeping to a Hobbit whose goodness and innocence is the only defence against its seductive force. I needed help in this daunting task. In New York I had met a young Italian architect, Rospo Pallenberg, who wanted to work in the movies.

I had been impressed by his high intelligence and unconventional mind. I asked him to co-write it with me. He came to Annamoe and we covered the walls of a large room with a breakdown of all the scenes in the three volumes. We made a detailed map of Middle Earth and an analysis of the characters. It took us several weeks. Much the most difficult part of the process was to devise a structure for the film. Shaping and condensing the mass of material was hard enough, but I also had to devise technical solutions to the special-effects problems. There was no computer then to generate magic, to miniaturise the Hobbits, to create monsters. The text is very visual, but at climactic points Tolkien would often resort to poetic evasion. As when Gandalf is vanquished: 'He fell beyond time and memory' – how do you film that? Eventually, we started writing. I wrote the first scene, Rospo wrote the second. We leapfrogged each other. At night we would study each other's work and make notes. My own valley is as close to Middle Earth as you can get in this depleted world. Rospo and I spent a wondrous six months in a mythic space. I once described the film-making process as inventing impossible problems for yourself and then failing to solve them. I relished the magnitude, the danger. I was ready to do battle. This could be the one, the ultimate movie.

During that time United Artists suffered a number of setbacks, including the failure of *Leo the Last*. *The Lord of the Rings* was an expensive project dependent on innovative special effects. By the time we submitted the script, the executive who had espoused it had left the company and no one else there had read the book. They had neither the money nor the conviction to make it. I took it to Disney and other places, but no one else wanted to do it. Tolkien had reluctantly sold the film rights to set up a trust for his grandchildren. He wrote to me asking how I intended to make it. I explained it would be live action and he was much relieved. He had a dread that it would be an animation film. He was comforted by my reply.

His death spared him the eventual outcome: UA gave it to Ralph Bakshi, the animator. I could never bring myself to watch the result. I tried to revive the project years later when Mike Medavoy was running Tri-Star. Saul Zaentz had produced the Bakshi picture and still held the film rights. Mike authorised me to offer him a million dollars. Saul said making the Bakshi film had been the worst experience of his life. He agreed to sell but would want nothing further to do with it. Despite this, he insisted on retaining the merchandising rights. Mike couldn't live with that, so the project collapsed again.

Now it has finally been made, wisely, as three films, at the other end of the earth and by another director as brave and foolish as I was. Had I made my version the world would have been denied the magnificent spectacle that Peter Jackson has created. I have seen only the first part, but it is of such scope and magnitude that it can only be compared to the building of the great Gothic cathedrals. My concept shrivels by comparison. For instance, to solve the half-size Hobbit problem I was intending to cast ten-year-old boys, give them facial hair and dub them with adult voices!

Tolkien was fascinated by the violence of ancient myth, yet lived the safe and privileged life of an Oxford don, and the terrors of his sagas are set against a nostalgia for a cosy bucolic England where decent people knew their place, authority was respected and there was no sex.

Despite my disappointment at the time, it was a valuable experience and it prepared the ground for the script Rospo and I eventually wrote, *Excalibur*. Many of the special-effects techniques I developed at that time were put to good use in *The Heretic*, *Zardoz* and *Excalibur*. Nevertheless, like most film-makers, I have spent more time on movies I have not made than on ones that I have. The deeper the emotional involvement, the greater the sense of loss. I was steeped in Middle Earth and letting it go was painful, but there was also relief, because we had devised an almost unmakeable script. It might have been that elusive transcendent movie, and it might have come crashing about my ears.

We finished *Leo the Last* and took it to Cannes 1970. *M*A*S*H* won the Palme d'Or. I got the Best Director prize. (I received the same award nearly thirty years later for *The General*.) *Leo the Last* was a hit in France and failed dismally everywhere else. It played one week in New York. It was scarcely noticed. I had that bleak feeling of worthlessness, of being found out, the same feeling I had when my father caught me lying about cricket. I had made four pictures and although the first three had got by, I had not made a commercial hit. I had seen several of my contemporaries fall away after a couple of misses. The brutal reality of the movie business is that if you don't make money for your masters, you are banished. The fear of never being allowed to make another film is the sword of Damocles that hangs over us. Kubrick once said to me, 'It's not that I want to make a hit, I just don't want to make a dud, and the only way not to make a dud is to make a hit.' I was chastened and decided I should put aside my quest for the ultimate movie and make something more conventional.

1970: *Deliverance*

Warners had taken an option on James Dickey's book *Deliverance*, but they had doubts about it. The head of production, John Calley, asked me to read it. He proposed that I write the screenplay, produce and direct it. Calley had been a producer himself, yet his policy was to have directors produce their own pictures. He was nurturing Kubrick and Sydney Pollack amongst others. He understood the process and knew that it was much simpler dealing with one person rather than adjudicating between director and producer – or between six or seven producers, as is sometimes the case today. Calley was your pal, but if things went wrong he was sometimes hard to locate and you could find yourself facing the severity of his boss, Ted Ashley. John had a passion for luxury cars and yachts and he bought and sold them. He was a beguiling raconteur, but when he got down to business he was in deadly earnest – yet at the same time, he never lost sight of how ludicrous it all was. In a town where almost all are neurotically obsessed with 'the industry', his ironic distance was original and refreshing. Before the first screening of *Clockwork Orange* I was talking with Calley in the street when Sydney Pollack drove up in his brand new Mercedes. Calley looked in the window. 'Gee, Sydney, you must be really secure not to need leather upholstery,' he marvelled.

Because he thought I had contacts with the IRA he asked me if I could get him a rocket launcher for his yacht. He thought the collapse of civilisation was imminent; he intended to take to the high seas and he would need to defend himself. Later he dropped out and lived in seclusion on an island off the coast of Maine, preparing for the apocalypse. He eventually got tired of waiting and went back to run Sony Pictures.

I read the novel with mounting excitement. I knew how to do it. Its themes coincided with my own: man's relationship to nature, the attempt to recover a lost harmony, the Earth's anger at the despoiling human race. At its centre was the rape of the city men by the mountain men. It was a metaphor for the rape of America. Lévi-Strauss in *Tristes tropiques* asks why Europeans who nurtured their land for centuries became rapacious when they came to America. In the story, four successful middle-class men from Atlanta want to canoe down a wild river before it is tamed and subsumed by a huge dam which will produce electricity for their air-conditioners.

It transpired that Dickey had written a screenplay himself. He had simply put the entire novel into script form. I wrote my own version and submitted it to the studio. Calley liked it and I went out to LA to discuss the logistics of making it. It was all very simple in those days. You didn't get reams of notes from the 'creative department'. However, Warners felt it was a picture of limited appeal and they did not want to spend more than two million dollars on making it. My English production manager, Charles Orme, and I had a brief discussion with the budget and production department at Warners, and then left for Atlanta to meet with Dickey. He lived in a comfortable suburban house in Columbus, Georgia, trailed around by his little round wife, Maxine, and her almost identical mother, Maxine 2. He spent much of his time trying to shake them off. I came to believe that this desire to escape domesticity was the impulse that drove him to write *Deliverance*.

Dickey was an imposing presence, his large frame still managing to carry his heavy flesh with some dignity. He had fierce wild eyes, a look he cultivated to give the impression of an inner poetic fire. His poetry readings were dramatic affairs. Sometimes he would falter, too moved by one of his own lines to continue, or at another point tears would undo him. It was thrilling stuff. The illusion suffered, however, when you saw him a second time: he would be spontaneously moved by exactly the same line and tears would flow at precisely the same point as before. The poet Robert Lowell said to me once, dryly, 'He reads them better than he writes them.' The poems themselves were raw and electric, but I later discovered that he had used up all his honesty in them and there was none left for his life.

We talked all evening, feeling each other out. He probed away at me. It so happened that *Catch Us If You Can* was being shown on television the next day. It was retitled in the States as *Having a Wild Weekend*. 'Is that a pornographic movie?' he boomed. 'No,' I said, '*Deliverance* will be my first pornographic picture.' The wife and mother-in-law cackled. 'He got you there, Jim.'

After a bottle of Jack Daniels had been rapidly consumed, Dickey took me aside and, with a look of fervent solemnity, said, 'I'm going to tell you something I've never told a living soul.' A long dramatic pause while he held my eyes with his, searching to see if I was worthy. '*Everything* in that book happened to me.' My mind raced across the story. Two mountain men killed with arrows, Bobby sodomised. I was shocked, shaken to the core. What was I getting into?

It was late by the time Charles Orme and I left Dickey's house for our hotel. Since he had made me swear to keep his secret, I naturally couldn't wait to tell someone. I spilled it all to Charles. 'Yes, he told me that too,' said Charles. 'He cornered me when I went for a pee.'

The next day we drove up into the Appalachian mountains with a couple of his pals. They brought canoes and bows and arrows, the elements of the story. As soon as Dickey got into a canoe I realised that *nothing* in that book had happened to him. He struggled awkwardly for a few minutes then tipped ignominiously into the river. He dragged himself up the bank and fell into a diabetic seizure, frothing at the mouth. We carried him to a farmhouse where he gulped down apple juice. I was more impressed by a man who could imagine this story than by one who could live it.

I began to see that the four characters in the story were aspects of his own personality. Ed was the advertising copywriter Dickey had once been, a man vaguely dissatisfied with a life of domestic ease. Drew played the guitar, as did Dickey, and was the artist. Lewis was an archer like Dickey, an obsessed outdoors man, with a fascistic belief that only the ruthless and the strong would survive the coming collapse of civilisation. Bobby represented the coward that Dickey revealed in many of his poems – the fear of flying, of pain, of demons, of dying. Just as *Point Blank* became a study of Lee Marvin, so *Deliverance* was to be partly about Dickey himself. In the course of the story the decent Ed evolves into Lewis the killer; he experiences the cowardice of Bobby and sees the goodness of Drew perish in the raging waters of the river.

It was tough to get Dickey to discuss the script. The book, the movie and his delusion that it had all occurred were somehow inextricably tangled up in the alcoholic mist that usually enveloped him. It was his story, they were his characters, it was his terrain and he was understandably reluctant to surrender them. However, we worked well in correspondence. His letters were cogent and rational and beautifully written and you could hear his voice, the lilt of his mind, as you read them. Very soon cracks appeared in our collaboration, and they soon widened into unbridgeable chasms.

The first difficulty lay with the opening. The first third of the novel explores the lives of the four men in Atlanta. Dickey cleverly evokes the indeterminate dissatisfactions of their comfortable lives. I decided to start the movie with the construction of the dam that will tame and kill this beautiful river, interposed with the four men arriving in the mountains with their canoes. I argued that the casting of the four men, their manner and behaviour would tell the audience most of what they needed to know and that their uncertainties should emerge in the course of the action. Dickey could not make the leap from novel to film. I wanted very much to have him with me, on my side; and in my letters I patiently argued the case, but could not wholly convince him. This was, as much as anything, a technical problem, a time issue, a pacing thing.

Things got rougher when we came to consider the core of the piece. Dickey's view is that the tamed, suburban Ed is fulfilled and strengthened when he is obliged to kill and survive. I wanted to say that the myth of regeneration through violence is an illusion. Far from finding his identity, I wanted Ed to be haunted, coarsened and diminished by the experience. The river, which no longer exists, still flows through Ed's troubled mind, I argued. I wanted to end the film with his nightmare of the hand of the man they had buried rising from water, like Excalibur in the hand of the Lady of the Lake, reaching up from the unconscious, an accusation. Was I justified in making such a fundamental change? I saw it as an interpretation of the text and I felt it could be read that way. When Dickey demurred, I was in a quandary. I did not want to make a movie which implied that violence was cathartic; but on the other hand, did I have the right to impose ideas that were not Dickey's? The problem hung there between us, unresolved.

We made a budget and Ashley and Calley said they would make it if I could find two major stars. I offered it to Lee. He knew he wasn't right for it and so did I, but I needed to make the gesture. He was in the same old one-bed beach house. He had finally escaped Michele Triola by running off and marrying his childhood sweetheart, the wonderful Pamela Feeney, and there she was. We had a great celebration together.

Jack Nicholson had just made *Five Easy Pieces* and was hot. I persuaded him to play Ed, but he said he would only do it if I cast his friend and next-door neighbour, Marlon Brando, as Lewis. I liked the idea and made the pilgrimage to Mulholland Drive to see the great man. He was about to make *The Godfather*, the first time he had worked in years. He said he intended to look at me for a while before we spoke. I guessed this was a technique he had picked up in the Tahiti archipelago where he had an island. The Palauans would never speak to you until they had spent time smiling and staring at you. I endured this test for fifteen of the longest minutes of my life, and eventually we conversed. He said he despised acting. He had learned to be a mimic as a child to get attention.

Acting was nothing more than mimicry. A bunch of tricks. I asked him about directors he had worked with. 'It's a contest of wills,' he said ominously. 'But who did you most enjoy working with?' I persisted. 'No question,' he said, 'Michael Winner.' I was startled. 'Why?' 'When I met him, Michael said, "Mr Brando, you are a great actor, I am not a great director, so please do whatever you like."'

After a couple of curious hours he said, yes, he would do it. 'How much do you want?' I asked, because I knew he didn't have an agent at that time. He said he didn't have a price any more. 'I'll take whatever you pay Jack.'

I called Jack's agent, Sandy Breslaw. He demanded five hundred thousand dollars. I said that was out of the question. This was one of those occasions when the studios get together and are determined to stop paying stars inflated salaries. 'I happen to know,' said Sandy, 'that Warners are paying Redford half a million to do *Jeremiah Johnson*.

I told Ashley and Calley the news. They were horrified. The Redford deal was supposed to be a closely guarded secret. There had been a dispute over another picture that Redford was supposed to do that Warners had cancelled. The half million included compensation for the other movie. But Jack was hot. They were thrilled that I had nailed him. They were wavering. I thought I'd better tell them about Marlon before they made a decision. Ashley had been an agent and he knew about these things. He was incensed. Marlon was box-office poison. He, Ted, would be ridiculed by every agent in town if he paid Brando that kind of money. In any case, at a million for the pair it made the picture too expensive. Find unknowns, they concluded, and make it cheap.

Ted Ashley took me aside. Would I do him a favour? A friend of his represented Steve McQueen. An agent is required to procure offers of work for his client every year or the actor is free to leave the agency. Would I meet McQueen? They had just told me they didn't want stars. He wasn't right for the part, I said. Ted replied mysteriously that he could guarantee that McQueen would not want to do the movie. They didn't want McQueen in the picture. I didn't want him. Nevertheless, playing the game, I met him for dinner at Mateos. To my relief it soon became clear that Ted was right: he was not interested in being in *Deliverance*. He had read the script, and although it bore my name, this did not inhibit him from saying, 'There's a germ of an idea here. Get yourself a decent writer to knock it into shape. Then I'll take another look at it.'

Neither of us wanted to be there. He made no effort to respond to my attempts at conversation. I tried various topics, but nothing stirred a response. I was uncomfortably conscious of his inner tension. He was wound up. The face was expressionless, yet the eyes warned that he could snap at any moment. Perhaps it was this tension that animated his features on screen, made him dangerous. Now he seemed marooned, beached. The effort to get where he was in his career had exhausted him. He was a star and he could do whatever he liked, but he needed something to hate to keep going. We plodded through the meal, lapsing into uneasy silence. Sugar Ray Robinson was at a nearby table with his wife and friends. Steve and I were inert rocks and their laughter was like ocean surf washing over us. Sugar Ray came over to our table. He stood on his toes in that familiar pose, swaying slightly as if ready to evade a punch, his huge smile taunting and teasing. His wit matched his speed in the ring and he launched into a story full of verbal jabs and feints. Steve seemed as bored with Sugar Ray's story as he had been with my mine. Undeterred, Sugar Ray kept going. He danced around us, softened us up with body blows of humour and just as he was going for the pay-off, the knockout, Steve cut across him. 'What do you think of Clay?' Sugar Ray slipped it with ease. 'He's slow.' It cost him a fraction of a second, then he hit us with the climax to his story. We were on the canvas, counted out.

Leaving this trail of movie stars in my wake, I set out to tour the regional theatres and auditioned hundreds of actors up and down the country. I found Ned Beatty working in a theatre in Washington DC. He was a devoted theatre actor who had never been in a movie or even a television episode. I cast him as Bobby. Ronnie Cox was another discovery. He played the guitar, which was essential for the role of Drew – but I could not find actors with the weight to play Ed and Lewis.

I returned to LA and reported back. I said I would try to find a couple of experienced but inexpensive actors for the roles. The budget was slashed back and I had very little to play with. I turned my attention to Jon Voight. He had been a sensation in his first film, *Midnight Cowboy*, but had since made a couple of duds and spent an enormous amount of time making, and then trying to salvage, *The All American Boy*. It had been directed by its brilliant writer, Charles Eastman, but the picture would not cut together. Voight had fought the studio to have Eastman direct the picture and he felt responsible for the wreck. He was in despair about his career. I wooed him. He resisted. He was too exhausted to do another picture. He felt he was too young for the role. He was too distraught to make decisions. His duty was to stay with *The All American Boy* and make sense of it. Maybe do some reshoots. I said, take a break from it, do *Deliverance* then go back to it refreshed. We talked for hours about the script. He had some very good ideas. He started to speak with an Atlanta accent, but he would not commit.

Meanwhile, I thought about Burt Reynolds for Lewis. He had the physique and the kind of posturing that fitted the Lewis character. Calley said that only someone unaware of American television would want Burt. He was a three-times loser, a trail of failed TV shows behind him. Richard Zanuck had joined Warners and he quite liked the idea of Burt. He became an ally and persuaded Calley. I offered Burt fifty thousand dollars with no back end. He took it. I went back to Voight. I spent an hour on the phone and he still would not make a decision. Finally I said, 'If you haven't made a decision in the next thirty seconds I'm going to hang up and cast someone else.' Jon's response was 'Why thirty seconds? That's completely arbitrary.' 'Jon, I'm about to hang up.' No answer. I hung up. My phone rang immediately. 'OK. I'll do it . . . but . . .' 'No buts, Jon.'

I asked Jim Dickey to come to LA for three days to go over the next draft of the script. I was in the midst of pre-production – casting, scheduling, putting a crew together. He holed up at the Bel Air hotel with a muscular dancer called Amy Burke. He wouldn't take calls and I never got to see him. We were due to fly back to Atlanta together and my last hope was that we might do some work on the plane. Amy came to the airport for a tearful farewell. Jim slumped into his seat and fell into a deep drunken sleep. An hour later he woke with a start and said emphatically, 'If I wasn't a *Baptist* and a famous *poet*, I'd *divorce* my wife and marry Amy *Burke*.' With that he closed his eyes and slept till the plane landed.

In Atlanta airport he was thrilled to spot Wilt Chamberlain, the black basketball ace who claimed to have slept with twenty thousand women. Dickey admired him on both counts. Jim was six foot three, but he had to look up at Wilt. Jim always wore a Stetson, and with his good-old-boy accent and his red neck he presented an odious image to Wilt. Jim said, 'Mr Chamberlain, I want you to know you have a lot of devoted fans in Columbus, Georgia.' Wilt chewed his gum and peered down disdainfully at Jim and said, 'On your way, cowboy.' Jim was thrilled and told the story against himself many times.

1971: Where Spring Spends the Summer

We made our base in Clayton, Georgia. As you entered the town there was a charming sign which read, 'Clayton, Where Spring Spends the Summer.' The upper waters of the Chatooga river ran nearby and that was the river I elected to use. River banks draw people to them and then look trodden down and used up. The camera ruthlessly picks up such evidence. I needed something wild and untouched. This river was flanked by such dense foliage, and its banks were so rocky, that it was impenetrable for much of its length. It was rugged and primal with flights of vicious rapids and jagged rocks. There were only certain points where you could put in canoes and even there you needed four-wheel-drive vehicles to gain access. Even so, when I took photos of the river with its blue water and green banks it still looked pretty and benign. I resolved to desaturate the colour in order to make it more ominous. It put me in mind of something the painter Constable said: 'Nature is too green and poorly lit.'

I studied John Huston's attempts at desaturation in *The Night of the Iguana* and *Moby Dick*. They were not wholly successful. Primary colours desaturate more slowly than mid-tones. In those films the reds and blues were still strong while the blander colours had almost completely disappeared. I decided to solve this problem by eliminating all primary colours from costumes, props, etc. Our camera tests showed that if diffusion filters were used, the image would disintegrate during desaturation. You needed a sharp, bald image. This meant that our rushes looked very bland and raw but we had to keep our nerve, knowing, or hoping, that it would look fine after the process.

I needed a tough and courageous cameraman. Vilmos Zigmond had not only filmed the Russian invasion of Budapest but had smuggled the footage out of Hungary with bullets flying around his ears. He was not going to be intimidated by a river.

The studio was still beating me up over the budget. I had cut back everything to the bone. I deferred half my modest fee. I even made do without an art director, except for one week. He came up right at the end to dress Ed's house, where there is a brief scene. The prop man and local labour handled all the construction and set dressing. I had a nasty setback from the camera unions, of which there are three – LA, New York and Chicago. It turned out that the Chatooga river is the state line between Georgia and South Carolina. I was told that when I shot on one side of the river I was subject to the NY union, but when I crossed to the other side I had to use a Chicago crew. We eventually reached a compromise whereby I employed a small Chicago camera team as a second unit. I had them do some wildlife shots, only two of which ended up in the picture. Since Vilmos was his own operator (an arrangement I much prefer), I was obliged to employ a camera operator who spent most of his time at the motel. These were added costs that I could not avoid.

Warners still demanded more cuts, or they would not make the picture. Dickey had played me a recording of 'Duelling Banjos', a traditional piece anonymously composed, which we intended to use in the early scene where Drew's guitar is challenged by a retarded boy's banjo. It is a powerful metaphor for the story and I had the idea that this musical theme should reverberate throughout the picture. Desperate to reduce the budget, I decided to cut the composer and the cost of the orchestral score and simply use that one tune played on those two instruments. We asked the local Appalachian musicians and hillbillies who was the best banjo picker. They all agreed – Eric Weisberg, a New York Jew who had acquired his great skill by listening to country radio stations. One afternoon in a local recording studio, we laid down every possible variation on 'Duelling Banjos' and that became the score. It brought the budget under the figure demanded by Warners and we got the green light to go ahead.

We rented several villas at the Kingwood Country Club. I rehearsed the actors in the mornings and they trained in canoeing and archery in the afternoons. Rospo Pallenberg wanted some practical experience of film-making so I brought him along as a general assistant. During pre-production I would give him tasks each day – find a special extra or a certain prop, or supervise the building of a bridge, or negotiate with a farmer about shooting on his land. However much work I gave him, I would always find him reading in a hammock by noon. He invariably found simple ways of getting things done. I said to him, 'Rospo, why don't you write a book on how to do things the easy way?' He considered it sleepily. 'That's not a bad idea,' he yawned. 'The first thing would be to find someone to write it for me.' Rospo had the advantage of an eccentric childhood roaming his grandfather's palazzo in Rome. Amongst the slew of cousins, he somehow got forgotten and nobody bothered to send him to school until he was twelve, so he avoided the dampening effect that education can have on the imagination. His mind makes hops and leaps over conventional thinking.

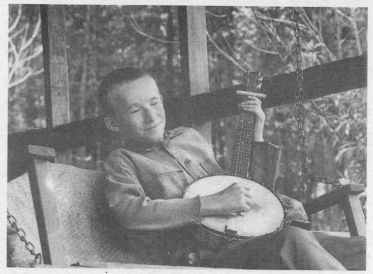

Deliverance: the boy with the strange, degenerate look

It was Rospo who discovered the boy who plays the 'Duelling Banjo' duet with Drew. I was delighted he had been able to find a kid with such a strange degenerate look who could also play the banjo. 'He can't play the banjo,' said Rospo. I was exasperated. 'So why is he here?' 'He looks right.' Rospo then produced another kid, very normal looking. 'He can play the banjo,' Rospo said proudly. 'I thought he could crouch behind the other kid and do the fretting.' 'Ridiculous, Rospo.' We continued to search to no avail. Reluctantly, I began to think about Rospo's ludicrous idea. We cut a hole in the back of the boy's shirt sleeve and inserted the left arm of the kid who could play. The boy kept his arm pinned behind his back and strummed with his right hand and the other kid did the fretting. Rospo's lateral thinking.

Dickey arrived at the Country Club in a spanking new powder blue Toyota jeep with Maxines 1 and 2 and a sensitive son. Dickey found the bar, claimed it and draped himself across it. I asked him to sit in at a reading of the script. Those fierce eyes burned holes in the actors. It was very tense. They squirmed and sweated and kept their eyes down on the text.

That night in the bar he called them to him one by one. 'Drew, come here, boy.' 'Bobby, get your ass over here.' He got each of them to swear an oath that they would never tell a soul that *everything* in that book . . . etc.

Burt was seething, waiting for his call. 'Lewis, I want to talk to you.' Burt ignored him. He was summoned again. Dickey waited, then drew himself up and went over to Burt. He leaned over him. 'Lewis, didn't you hear me calling?'

'My name's Burt. I answer to Lewis when I'm playing him.' Dickey smiled approvingly. 'That's *good*. That's Lewis talking. Don't *mess* with Lewis. *No one* – and I include Brando, we could have had him, you know – *no one* could play him better than you. You *are* Lewis.'

I began rehearsals. Dickey sat in. The actors were intimidated. We talked about the text, the scenes, the characterisations. It was awkward. No one would commit, take a risk. I took Dickey aside. I said the actors needed to explore their roles and his presence was inhibiting them. I invited him to come in at the end of each day and we would review progress with him. The rehearsals progressed. We would see Dickey through the window pacing outside, waiting for the appointed hour. He would burst in with a statement. 'Do any of you know, *really know*, how *good* this is? It's *better* than good!' or 'Ed, I'm going to tell you something important. When Lewis breaks his leg, *you* have to *become* Lewis. *Become* him.' His tone was emphatic. He heavily italicised key words. In his letters too. How did that lean prose, that incisive poetry come out of this shambling, bombastic, hyperbolic man? He fascinated me, his know-ingness, the theatricality, those eyes, the voice, the accent. I decided to cast him as the Sheriff, a man with a weary knowledge of the depths of the human soul. He was delighted and it gave him a function, a connection.

Despite this arrangement, the situation deteriorated as the first day of shooting came closer. Dickey plagued the cast and crew in the evenings. Burt was ready to explode and he was also getting impatient with Voight. Jon wanted to analyse every scene, every gesture, every nuance. He had lost his acting nerve and by examining all possibilities it delayed the need to make choices, to commit. His first approach to a scene was always brilliant, astonishing. Because it came easily, he didn't trust it. He would worry it to death and my task was to coax him back to his origi-nal response, but the high intelligence he brought to his probing was always valuable. Burt hated rehearsals. His approach was to look for a trick, a bit of business to get him through each scene. When Jon and I pressed him to examine his emotions, he became uncomfortable and hostile. Or funny. He could deflect anything serious with his wit.

Burt and Jon were a good match. As Jon forced Burt to think a little deeper, so Burt pushed Jon into being more spontaneous. Burt continued to focus his insecurities on to Dickey's looming presence. He and Ned Beatty urged me to send him away. Ronnie Cox had fallen under Jim's spell and was against him leaving. Jon could see both sides. It exactly reflected the attitude of their characters in the ethical debate following the killing of the mountain man, as to whether they should go to the police or cover up the crime. To complete the analogy, Jim was beginning to behave like the mountain man, getting ever drunker and more objectionable. I had to do something. I told the actors I would talk to Dickey. I left the rehearsal room and went to the bar where Jim was having his pre-lunch drink. The barman took me aside and whispered urgently, 'I think you should know what Mr Dickey just told me.' 'It all happened to him?' I said. He looked startled, then a sheepish grin. Of course, he should have known.

I told Jim we were all inhibited by his presence. It was going to be a tough shoot. I needed a high level of concentration from everyone. He had to trust me to do justice to his book, but I needed to be left alone.

'I want you to leave, Jim. Go home and come back to play the Sheriff.'

'If I go, I ain't coming back,' he said. 'Get yourself another boy.'

I insisted that he play the Sheriff. I knew his heart was set on it.

'By then they'll all be into their roles and more secure,' I said.

He drew himself up. There was a dangerous look in his eye. I thought he was going to hit me.

'You're just an opportunistic Englishman.' It felt like a written, rather than a spoken line, and I guessed he had put it in a letter to someone. A long pause, then, 'If I'm leaving, I want to say goodbye to the boys.'

We walked in silence to the rehearsal room. The actors looked up anxiously as we entered. Jim glared down at them.

'It *appears*,' he italicised, 'that my *presence* would be most *efficacious* by its *absence*.' He let that sink in for a long moment, turned on his heel and left. Burt looked perplexed. 'Does that mean he's going or staying?' You could never be sure with Burt whether he was being dumb or acting dumb. His deprecation of self finely balanced his macho posturing. On the last day of shooting Burt said, 'I was in this movie under false pretences.'

'Why do you say that?'

'I can't act. I was just faking it.'

Shooting *Deliverance*, Shooting
the Chatooga

We were well prepared. I had canoed the river myself several times. There were stretches of rapids that were rated too difficult to run in an open canoe. Those were the ones I planned to shoot (in both senses of that word). We were using a traditional Indian wooden canoe and an aluminium one. We smashed up six wooden canoes in the course of the picture. I needed to 'learn' the river and I swam through the white water in a wetsuit, allowing the flow to guide me between the rocks, staying loose and supple and resisting the temptation to tense up and fight it. I wanted to abandon myself to the river, to become the river. My childhood on the Thames had bequeathed me an ease in water. I loved the Chatooga, its wild torrents, its precipitous falls, its peaceful passages. I was at home, and the actors sensed it, and it gave them comfort. I felt that the river embraced me too. It put me in a state of grace. The film fell into place in my mind. I experienced one of those magical episodes where I could do no wrong.

Which is not to say I was unscathed. We all had spills at one time or another. Ned Beatty's easy warmth masked a deep-seated rage which could detonate whenever his short fuse was lit. It made us all wary of him. The fact that he was going to be sodomised led us to treat him with the tolerance you would show someone with an incurable disease. It was his first movie. He was in uncharted waters in more ways than one. I had to guide him through the unfamiliar technique, but his performance was unerring from the very beginning. There was never a false moment. He knew the character. It belonged to him.

Ned sat in the front of the wooden canoe. He despised and feared Ronnie Cox's uncertain steering at the back. As they approached a steep and dangerous set of rapids, where it was important to enter at the right point and angle, Ronnie slewed the boat round. In a self-destructive rage, Ned hurled his paddle into the river. The canoe turned over and broke in two as it smacked broadside into jagged rocks. Ned somersaulted down the rapids and was caught in a hydro at the base of the falls. This is an unpleasant sensation, like being spun in a washing machine. You lose any sense of which way is *up*, so your struggles might be taking you deeper into the river rather than to the surface. My two professional divers went in after him. They got into the hydro but he was

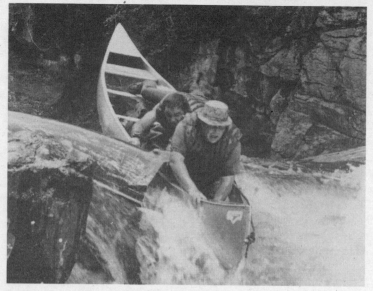

Shooting the rapids: Ned Beatty (front) and Burt Reynolds

gone. A long ninety seconds elapsed before he surfaced way down-stream. I asked Ned what had gone through his mind when he thought he was drowning.

'I thought, how will John finish the movie without me? My next thought was, that fuck will find some way to make it work, and that was when I became determined to live, and I fought my way up to the surface.'

On some stretches of the river, the ones I liked best, the banks were impenetrable. The unit would put us in at one point and meet us down-stream at the end of the day at the next spot that could be accessed. We would set off, four actors, two canoes; Vilmos, Art Brooker, the grip, and myself in a rubber dinghy with the camera. We took our lunches in a waterproof bag. Because of the roar of the water, we made no attempt to record usable sound; the dialogue was all added later at Reeves Studio in New York, which had just pioneered ADR – Automatic Dialogue Replacement.

Before that, adding dialogue after filming had involved breaking down the film into thirty-second loops which went round and round in the pro-jector until the actor synchronised his dialogue. Then the next loop was threaded up, and so on. ADR rocked the film back and forth without breaking it into loops so that a whole sequence could be played back, checked and re-recorded until it was perfect. Voight, like many 'method' actors, was bitterly opposed to looping. He felt you could never duplicate the emotion of the moment. But ADR made an art out of a necessity. When Voight understood how a performance could be shaded and nuanced in the studio after the event, he became a passionate convert. I have never failed to convince an actor of its efficacy. It was the old loop system that got post-synch such a bad name: Peter O'Toole famously said that his idea of hell would be to spend eternity looping his entire life in thirty-second segments.

The secret to the river scenes in *Deliverance* is that they were shot on a manoeuvrable unblimped Arriflex camera, wielded by a cameraman and a director up to their necks in violent water. Recording sound slows things up. By dubbing in the sound afterwards, we broke the tyranny that the word exercises over the picture. Most Italian films are made that way. Fellini once said to me, 'John, if the Americans find out about dubbing, we are finished.'

On my trips down the Chatooga during pre-production I searched the banks for a place in which to shoot the rape scene. I knew that if I could find the right setting, I would know how to shoot it. Rospo found it in the end, a place of tangled black laurel where only a bilious green light penetrated. There was a deep floor covering of coarse leaves on an undulating surface. Beyond the laurel were dense trees. I contrived to have the mountain men emerge from them. I strove for the illusion that they had actually come out of the trees themselves, like malevolent spirits of nature seeking retribution; for it was to generate power for men in Atlanta like their victims that this wild river was to be sacrificed.

I had shot the preceding scenes in rhythmic cuts as the four men canoed joyfully down the river. By contrast, I made the confrontation scene – in which they and the mountain men circle each other like dogs, eventually leading to the rape – in a single six-minute shot. The absence of a cut creates an unconscious tension in the audience. Is this a mechanical manipulation? I would argue not. I was attempting to reproduce the sensation we experience in frightening situations, when time feels suspended.

In his autobiography, Burt Reynolds tells how he had to wrench Bill McKinney (the rapist) away, because he was actually about to penetrate Ned Beatty. Utter nonsense. Bill McKinney was a skilful and disciplined

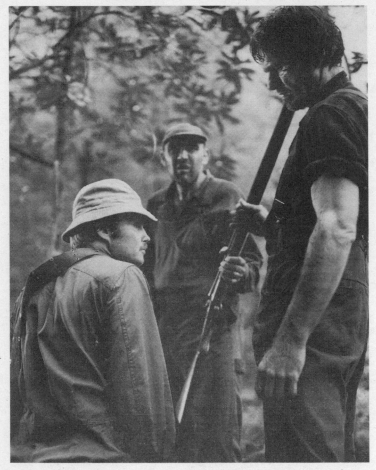

Jon Voight confronts the mountain men: Herbert 'Cowboy' Coward
and Bill McKinney (right)

actor. He and Ned came to terms with what they had to do. They spent
a lot of time together. It was as though the act they were about to perform cut them off from the rest of us. We rehearsed and shot it like any
other scene. It was carefully worked out and calmly executed. Thirty
years on, people still call out to Ned in the street, 'Squeal like a pig!'

Some years later, Stanley Kubrick called me. He was thinking of casting McKinney as the sadistic drill sergeant in *Full Metal Jacket*. 'What's he like?' asked Stanley. 'He's got to be a scary guy.' I told him that Bill was a fine upright fellow and that what Kubrick had seen on the screen was acting. 'That is the most terrifying scene ever filmed,' he said. 'He has to be a monster to be capable of that.'

Bill did several auditions on tape and finally got the job. He was at LA Airport on his way to London to make the film when he was called on the PA. Kubrick had cancelled. Bill got paid, but lost the job. Kubrick could not face meeting him.

As a further test of Bill McKinney's acting skill, I required him to die slowly and then 'act dead' during the long ethical debate that followed his killing. He achieved this flawlessly, holding his breath for up to two minutes at a time. The American Ratings Board threatened an X certificate if I did not shorten the scene of Bill dying. My case was that it was important that the four men witnessed the horrific reality of killing a man, an act that Lewis saw as the romantic fulfilment of manhood. I enlisted the press in my wrangle while the studio waited nervously in the background. The censors' objection to the dying scene was a cover for their real concern, which was the male rape. I pointed out that if they allowed us to see women being raped, how could they object to the male version? They didn't want to fight on those terms. Barbra Streisand called me, asking to see the movie before cuts were made: 'I want to see a man raped for a change.' Eventually, a face-saving compromise was reached, in which I cut six frames, a quarter of a second.

The other 'mountain man' was played by Herbert 'Cowboy' Coward. Burt put me on to him: they had worked on a dude ranch together way back. Cowboy was a man of simple tastes. In the evening he would fill the bathtub in his motel room with ice cubes and throw in a dozen cans of beer. He sat on the toilet seat and worked his way through them. In the film, after Voight has killed him with an arrow, the body is lowered down the cliff on a rope. I lined up the shot with a dummy, and told Cowboy to watch the rehearsal. 'You have to hang there motionless, Cowboy. Whatever happens, don't move a muscle.' Cowboy, still woozy from last night's beer, looked blearily at the dummy swinging in the chasm below and said, 'I guess if he can do it, I can do it.' And he did.

As the picture progressed, Voight gained in stature. He rose to the ever-increasing demands of each scene. He is the real thing: intelligent

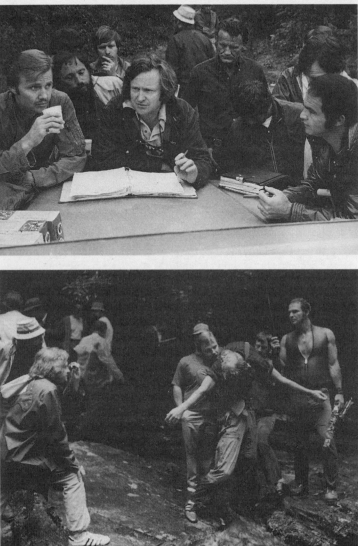

Deliverance: Directing on location

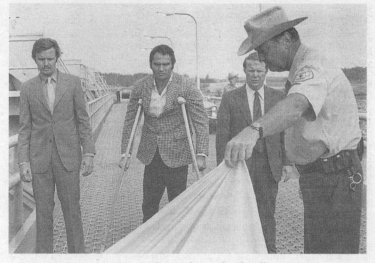

James Dickey (right) as the Sheriff

and intensely intuitive, skilful, yet with that mysterious something that great actors have, the ability to transcend acting, the ability to *become*.

Jon tells amusing stories of my recklessness and risk-taking on *Deliverance*. But I knew the river, knew how far I could go. The rapids and cataracts were not the problem, it was the emotional depths I was dragging him into that he feared. He says that I saved his life by persuading him to do the picture, then did my best to kill him while making it.

Burt found emotional depths in himself for the big scenes while still pretending not to. In a scene where he and Jon had to appear out of breath, Jon asked me for a two-minute warning before we were ready to make each shot. Jon would then sprint through the woods and come back, chest heaving and covered in sweat. Observing this, Burt asked me for a thirty-second warning. He sprayed himself with water vapour and simulated panting, making sure that Jon saw what he was doing.

Towards the end of the shoot, Dickey returned to play the Sheriff. He was very nervous and fairly sober. I showed him some sequences we had cut together and he professed himself pleased. I had lived his fiction and survived. He said, 'I honour your *endeavour*. You've proved yourself *worthy*.'

A Hit Movie

On impulse, Christel and I decided to return to Europe by boat. We got berths on the *Queen Elizabeth*. The agent said, 'You're in luck. We just had a cancellation.' We took the train to New York and discovered it was the last time the old ship was to leave Manhattan. People had booked for months to be part of it. Some of them had spent their honeymoon on its maiden voyage. Fireships saluted us with water cannon, there was a flotilla of yachts and bagpipers on tugs, helicopters and light aircraft accompanied us out beyond the Statue of Liberty. It was moving and sad.

I edited at home in Ireland. The Ardmore Studios are just twenty minutes away from my home in the Wicklow Hills. When I had a cut, I took it to Burbank to show to Warners. At the end of the screening there was silence. The studio executives got up and walked out without a word. They gathered in Ted Ashley's office. I walked in and saw the long faces.

'So you didn't care for it,' I said.

'It's not that,' said Ashley, 'but it has just been pointed out to me that there has never been a hit picture in the history of Hollywood without a woman in it.'

'Ah,' I said, 'I wish you'd told me before I started shooting.'

Calley whispered, 'Shock affects people in funny ways.'

I had a screening for a few friends – Lee and Pam Marvin, Isherwood, Rospo, Voight, Burt, Ronnie, Ned. Again the utter silence and people hurrying out, avoiding my eye. We assembled for dinner at the home of my lawyer, Ed Gross, in Beverly Hills. Joan Didion and Gregory Dunne arrived late and distraught. It was raining. Joan's fragility was shattered by the movie, and to make matters worse, they had had a puncture on the freeway, a horror she had described in *Play It As It Lays*. Writers are often stalked by their own fictions.

Burt was living with the singer Dinah Shore at the time. He describes in his autobiography how everyone at the party assured him he would win the Academy Award for his one big speech alone. He tells how I took him on one side and said I was going to cut that very speech as it unbalanced the picture. On the way home in the car, he told Dinah the bad news. They cried all night, he said. There *was* such a speech in an early draft of the script, and Burt would have read it. In succeeding drafts it got whittled down. It was a statement of Lewis's philosophy, telling the audience what the movie was about. What we finally shot was a very brief version of it. It still jarred and I did tell Burt it would have to be cut. In his mind it must have been that long bombastic rant from the early draft that I had excised, thus denying him his Oscar.

Burt got a lot of attention from his performance. He posed naked in *Playgirl*. He did all the talk shows. He was a star, a sex symbol. Women were throwing themselves at him. He said it was all very well but these women were invariably disappointed. They expected transcendent orgasms, violins, earth movements. 'The problem is, I'm just a fumbler like everyone else,' he said. In fact, Burt was not interested in casual sex. I had lunch with him at Scandia's restaurant on Sunset Boulevard on Christmas Eve of the year *Deliverance* came out. His car was loaded with gifts which he intended to distribute that afternoon. Many of them were for ex-lovers. I was impressed that he was on such good terms with them. He explained his secret:

> For me it's about love. I fall in love. All the way. I can't make love without love. But I've learned over the years that there comes a time in every relationship when it passes its peak and starts to go downhill. You have to be honest and recognise the signs. When I do, I arrange a romantic dinner. I talk about all the wonderful times we have had together. I pay the check. Then I tell her it's over. I get up and walk away without looking back. That's important. Never look back. Now, don't forget, I'm in love. It's agonising. I have to fight the temptation to pick up the phone and call her. I'm a wreck. But I've learned that the pain only lasts between twelve and fourteen days. So when we recover, all we have are beautiful memories. Now if you let an affair run its course and it all ends in recriminations and bitterness and tears, you end up hating each other.

I was fascinated by this twelve to fourteen days. Was it like giving up cigarettes? Did he not experience a few pangs beyond the two-week mark? 'Not if you go cold turkey,' he said.

I tried to persuade Mo Ostin, head of Warner Records, to put out 'Duelling Banjos' as a single. He treated me to a lecture about the music business.

> To sell a record you have to get radio stations to play it. Nobody will play 'Duelling Banjos'. Country music is all about the words. Your piece has no words. The rock'n'roll stations won't play it. Is it middle of the road? It certainly is not. So who's going to play it?

Nobody's going to play it. So we're not going to do it.

I pressed Ted Ashley, the head of Warners, to intervene. Eventually they agreed to put it out as a single in a test area, somewhere in the Midwest. Within two weeks it was number one in the whole country and every station was playing it. There was no composer involved, so all the royalties went to Warners and Eric Weisberg. The studio's profits paid for the budget of the movie. Eric became a rich man. My reward was a gold record which Warner records sent me in a nice frame. It was stolen from my house in Ireland, almost certainly by Martin Cahill, the General. When I made my film of his life, I wrote in a scene of him stealing a gold record and his disgust at discovering it was vinyl sprayed with gold paint.

Dickey haunted the movie houses, watching the picture over and over. He would hang about outside and talk to the people waiting in line.

> Boy, are you going to get your money's worth! And then some! I'm Jim Dickey. I wrote the book. I wrote the script. I acted in it. The only thing I didn't do was direct it, and [out of the corner of his mouth] I even did some of that.

He would talk to the screen. When Burt was lining up his arrow on the mountain man, Dickey would yell, 'Kill the son-of-a-bitch.'

As the success of the picture fed his fantasies, his claims got wilder. He told several people that he had had a homosexual affair with Burt in order to 'save the movie'. Many years later Dickey's biographer, Henry Hart, called me. I told him the story of Jim claiming that everything in the book had happened to him. I said he had nothing to prove: after all, he was a genuine war hero, having been a fighter pilot in the Korean war. 'That wasn't true either,' said Mr Hart. He called his book *The World as a Lie: James Dickey*.

I loved Jim for his excess. He was us writ large. My little lies were his monstrous ones, my hypocritical modesty was his wild boasts, my drinking was his drunkenness. Although at the time he would say to everyone, 'Have you seen the movie? It's better than the book,' towards the end of his life he disowned it and tried to get it remade 'properly', using his script.

Deliverance was nominated for Academy Awards for Best Picture, Best Director and Best Editing. There was not as much fuss about the Oscars back in 1972. I was already working on the script of my next picture,

Zardoz, and I decided not to make the trip. *The Godfather* was also nominated. It was a better picture than *Deliverance* and I was sure it would win.

The death of the British film industry has been announced at regular intervals since I started making movies. In the post-war period David Lean, Carol Reed and the team of Michael Powell and Emeric Pressburger were making big pictures. Ealing comedies abounded, and Rank was financing pictures entirely out of its own coffers. All that collapsed, and we have never recovered. We now make movies financed by television and rely on American pictures to fill Pinewood and Shepperton studios. They come to Britain when the dollar is strong and go to Canada when sterling is too expensive.

The choice for a British director is to stay at home and do small pictures, or to go to Hollywood and make big ones – or to do a bit of both, as I have done. There is certainly no stability or continuity. Our lives are frittered away on movies we fail to make.

There was a moment when this could have changed. Dick Lester, director of *The Knack*, hatched a clever idea. He recruited the leading directors working in Britain at that period: Joe Losey (*The Servant*), Ken Russell (*Women in Love*), John Schlesinger (*Darling*), Karel Reisz (*Saturday Night and Sunday Morning*), Lindsay Anderson (*If...*), Tony Richardson (*Tom Jones*), himself and me. We would each make three pictures over six years. Each film would cost a million dollars, which was a decent budget at the time. We would have carte blanche. There would be some arrangement whereby we shared in each other's profits, if any.

United Artists was the only taker, but they imposed a condition: they wanted the right to exclude one of the names. Dick called a meeting and we assembled at Joe Losey's house in Chelsea. Joe was a fugitive from the McCarthy blacklist, and was notoriously and understandably paranoid. He was sure he was the one they wanted to exclude. Before Dick could present the case, Joe said: 'There shall be no blacklist. It is all or none!' Sheepishly, we agreed, and the deal fell through.

In fact, it was Tony Richardson they would not have. After the sweeping success of *Tom Jones*, he had made several duds for United Artists, and they would not stomach him. Imagine if those eight directors had made those twenty-four films over six years, working unimpeded, and with financial security. How different things might have been.

1973: *Zardoz*

I was hot. I had made a hit, a genuine blockbuster. The picture had not been expensive. The studio had made lots of money. I had earned myself the power to make what I wanted. Warners had bought the film rights to *The Exorcist*. Calley asked me to make it. Would I read it and give him a fast answer? I found it repulsive. I told Calley it would be a film about a child being tortured. Calley said, 'You're such a snob.' This was a huge bestseller. What business did I have to moralise? He asked me what I wanted to do next. I told him my idea.

In a sense, it was an extension of the theme of *Leo the Last*, the rich exploiting the poor. We, the people of the developed world, are extending our lifespan through advances in medicine, while the majority of the world is getting poorer and more abject. I wanted to project this tendency into a future where immortality had been achieved. How would this elite protect itself from the huddled masses? Living in Ireland the answer was all around me. The Catholic Church had controlled and oppressed a nation in a way that England had been unable to achieve through force of arms. So my elite would invent a religion. Calley was intrigued. I went home to write it.

As I invented this possible future, I became entranced by its complexities and the old hubris reared up. If people are immortal then reproduction is unnecessary – indeed, undesirable. In such circumstances, does the sexual drive survive or atrophy? I devised categories, imagined how different temperaments would respond to endless life: the Apathetics who had lost interest in living, the Renegades who wanted to die. Crimes were punished by 'ageing' – by one, five or ten years, depending on the seriousness of the misdemeanour. Consequently, the Renegades were mostly ancient whilst the Eternals were perpetually youthful. There were, of course, no children.

Outside this idyllic commune, the Vortex, lay the Outlands, peopled by the Brutals. Zed was a Brutal of great physical and mental prowess. He discovers that the God who rules them, Zardoz, is a version of the 'wiZARDofOZ', a terrifying stone head that flies across the Outlands and commands their lives. This trick has been devised by Arthur Frayn, a Merlin surrogate. Zed uncovers this elaborate conspiracy and penetrates the Vortex to wreak revenge on his masters. Zed's objective is to destroy a place which he believes has become a perversion of nature, and of life. In death, there is a beginning.

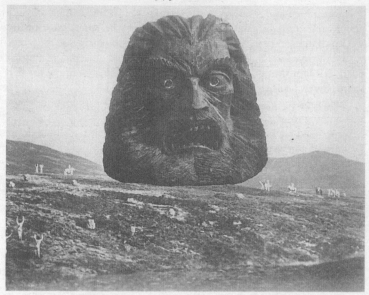

Zardoz: The stone head that flies across the Outlands

Calley read it and passed. My agent at ICM, Jo Wizan, pitched it to the studios. They were perplexed. One studio executive said, 'Jo, we'd love to have a Boorman picture, but I just don't understand the script. If you can explain it to me, we'll do it.' Jo, who had no idea what it was about, panicked. They were sitting face to face, but Jo said, 'Not on the phone.'

David Begelman was the head of the ICM agency, a man of great dignity and gravitas. He was so sincere, it was almost real. David stepped in. 'What's the lowest figure you can make it for?' he asked. 'One million dollars,' I said boldly, a pledge I would live to regret. David considered the problem, and came up with a plan. It was a last hope. Gordon Stulberg was the new head of 20th Century Fox. He needed a product. David called Stulberg and said, 'Here's the deal. You send Gerry Henshaw (his head of production) to London. He will have an hour and a half to read the script in our office. The budget is one million dollars all in, a negative pickup. You have no approvals. Gerry must give us a simple yes or a no.'

It was a high-risk strategy, but it was our last throw. Behind David's air of calm control lurked a reckless gambler who spent most of his weekends in Las Vegas. My script was a chip he was placing on the table.

Gerry arrived at the ICM office in London. David greeted him courteously, led him into an office and sat him at a desk, bare save for my script. Gerry, jet-lagged and nervous, began to read.

David took me to lunch. I was too anxious to eat. He assured me there was nothing to worry about. It was going to be fine.

We strolled back and sat in the anteroom. I stared at the closed door. David read a newspaper. We waited.

The door was flung open. Gerry stood before us. His arms hung at his sides. In his shaking hand was the script. The pages fluttered and hissed. He looked down at it with wild eyes, as though it might leap up and bite him. He was sweating profusely. Before he could speak, before he could say yes or no, David went to him, his hand extended, smiling, confident. He said, 'Congratulations, Gerry.' Gerry slumped. David's charm covered him like honey.

Some time later David became head of Columbia Pictures. He forged cheques to feed his gambling habit and was disgraced, sentenced to community service. He survived that and functioned as an independent producer, but in straitened circumstances. He could not bring himself to live at a more modest level. I was at his house shortly before he died. He still had a screening room, servants, the lifestyle of a potentate of the film community.

We went to a symphony concert together. He insisted on paying for everything. Shortly afterwards, he shot himself in a hotel room. If he had sold his house and paintings and moved to something more modest he could have paid off his debts. I like to think there was only one bullet in that gun and the great gambler was playing a final game of Russian roulette. Without his bold gamble there would be no *Zardoz*.

I wanted Bill Stair to design it and Tony Pratt to be art director. We had to invent a future, make a coherent society. My plan was that Bill, in full flow, would throw out the ideas, and Tony would implement them. A mistake. Although Bill wanted the status of designer, and I wanted him to have it, responsibility came with this, and he panicked at the prospect. As we worked through the script, he sat rigidly, taking notes, fear in his eyes, his imagination frozen, his brain seized. We were working in my house in Ireland. By the third day, Bill was in a complete funk. During that night I was woken by his screams. We all got up and went to him. He had scratched his eyes in his sleep, and they were bleeding. We dashed him to hospital: the damage was superficial but his eyes had to be bandaged. An absence of vision was something of a handicap for a designer. Tony took over and Bill reverted to his role of floating free spirit. He sat smiling under his bandaged eyes, and his ideas flowed freely once more.

Zardoz was a negative pickup: Fox would pay the million dollars when I delivered the completed film. I had to bear the cost of borrowing the money as well as paying for a completion bond, which would insist that ten per cent of the money be put aside as a contingency. This meant that what I could actually spend on the picture was eight hundred thousand dollars. This left no money for fees to the writer, director and producer – me.

I offered the leading role of Zed to Burt Reynolds. He accepted, but fell ill and had to back out. Fox wanted me to consider Richard Harris, since they had had a success with him in *A Man Called Horse*. I felt he lacked the bulk and muscle for the part, but I agreed to meet him. His house in London was mock-medieval, decorated with props from *Camelot*. It was chaotic. Children were playing, dazed friends wandered in and out, there were people demanding money. It was impossible to talk. Richard said he would be in Dublin on Saturday for a rugby match. We could meet there. I said come to Sunday lunch in Annamoe. He agreed. One o'clock came and went. We waited. At three o'clock we finally ate without him. There was no word nor sign of the man.

On Monday I spoke to Gordon Stulberg. I said, if he can't show up for the audition what will he be like once he's got the job? It was many years before our paths crossed again, but when they did Richard apologised graciously. He had had a heavy night after the match. He was hung over. It was well past noon. He hailed a taxi and told the driver to go hell for leather. He had to be in Annamoe by 1 p.m. When they were halfway there, the driver offered him a newspaper. He looked at the date. It was Monday. He said, 'Turn back to Dublin and stop at the first pub.'

I decided to try for Sean Connery. He had had enough of being James Bond, but was finding it hard to forge a career beyond it. Despite having made other movies in between, like *The Hill*, he was thought to be too closely associated with 007 to play other roles. I paid him a hundred thousand dollars. He had a car and driver in his contract. He asked me how much that cost me. I said a hundred and fifty pounds a week. He said, 'I'll drive myself and split it with you.'

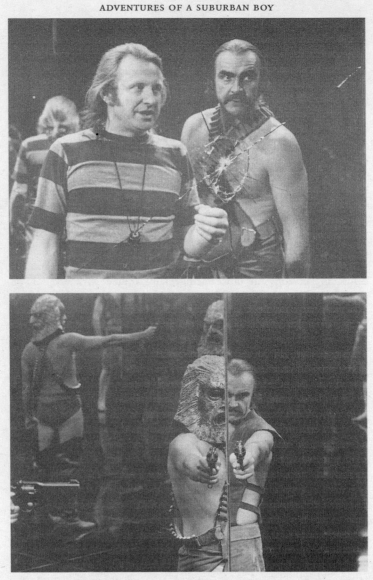

With Sean Connery on the set of *Zardoz*

He lived in my house for several weeks. He was a model guest: entertaining, thoughtful – he moved around the house turning off lights, a frugal Scot. He has an extraordinary memory and the stories of his childhood were made vivid by intense detail. Before dinner he would retire to his room and write poetry. He was at ease with himself, at home in his body, he knew exactly who he was. He had played many nationalities in his career but they all had a Scots accent. In *The Wind and the Lion* he was an Arab. They had to slip in a line telling us he had been to school in Scotland. He won a Best Supporting Actor Oscar for *The Untouchables*, playing an Irish cop with a Scots accent. I once asked him if he ever thought of using a different accent. He said, 'If I didn't talk the way I talk, I wouldn't know who the fuck I was.' This is the mystery: the movie star can play different roles yet remains himself, whereas the character actor inhabits his parts, is lost in them, and has no idea who he is.

Sean never had an entourage and didn't allow his fame to cut him off from the world. We went to an international soccer match in Dublin during his stay with me. As we were leaving the stadium, he was recognised: his name rippled and repeated and became a tribal incantation. The crowd began to press in from all sides. We were at the vortex of a crush of bodies. It was frightening.

Sean raised an imperious arm. His voice boomed out: 'Stand aside! Make way! Coming through! Move away!' The Red Sea of faces parted, a corridor opened before us and we walked to safety.

A future community posed a problem: that of diction and behaviour. I decided on a language that would be simple, as unidiomatic as possible, cold and neutral. Certain archaic words and neologisms were used merely to create a sense of strangeness, a particular rhythm. I was looking for actors and actresses who, though young, already had signs of maturity on their faces. Charlotte Rampling and Sara Kestelman fulfilled these conditions; both of them, in addition, have beautiful voices.

When I am making shots, I find it difficult to talk coherently to actors; that all has to be settled beforehand in rehearsals, because at this stage I'm interested in images, in the juxtaposition of shots, in surfaces, externalising the story. What matters to me then is the position of the actor in the shot, his movement within the frame, the sound of his voice. I am not concerned with what he is thinking and feeling, only what I can read in his face, what I can hear in his voice. Oddly enough, when I write a script, I don't see it in terms of camera shots. It is still internal.

Each stage of a film involves abandoning the previous stage. There's a gulf between the script and the shooting, then between the shooting and the editing. When you are shooting, the script becomes a kind of dead skin that you shuffle off. At the end of the shoot, you finally have some footage, to be sure, but it's a clumsy, shapeless monster which unfolds before you. It's only on the editing table that one eventually has the feeling that the film exists. Each stage is a struggle against the preceding one. When I direct, I never indulge the screenwriter in me; the editor, in turn, becomes very critical of the director.

I had the great Geoffrey Unsworth as cameraman on the film. He was a soft-spoken, courteous man, with the air of a distracted wizard. When colour arrived, cameramen continued to light as they had done for black and white, using shafts of direct light to separate objects and differentiate the various planes. Film is two-dimensional: lighting and camera movement are concerned with creating the illusion of a third dimension. In the black-and-white days on a typical set you would see a forest of black flags, arranged to allow slivers of light to pinpoint particular spots. Geoffrey, however, realised that colour did the job of distinguishing objects from each other, and that direct light made the colours very harsh and brash. He devised a radical new approach to colour lighting, using only indirect soft light. He combined this with diffusion filters, wide-open apertures in the lenses, and smoke on the sets, to soften and bind the elements together. It was the absolute contrary of the former style, attempting to meld the characters and the settings together, rather than differentiating between them. The result resembled an impressionist painting.

The studios hated this technique. Subjected to mass, high-speed printing, the picture would tend to collapse into a fuzzy mush. It also looked murky on videotape and television. Today, the American studios demand a crisp, sharp image, although all cameramen now use Geoffrey's method of indirect lighting. Geoffrey was finally vindicated with an Oscar for *Cabaret*, that astonishing hybrid descendant of Isherwood's Sally Bowles stories. The book became the stage play, *I Am a Camera*, which became a film, which became the Broadway musical, *Cabaret*, which became the movie.

With our meagre budget, all the extensive special effects were done in the camera using old techniques, like aerial image (blending two images through a reflective glass in front of the camera) and in-camera superimpositions. The research I had done for *The Lord of the Rings* proved invaluable. Tony Pratt was very inventive and Bill's touches were everywhere. Bill devised graffiti for the Outlands. 'Not to be born is best' was one close to his heart. The absence of death made the film a meditation on death. It explored the possibilities of human evolution, and the consequences of eliminating the procreative urge, which drives so much of our lives. I shot the picture on locations close to my home and in Ardmore Studios. Christel designed the costumes and my four children appeared briefly, in a flashback to a time, a hundred years back, when there were young children in the Vortex.

The script was overloaded and the production undernourished. More money would have given this vision of a future world more substance. It was too ambitious for its own good, but it is the ambition, its engagement with important ideas that redeems it. Despite its weaknesses, there are some good scenes and it was technically innovative in its day. Geoffrey's work is uniformly excellent.

Zed eventually destroys the Vortex, giving the Immortals the gift of death. He survives with Charlotte Rampling and they have a child together. The final sequence is done in a single shot with a fixed camera. Sean and Charlotte are sitting side by side in a cave with the baby. The baby becomes a child, the child becomes a youth, gets up and leaves them without looking back; they get older, then become ancient, and finally just their skeletons remain, which eventually crumble to dust. Only then does the camera move. It tracks in to a handprint on the wall of the empty cave, like the cave painting of primitive man in Lescaux, suggesting that this future world could have been in the past, and that as that civilisation ended, ours began.

This shot took an entire day to shoot. The actors had to be removed and make-up applied incrementally to add the years. Sean has a delicate skin and hates make-up. He had to endure it all day. He became more and more irascible. This was the last day of shooting. We had the wrap party that night. Sean had a golf tournament to go to the next day. I had to hold him until the morning for the laboratory report. The call came at 6 a.m. There was a fault in the film stock. It would have to be redone. Sean was apoplectic. He stormed and raged, but it had to be done.

We reassembled with our hangovers and started again. A long day, hours of make-up, Sean smarting from his suffering skin. Finally it was done. The clapper-loader took the magazine from the camera to prepare

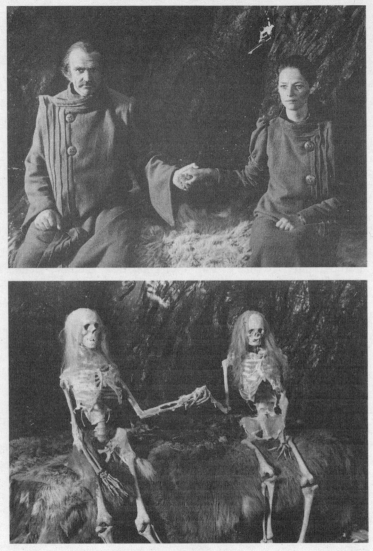

Zardoz: the gift of death

it for the lab. A few minutes later he came to me, trembling and ashen-faced. He looked so devastated, I thought someone had been killed or that the Third World War had started. I was almost relieved when he admitted that he had opened the can by mistake and exposed the film to daylight.

Sean would not believe me. 'Is this your idea of a joke?' he fumed. Finally convinced he would have to do it for a third time, he erupted. It was a terrifying sight. He roared, he ran amok. He went after the clapper-loader. He tried to kill him. It took four strong men to subdue him.

Twenty years later I was drinking coffee in Starbucks in Venice, California, when I was approached by a man with a familiar face. I couldn't place it. He reminded me that he was the clapper-loader who had exposed the film. He had fled the country immediately after this catastrophe, changed his identity, and was now a cameraman shooting commercials in LA. As we parted, he said, with an ironic smile, but also with a trace of fear, 'Sean's not in town, is he?'

Fox did an honest job in promoting *Zardoz* but it crashed at the box office. Reviews were at best lukewarm, at worst scathing. It came and went, but gradually gathered a cult following. Whenever it showed in America, devotees would show up, often travelling long distances in a hired bus.

The Immortals baked loaves of green bread: whenever I checked into a hotel in New York or Los Angeles, a green loaf would be awaiting me.

1976: *The Heretic*

I had made *Zardoz* without a fee, hoping that its low budget would ensure me some profits. That was now not going to happen. I had done two years' work and earned nothing. John Calley's judgement had been proved right. I was chastened. It dashed my hopes of making a film based on the Arthurian legend. I had rewritten my treatment and pitched it around town, but the studio executives read it with backward glances at *Zardoz*.

Calley gave me a two-page treatment for *The Heretic*, written by William Goodhart. It was not so much a sequel as a response to *The Exorcist*. I found it extremely compelling. It was based on Teilhard de

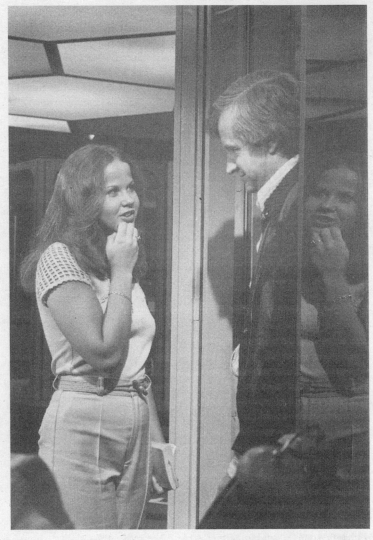

The Heretic: me, with Linda Blair

Chardin's intoxicating idea that biological evolution was the first step in God's plan, starting with inert rock and culminating in humankind. In the next stage, (predicting the Internet) he believed that technology would provide the means of linking all minds, covering the earth with a vast 'thinking skin': mankind would experience a spiritual convergence and eventually become one with God. He feared that this new power could be used for evil as well as good. In Goodhart's story, following this idea, a machine called the Synchroniser allows people to enter each other's minds. It was based on experiments in mutual hypnosis done in the thirties. Goodhart's clever conceit was to suggest that Regan – the young girl from *The Exorcist* – was one of these evolving humans, capable of a new sort of contact with others, but that this spiritual goodness attracted great evil, hence her ordeal.

I was tempted. I would get a substantial fee. I would have a large budget and resources at my disposal to make what amounted to an experimental metaphysical thriller involving innovative special effects and huge sets. Millions of people had enjoyed watching a child being tortured in *The Exorcist*. *The Heretic* would be the antidote, a film about goodness rather than evil. I should have known better. Kubrick told me the only way to do a sequel to *The Exorcist* is to give them even more gore and horror than before. No one is interested in goodness.

Goodhart delivered his screenplay. It was disappointing. Working with him proved difficult. Long discussions were required to get him to change a comma. I wearied of the process and asked Rospo to help. He and I started working on the script.

In the story, a priest, Father Lamont, has been assigned by the Vatican to investigate the exorcism of Regan MacNeil. Regan was experiencing alarming flashbacks to her exorcism and was now being treated by a psychiatrist, Dr Tuskin, who was using the Synchroniser to achieve this Teilhard de Chardin kind of contact. The priest has lost belief in God, but rediscovers a spiritual connection through the Synchroniser. In doing so he confronts powerful forces of evil.

My ambivalent attitude to Catholicism made this idea of a spiritual investigation very seductive. I was also intrigued by the idea of a relationship between a young girl and a priest, the poignancy of irresolvable sexuality, something I had witnessed in Father Maguire.

I asked Jon Voight to play Father Lamont. He had studied for the priesthood in a Jesuit seminary before he left to become an actor. He was intrigued. He had a lot of ideas, particularly about the ending. I was trying to keep Bill Goodhart involved and I arranged for him to meet with Voight. Bill was upset by Jon's free-wheeling improvisations and became even more defensive. I, conversely, am always stimulated by the input of actors. A movie grows out of these convergences: this is how we breathe life into it.

I wanted Goodhart to do a rewrite based on the new structure Rospo and I had developed, but he couldn't find a foothold, it was too different from his own sensibility. He was a playwright, accustomed to renting out his words, whereas a screenwriter sells them outright. We would spend hours arguing over a line of dialogue, whereas anyone involved in making pictures knows it will probably be changed several times in rehearsal or on the day it is shot – or even in post-production in the re-recording studio. Or it may be cut altogether. I admired Bill, though, and I promised him I would be true to the spirit of the story he had written.

Voight was playing *Hamlet* at that time. He was extraordinary, one of the very best of the dozen or more I have seen in my lifetime. It was a painful, tortured portrayal, and the madness utterly convincing. It is an overwhelming ordeal for any actor. Hamlet's doubts, combined with Jon's own, made it doubly difficult to get a decision from him.

After *Deliverance*, Jon had married his sweet girlfriend Marcheline. They invited us to spend the following Christmas Day with them in LA. Marcheline had a tree loaded with presents and our four children gorged on their extravagant largesse. As it got to meal time and beyond, I was alarmed that no aromas were coming from the kitchen: there was no sign of Christmas dinner. Eventually, I raised the issue. Marcheline's big innocent eyes widened: 'I thought we could go down to Baskin Robbins.' I was horrified, but my children always claimed it was the best Christmas dinner ever – an orgy of ice cream.

They now had two children themselves: a boy, and a shy, demure little girl who would grow up to be Angelina Jolie. Jon had lived out this sentimental idyll of babies and toys. Their house was an impractical fairyland. Jon was a kind and caring husband. He is a deeply spiritual man, but he has a dark, shadow side. Father Lamont's wrestle with evil was something that he connected with and feared. Yet he could not make up his mind.

He was still in the grip of *Hamlet*. He had fallen in love with the young actress playing Ophelia. She was a wild free spirit, a redhead with a fierce temper and unpredictable sexual appetites. She found his obsession with her oppressive. She was fickle. She would come and go. Jon was demented. He had always been devoted to his family and now he was torn apart. The dark side was demanding its due. The serious, perceptive, responsible man could quickly shift to a teasing and mocking one, who refused to take anything seriously. He is a brilliant and cutting mimic. His impression of me is devastating.

Shortly after *The Heretic*, he wrote a script with Dore Previn. I arrived at the Chateau Marmont after the long-haul eleven-hour trip from London. Jon and Dore were waiting with the script. They said they would sit downstairs while I read it. I was much too tired and promised I would do so as soon as I woke up. Reluctantly, they left. Nevertheless, I was intrigued, and after taking a shower, I opened it up. It was about two brothers. One was a steady, reliable family man, the other a Beverly Hills doctor leading a life of drugs and sex, who was involved in a destructive affair with a bisexual redhead. My phone rang. It was the redhead. She was downstairs. 'That script is my fucking life. It's not his. I want it back. I want my life back.' She stormed up and tore it from my hands.

Father Lamont's contest between his goodness and his evil was close to Jon's own, too close. After much agonising, he decided not to play the role. His torment continued over the next few years. He renewed his spiritual quest. He studied the Bible. It led him to Judaism. He lived frugally, gave generously, was celibate, did not work for several years as he struggled with his demons. It would be more than twenty years before we worked together again on *The General*. By then he had made peace with himself, and with the God of Abraham. The doubts and fears that inhibited his acting were resolved, and he had become a bold and intrepid actor, taking risks, allowing his intuitive talent full rein – the best actor of his generation, and as kind and caring a man as I ever met.

Everyone told Burt Reynolds he was going to win the Best Supporting Actor Oscar for *Boogie Nights*, and Jon felt his anguish when he didn't. Jon was shooting a film the next day but he made several calls to the Four Seasons Hotel where Burt was staying. Burt was refusing to take calls. At the end of the day, Jon took himself to the hotel and demanded that his call be put through. Despite their instructions, they wilted before a movie star. Burt's girlfriend answered. She said Burt didn't want to see anybody. He had been in bed all day with nausea and hadn't eaten. In fact, they had only now ordered some bland food from room service. Jon borrowed a waiter's uniform and wheeled the trolley up to their room. Burt was in bed reading a book and the girlfriend was on the phone.

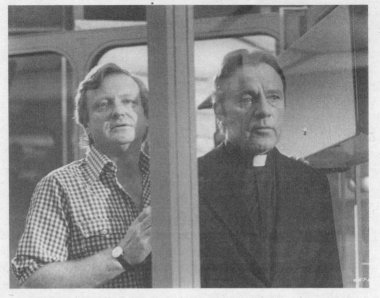

Me, with the weary and burnt-out Burton

Neither looked up. In a heavy French accent, Jon said, 'Ah, it ees Bot Renoolds.' He leapt on the bed and kissed Burt on the mouth. He got Burt laughing again. They spent a happy evening together.

When Voight was in London making *Mission: Impossible*, my daughter Telsche was suffering from cancer. He visited her every evening and never failed to make her laugh too.

I always saw Lamont as a young priest. I tested Christopher Walken, but Ted Ashley felt that the scale of the movie needed a bigger star. David Geffen had just become an executive at Warners. He pressed for Jack Nicholson. Much as I admired Nicholson, I couldn't see him in the role. If Jack made a pact with the devil, you'd think that was where he belonged.

Richard Burton's name came up. I resisted the idea. Ashley asked me to go to New York to see him on stage in *Equus*. Everyone was impressed that he could get himself on stage every night in such a demanding role. I had to admit he was mesmerising. So the passionate young priest became a weary and burnt-out one. Another rewrite. What had been an original character became something of a cliché. Then

Lee J. Cobb died. Detective Kinderman, the character he played in *The Exorcist*, was central to our script. A bigger story problem. No sooner did we shore up the story, when down it would tumble on our heads. I cast Louise Fletcher as the psychiatrist. She had just won an Oscar for *One Flew over the Cuckoo's Nest*. She had an air of authority. She was tall and regal. Burton said to her, 'I'm a Welsh dwarf and it's always my fate to be cast with tall leading ladies. Sophia Loren not only towered over me, she insisted on wearing six-inch heels, even when they were not in shot. She said if she took them off it changed the shape of her body.'

Ellen Burstyn was determined not to reprise her role of Regan's mother and nothing would make her change her mind. Max von Sydow also refused. He hated the first film, the torturing of the child, and thought it morally destructive. The links with the first picture were diminishing. I was getting desperate. I met Max and argued that by making the sequel he could perhaps repair the damage he had helped to inflict. He said that kind of Jesuitical sophistry made no sense to a practical Swede. He had a goodness and kindness that I felt was vital to the film and eventually I talked him round.

To give the picture a heightened dream-like style, we decided to shoot the outdoor African sequences in the studio rather than on location. I set up a colour palette for the film eliminating all blues and greens, the colours of comfort and hope. Their absence would make the audience uneasy, deprived, the way you feel in a city under grey skies where there are no trees. It externalised the notion of our world plunging into a technological nightmare of smog and desertification, and thus set up the desire for some kind of redemption.

We were tackling huge aesthetic and technical problems, and doing experimental things on an epic scale, in the context of a big-budget Hollywood studio picture. I knew how hard this would be to pull off. Yet again I was trying to do too much. The bigger a movie gets, the less original it tends to become. My aesthetic theories and colour codes seemed like indulgent whims to the crew of hardened cynical technicians. But we persisted. We were constantly obliged to rewrite as problems arose and new solutions were needed. Bill Fraker, the cameraman, was tested to his limits, having to light exterior scenes on indoor stages. And everything that could go wrong did go wrong, technically and personally.

We rented a house in Westwood and hired a tutor to attend to the children's schooling. Daisy, who was ten, complained of excruciating pain in

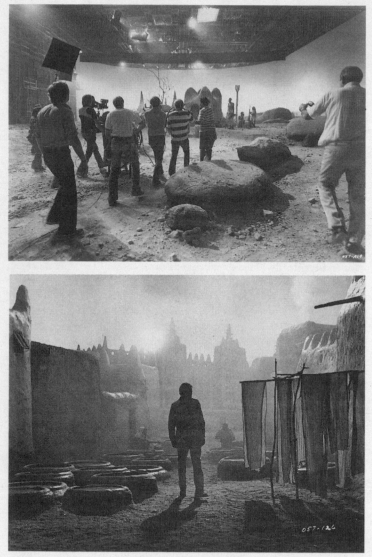

The Exorcist: Shooting the African sequences in the studio

her shin. It was swollen. X-rays revealed it to be a tumour in the marrow of the bone. We were devastated. Were my daily dealings with evil forces somehow unleashing these tribulations? She was operated on. The bone was split open and the tumour removed. We awaited the verdict. Christel was distraught. I watched her suffer and wished I could take the pain upon myself. Alas, pain is not transferable. It defines our aloneness.

I went on working and felt guilty for allowing these huge but trivial movie problems to distract me. The news came. The tumour was benign. Daisy was still in agony from the trauma to the shin bone. She needed morphine to make the pain endurable. She screamed for the drug and had a hard time coming off it. Meanwhile Katrine, now sixteen, broke her big toe, and felt that Daisy's more dramatic agony deprived her of the sympathy she deserved.

The sheer scale of the picture slowed us down. Lighting ate up much of the day. Special effects held things up too. When there is a lot of waiting, momentum is lost. It is particularly hard for the actors to maintain concentration and energy. Burton had a reputation for being difficult. On the contrary, I found him completely professional. The only demand he made was that I should go personally to call him from his trailer when I was ready for him. That was shrewd. He knew from experience that nervous assistant directors would tend to call actors early so as not to get caught out and earn the ire of the director.

Richard kept his drinking to the weekends. However, he made no contribution to the enterprise. I told him what was required and he did it. If I asked him to adjust his reading, he simply changed it without comment. He expressed no preference, he had no view of the character, and it was, I suspect, of no interest to him. He acted from the neck up, face and voice. His body was rigid, completely inexpressive. When alcoholics are on the wagon there is a hollowness about them. Some of their humanity drains away when they pour the booze down the sink. I persuaded myself that this emptiness could work for the film. He said, 'This is my sixtieth film. I've never seen any of them except the first two. I was shocked. I was looking at my father's face. Unbearable.'

Linda Blair, who played Regan, was incapable of arriving on time and lingered ever longer in make-up. One day she said to me, proudly and without irony, 'John. Did they tell you I was only ten minutes late today?'

I began to suffer back pain and high fever. I dragged myself through each day's work. Nothing would shake the fever. It was coming up to the Fourth of July holiday. A rash broke out all over my body. At the end of

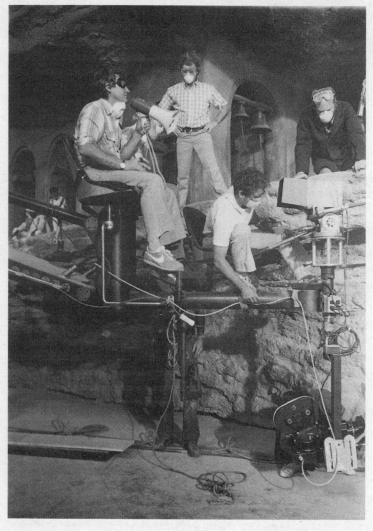

'We had brought in sand to the studios for our African sequences.'

that day, that Friday night, I checked in to the UCLA medical centre. They got very excited when they saw that the rash covered the palms of my hands. They diagnosed syphilis. They told me that the law required me to write down all my sexual contacts for the last five years. They took blood tests and I went home and crawled into bed. I told Christel they thought it was syphilis. Her response was immediate: she said I must have my own knife, fork and plate.

The tests were all negative, but my temperature was now up to 103. Ed Gross, my lawyer, sent his doctor, Elsie Georgi, over to see me. She had run a New York haulage business to put her younger siblings through school, and did not study medicine until she was in her late thirties. She was a bitter foe of luxury medicine, and claimed that unnecessary interventions and treatments were killing off the ageing rich. She was a famed diagnostician. She said, 'You've got valley fever. It is a fungus found in the desert, and becomes active when the grit is disturbed.' We had brought in sand to the studios for our African sequences. Elsie put me in the hospital and they packed me in ice to keep down the soaring temperature. Elsie arrived at my bedside. She said, 'There's no treatment for what you have, so I've made you some pasta.' She explained that the fever would persist until the body calcified the fungus in my lungs. I would then have to have a lumbar puncture to discover if the fungus had travelled. 'And if it finds its way to the brain it kills you.'

'There's no treatment?' I asked.

'There is a drug,' she admitted ruefully, 'but it brings about premature ageing, so it's just a delaying tactic.'

Ed Gross had a phobia about needles and infections. He called and I told him about the lumbar puncture, how I had to lie in a foetal position with a needle inserted into my spinal column for twenty minutes, because the fluid had to be extracted very slowly. A sudden movement could snap the needle. I heard a moan as his phone clattered to the floor. I could hear the sound of furniture overturning as he fainted away.

While I was convalescing, I heard from a friend that Mae West wanted to sell her beach house in Santa Monica. I called her and she arranged for me to view it. It was built in the thirties by a German architect. Although Mae West was in her eighties, she offered me a private twenty-year mortgage. She must have believed she was immortal. She hadn't used the house for many years. There was a caretaker and she would go down and take tea with him each Thursday afternoon. He showed me around.

White carpets, white grand piano, a big white TV console with a tiny screen. The kitchen and bathroom fittings were original. I had stepped back into the thirties. There were pictures and drawings of her on every wall. Over a curving staircase was an extraordinary mural – vigorous young men cavorted and struck muscular poses, their erect penises picked out in gold leaf.

I described it all to Isherwood and Bachardy. They were in a lather of excitement. They begged me to take them to the house. I arranged to see it again and took them along. Among the gay community there was the belief that Mae West was a man – they searched the house for evidence, but to no avail.

When I took Christel to see it, we walked around the perimeter of the garden, which was walled off from the public beach. A wino was sleeping against the gate. It was enough. She said no.

It was at this time that Mae West, after years of retirement, re-emerged to play a role in *Myra Breckinridge*. A party was organised in her honour and the A-list attended. Every star, every major director turned up to pay homage. There was a line, and everyone shuffled along to take their turn in shaking her hand and exchanging a few words. People were astonished at her brilliance, her acute awareness of contemporary movie-making, her judgement, her wisdom. It transpired that she had said exactly the same words to everyone: 'Loved your movie. Loved your movie.'

It was a month before I got back to work, and I was still weak. The feeling was getting around that the picture was jinxed. Louise Fletcher's husband fell seriously ill. She herself was rushed to hospital for a gall bladder operation. 'That's what happens when you play around with the occult,' a prop man told me.

We built a huge Georgetown street set on the stage for the climax. It was much admired. It is often the way with street sets: people are impressed with their size, but once it is on film, it is simply a rather small street. Lee Marvin came to visit. He was drunk and harboured a grudge against Warner Brothers. They had cheated him in some way. Steve Ross, head of Warners, was in awe of movie stars. His father had had funeral parlours and Steve devised the idea of using the undertakers' limousines at night to ferry showbiz people around New York. It was the foundation of his fortune.

He came down to the set to meet Lee, who shook his hand, then forced it down until Steve was kneeling in our fabricated Washington gutter.

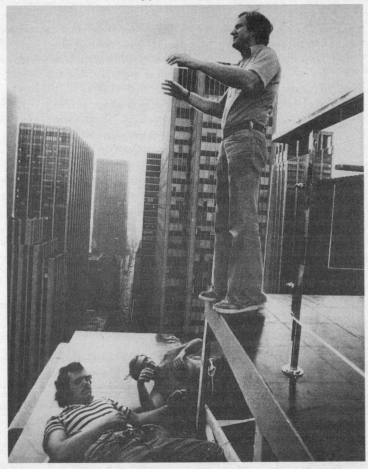

The Exorcist: Lining up the shot – without a harness

'That's where you belong,' said Lee, ever alert to a visual metaphor. Steve was thrilled to be humiliated in this way. He crouched there, giggling. Lee wasn't through with Warners. He went roaring up to the executive offices. Calley was on a sabbatical and Guy McElwaine had taken over as head of production. Lee, replaying a scene from *Point Blank*, demanded to see him. The secretary enquired politely what his business might be. 'I want my money.' She called through to Guy, who wisely refused to see him. Lee hammered on Guy's door. No response. He burst in. Guy had taken the precaution of locking himself in his bathroom. Lee rampaged around the empty office, then lay down on the sofa and went to sleep. Eventually Guy ventured nervously out of the bathroom, crept out of his office and went home.

We moved the unit to New York. The union would not allow us to bring our crew. We had to pick up their people. We built Regan's family apartment on the roof of the Warner building: appropriately, the street number is 666. Driven by her demon, Regan sleepwalks to the edge of the roof garden and is on the point of falling. I wore a harness attached to a rope so that I could lean out safely and teeter on the edge as I lined up the shots with my viewfinder. At the end of the day I found that the other end of the rope had not been secured. Lee would have seen that as a metaphor for film-making itself – your invulnerability is illusory. The picture felt like a masterpiece, a breakthrough, but I was soon to plunge off the building.

Burton was planning to marry Susan Hunt, who had abandoned her racing-driver husband for fast-living Richard. Their divorces finally came through and Richard informed me that they were to be secretly married. He invited me to join them afterwards at the Lombardi Hotel. When I arrived with my daughter Telsche, the hotel was besieged by press and public. The wedding was the worst-kept secret. We found it was impossible to get through the mob. We called from a payphone and they came out and cleared a path for us. We found the couple sitting at a table with only eight guests. A meal was served. Richard was drunk and did not eat. He was a great raconteur, but in his cups the stories rambled interminably. They brought in a hastily improvised wedding cake. It was made of ice cream and the figures of a bride and groom were stuck into the top.

Burton launched into a story about his Welsh childhood. He was like a rambling Dylan Thomas. It was *Under Milk Wood* with no end in sight. The wedding couple on the cake began to sink into the melting ice cream. Telsche took pictures on her instamatic. Susan said, 'Come to bed, Richard.

I promise not to rape you,' but his story had miles to go. I was transfixed by the sight of the wedding couple disappearing, drowning in the cake.

So secretive had they been about the wedding that there were no photographs. Telsche's pictures were the only record. I handed over the undeveloped film so that any subsequent leaks could not be laid at my door.

While we were shooting in New York, new sets were being built back at Burbank. When we got back, nothing was quite ready. We scrambled to find something to shoot. I felt the end would never come. Rospo's wife, Barbara Pallenberg, was commissioned to write a book about the making of the movie and it has more horror in it than the film itself. I have just been rereading it, and reliving the pain. I had forgotten, repressed perhaps, many of the crises that we faced. My oft-quoted definition of film-making as inventing impossible problems and failing to solve them yet again had come back to haunt me. The scale of it, the vaulting ambition, the succession of accidents and misfortunes, were always pushing us to the verge of disaster. Yet living on a knife's edge must be where – unconsciously, perhaps – I need to be. In the comfortable, protected world of the privileged there are few situations where we can test our mettle, discover our absolute potential, and even exceed our limitations. Film is war, quoth Sam Fuller. When I am casting crew, one of the questions I ask myself is, would you want him or her at your side if you were going into battle?

I was wounded and weakened by valley fever and I never got my full strength back. The principal photography finally limped to an end. There remained elaborate model shots of an African village to be done. I decided to shoot them at home in Ireland and they filled the big stages at Ardmore Studios. Garrett Brown, the inventor of the Steadicam, glided across the models simulating the locust/demon's point of view. He was using his prototype camera and had shot scenes for me back in Burbank. He had taken his invention to Panavision, but they rejected it before going on to develop a version of their own. He was lining up his device on stage 16 when he saw Robert Gottschalk, the president of Panavision, taking pictures of the Steadicam from the shadows – a little industrial espionage. Garrett had just strapped on the camera. He shouted at Gottschalk, who scampered off the stage. Garrett turned on the camera and ran after him. We all enjoyed the next day's rushes of Gottschalk running for his car. Garrett kept the film as evidence. Although Panavision made their own version, it never worked. They were stymied by Garrett's patent. However, the US military have the right to appropriate any patent that may be of use in weaponry. They used the Steadicam harness as a gun mount in helicopters. Garrett, a pacifist, saw his invention become a killing machine.

As always, I edited the film at Ardmore. The family gathered back together, and we got back our strength in the healing hills, and took comfort from the trees and flow of the river. Then, all too soon, I was back to Burbank for the track laying and sound mix. The mixers all complained about a young director who preceded me in the dubbing theatre. He constantly changed his mind and insisted on re-cutting the picture during the mix, confusing everybody. I ran into him. He was small and softly spoken. He was about to turn the movie business on its head. George Lucas was fretting over *Star Wars* as I struggled to shape *The Heretic*.

Rospo's wife, Barbara, was always at my side, watching, sharing the tribulations. We were in daily intimate contact, as close as lovers. She had seen all that I had seen and felt it as deeply. It struck me that the probing interview, the professional study of one person by another, is the post-modern relationship. Just as I fell in love with Alison as I probed her life, so Barbara and I became bonded by what she knew of me, and the journey we had taken together through the making of this movie.

There were lines around the block waiting for the film to open. *The Exorcist* had been a phenomenon. They had screamed, passed out, vomited on the seats. They were ready for more. What they saw outraged them. They threw things at the screen. There were mass walkouts. They found the ending particularly offensive. Warners panicked. I made a hasty attempt to re-cut the last reel, and we pulled the prints and changed them overnight. The press hounded me. How did I feel about making such a disaster?

Rospo, Barbara and I watched as the ambitious work we had laboured over was torn to pieces by the mob and ridiculed by the critics. This is what Pauline Kael wrote in *The New Yorker*:

> The picture has a visionary crazy grandeur (like that of Fritz Lang's loony *Metropolis*). Some of the telepathic sequences are golden-tone and lyrical, and the film has a swirling, hallucinogenic, apocalyptic quality; it might have been a horror classic if it had had a simpler, less ritzy story. But, along with flying demons and theology inspired by Teilhard de Chardin, it had Richard Burton, with his precise diction, helplessly and inevitably turning his lines into camp, just as the

cultivated, stage-trained actors in early-thirties horror films did. Like them, Burton had no conviction in what he was doing, so he couldn't get beyond staginess and artificial phrasing. The film is too cadenced and exotic and too deliriously complicated to succeed with most audiences. But it's winged camp – a horror fairy tale gone wrong, another in the long history of movie-makers' king-size follies. There's enough visual magic in it for a dozen good movies; what the picture lacks is judgement – the first casualty of the movie-making obsession.

I was found out, humiliated. I limped home to Annamoe. This would surely end my career. As ever, I had tried to do too much, put too much in, been too ambitious. As Ms Kael said, my judgement was faulty – I had taken something on without thinking out the consequences. And letting Voight slip through my fingers and casting Burton against my instincts was another mistake.

1977: The Mystery of Memory

My son Charley was badly dyslexic. I took advice from the experts, read up on it. The more I learned, the more complex it seemed. This disability can take many forms. The process of learning in a young child apparently causes chemical shifts in the brain which open up the short-term, and then progressively, the medium- and long-term memories. In the dyslexic this process is impaired. The only effective treatment is one-to-one attention, endlessly repeating the words until they stick, grinding away, forcing that chemical change to occur in the brain. In times past when everything was taught by rote, dyslexia didn't show up as much as it does in modern methods of teaching. One of the experts said to me, 'Who do you suppose would have the motivation and patience for this grinding one-to-one teaching?' Only a parent.

I decided to devote a year to teaching Charley. I suppose it was also a way of opting out of movie-making. My nerve had gone.

It was frustrating for Charley. He would learn a word, repeat it, write it down, spell it, know it. We would go on to the next word. By the time he knew that, the previous word was forgotten. Little by little, by tiny steps, we made progress. He would do anything to avoid the work, to delay it, to shorten it. He became skilled in distracting and amusing me. We laughed a lot, but he also raged against his dysfunction. I drew heavily on my army experience of teaching illiterates. I remembered how nervous tension would build up as they struggled to learn, and how it helped to get them moving, physically; so Charley and I would throw a ball back and forth as he spelt out words. Singing the letters to a familiar tune also helped. We could only work in short bursts. Mostly, we played together. It was a beautiful time. Like all kids he was insatiable for stories, and I never tired of making them up. We took many journeys with Merlin and Arthur, and when I saw the wonder in his eyes, I would feel the old itch to put it on film – then I would remember . . .

Faced with this dysfunction, what astonished me was not that Charley had a problem, but that most people could so easily grasp the meaning of these little symbols and shapes. I yearned for some sort of synchroniser so that I could transfer my vocabulary directly to my son. Teilhard de Chardin charts the evolution of man, this groping towards consciousness, this struggle of the mind to comprehend God; Chardin acknowledges all the failures along the way – the casualties, the impaired, the Blobs – who never countenance such aspirations. Yet working with Charley, I felt I edged a little closer to the mystery of memory. It is only when it fails that we appreciate its complexity. When someone loses the ability to recognise faces or distinguish between them, we realise what a prodigious feat that recognition is. 'I never forget a face,' people say casually, without realising how wonderful that is.

Luis Buñuel in his memoir, *My Last Breath*, notes his failing memory and equates it with dying. Memory is a definition of life. The lowliest plant or insect remembers what it must do. One of Jorge Luis Borges' stories tells of a man who has absolute and total recall. He finds it insupportable. Each morning he must commit to memory the sky, each formation of clouds, everything he looks at is completely new. The vividness of a child's vision, seeing things new, gives way in the adult to the ability to generalise – not specific clouds but a cloudy sky, not a hundred faces, but a crowd. Thus the world becomes less real and more abstract. As we get older the generalisations get broader, a week passes, a year passes, marked only by a vacation, a death, a journey. The camera cannot generalise. The eye, looking at a London street in November, will see a monotony of greyness; if you photograph it, the dominant feature will be the red bus.

At the end of that year we sent Charley to a Quaker school in Banbury that specialised in dyslexia. His first letter home, which must have taken him an age to write, broke our hearts. 'I've only gone one friend,' he wrote, 'and I don't think he likes me.'

His twin sister, Daisy, pined for him, so she followed him there. They learnt to love the school. Charley phoned me one day to wish me a happy birthday. I told him I was impressed that he remembered. He said he hadn't actually remembered. It was in the newspaper. 'Well,' I said, 'I'm delighted you are reading a newspaper.' 'Well, I didn't read it myself. One of the other boys told me.' They found the Quaker practice of daily communal silences excruciating, yet when they left school the silences were what they most missed.

A year had passed since the release of *The Heretic*, yet I still imagined fingers were being pointed at me, and that people were whispering behind their hands: 'There's the man who made *The Heretic*.' Ridiculous, of course. By now, who remembered it? A lot of films fail and lose millions of dollars and pass unnoticed, but some movies like *Heaven's Gate*, *Cleopatra* and *The Heretic* become infamous, notorious failures. In fact, Warners did not lose money on *The Heretic*. They were covered by advances from theatre chains.

Nevertheless, I was still desolate, and glad to accept an invitation to the Moscow Film Festival in the hope that my shame had not penetrated the Iron Curtain. I took my daughters Telsche and Katrine. They were seventeen and sixteen, irreverent and teasing, ridiculing my gloom. We stopped in Vienna on our way to Russia and I was determined to teach them the rudiments of dialectical materialism before they set foot in the USSR. We were awaiting a train to take us to the Vienna Woods. I told them that Marx had defined money as accumulated labour. Telsche said, 'Well, I don't think it is.' I said, 'It doesn't matter what you think, I'm trying to tell you what Marx thought.' The argument became heated. I gave her a gentle push, but like a striker trying to steal a penalty, she staggered back and contrived an elaborate fall into a stall of flowers. I was seized by a railway policeman. The train pulled in and the girls jumped on board, waving and grinning at me as it pulled out, while I tried to convince the witnesses that it was my own daughter whom I was properly chastising.

When we got to Moscow the last thing anyone wanted to hear about was dialectical materialism. Everyone we met was deeply disillusioned with Communism. One student told me that he and his friends were convinced that Communism was a western plot foisted on Russia to keep it weak.

Our interpreter took us to Mosfilm's vast studios where a lavish costume drama was being filmed. As we arrived, they were about to shoot a scene involving hundreds of extras. When the director was told I was present, he stopped the work and came over to greet me. 'Come, we will drink a coffee together.' I said, 'But you are ready to shoot.' He brushed that aside, sat me down, and coffee was brought. I glanced anxiously at the waiting cast and crew. 'Don't worry. In Russia, money no problem. I take what time I need.' He looked relaxed and happy. What a contrast to my daily stretched-out tension of trying to make every moment count, of pushing the crew, of having one eye on the clock, of having to make daily compromises.

In order to get him back to work I asked him to write down his address. I promised to write to him, invite him to Ireland. Our interpreter stepped in to help. She had an extraordinary command of English, but she had never been to an English-speaking country and had been taught English by interpreters who also had never left Russia. She was anxious to pick up colloquialisms from my daughters. She cast around for something on which to write. 'Do you have a piss of paper?' she asked. When Telsche and Katrine convulsed with laughter, she said, 'Oh, I have used the wrong expression. I should have said a shit of paper.' That was even better.

A very young Isabelle Huppert was there with her first film, *The Lace Maker*. She wanted us to see it. It was playing miles out in the suburbs. We took a taxi. It started to rain. All the vehicles came to a halt. The drivers, including ours, got out and fitted their windscreen wipers. They were in such short supply that they had to keep them inside for fear of having them stolen.

The cinema was mobbed. Hundreds of Muscovites besieged the box office in a hopeless quest for tickets. We fought our way in and the chaos was such that the screening was delayed for more than an hour. We soon learnt that this was the norm in the festival. Isabelle and the director went up on stage and were interviewed interminably. Isabelle came back and sat beside us and finally the lights went down. Up came a Bulgarian film with Russian subtitles. No one complained. No one apologised. Isabelle ran out in tears.

At the end of the festival there was a reception at the Kremlin Palace. A long buffet table was laid out with food and bottles of wine. Half-starved as we were by the chronic food shortages, we fell upon it. Everything was quickly devoured and drunk, except for one cluster of a dozen wine bottles that nobody touched. I was talking with the chief interpreter, who had spent a year travelling throughout the USSR showing *Deliverance* to elite groups. She had done a live translation of the dialogue. She knew the picture as well as I did. I asked her about the left-over wine.

'That was Stalin's special reserve wine,' she explained *sotto voce*. 'What you have to understand is that every gesture, every action in Russia is political. If you drank that wine you would be endorsing Stalin's policies. However, it is the best Georgian wine and you are an ignorant foreigner, so why don't you take a couple of bottles and bring them over here where we can all drink it.' Nervously, I reached out for the bottles. All eyes turned on me. I poured it with reverent care. I thought of the twenty million he had killed. It was a rich, dark red. It was like drinking blood.

The heroes of the Soviet Union are buried by the Kremlin Wall. I made the tour. The important ones have their faces sculpted on their tombstones. There was one that looked vaguely familiar. When I looked more closely I saw that it was Stalin, but not with the familiar, arrogant expression; instead, he was wearing a humble, apologetic look. The guide did not mention him – presumably that would have been a political act.

I went to visit the humble apartment of the great director, Sergey Eisenstein, now a museum. Whenever he had his photo taken during his period in the political wilderness, he always held a copy of *Alice in Wonderland* in his hand, in clear view of the camera. More subtle semiotics. We were each afforded the privilege of sitting at his desk for a moment. I wrote in the visitor's book on behalf of several directors making the pilgrimage, 'We, who stand on his shoulders, now sit in his chair.' As I sat there, his images flowed through my mind's eye. I thought of his rhythms, his montage, of his work with Prokofiev in forging a theory of film scoring, the wit and lightness he achieved in the midst of vast epics. He smiled at me out of many photographs crowding the walls. It was an epiphany. It was as if he was saying, 'You must keep going. You have to make your transcendent movie.'

It arrived in the post . . .

1977: *Broken Dream*

. . . I opened the package. It was from a French producer, Claude Nedjar, whom I had met in Cannes. It was a slight, very French, mystical book set in some future or past Ireland. It hung in the mind, preyed on my imagination. One morning I awoke, having dreamt the entire movie that it could become. Inevitably, I could recall only fragments of it, but I was sure it could be teased out of the unconscious. It left me in a state of high excitement. My year in the wilderness was over.

Neil Jordan was a young writer who had published a book of short stories in which he revealed a unique visual imagination. I asked him to collaborate with me on the screenplay. We called it *Broken Dream*. We met each day and wrote it together in an office in Ardmore Studios. We shared out the characters. I had the voices of some, he of others.

A young magician, Ben, and his lover, Nell, travel the land performing in little theatres. It feels like the past – no cars or electricity, but it transpires that this is the future when fossil fuels have been exhausted, and people are living a simple life. The boy is sent for by his father, Old Ben, a blind magician, who tells him he has mastered the ultimate trick: how to make objects disappear. He wants his son to learn it and perfect it. When he has mastered it, Old Ben tells his son to make him disappear. He wants to cross to the place where the objects go, to form a bridge so that others may follow. Young Ben's lover, Nell, and indeed anyone who witnesses the crossing over, yearns to go too. It is a metaphor for all our endings, for death and the possibility of redemption and transcendence. The world is running down, coming to a close. Ben must try to send the people over to the other place, before the world ends. This apocalyptic vision reflected the state of the world at that time: the realisation that fossil fuels were finite, the pervading sense that the planet was in terminal decline.

The writing of the script became a two-month tutorial in film-making, and Neil absorbed it. He was inarticulate, guarded, tense. People were careful in his presence, wary. He was numinous, with visionary insights, yet found it painful to conduct the ordinary exchanges of everyday life. It was more than shyness, it was a kind of anguish, a dysfunction. It was as though he was nothing and his gift was all. He was self-effacing, yet his talent was assertive. We wrote a beautiful script. I dared to hope it could be what I had imagined in Eisenstein's chair – that elusive grail, a film that transcended film.

Needless to say, no one would finance it, but even after many strenuous and costly attempts to make it, I never gave up on it. After every subsequent film I made, I would pull it out of the drawer and try again. More than once, we got as far as pre-production, casting and designing, before it foundered. River Phoenix was to have played Young Ben, but made his own crossing in the arms of heroin. The problem was that it was an art film that required a mainstream budget. That contradiction was its nemesis. After Neil's involvement with this project was long gone, I rewrote it several times. I tried to make it simpler and cheaper. It didn't work. Then I made it bigger, more mainstream, but I failed to conceal its subversive, surreal intentions. The studios knew I was cheating, and the spectre of *The Heretic* and *Zardoz* hovered over my efforts.

Most directors have an alternative filmography. The films they did not make that might have taken the place of the ones they did. I discussed this with the great Italian director, Michelangelo Antonioni, when he came to dinner at my house in Ireland around that time. We were exchanging painful stories about producers and our unmade and unloved movies. When he was trying to make *L'Avventura,* Dino De Laurentiis heard about it. He called Antonioni and arranged an airline ticket for him to fly to Rome. He said, 'You tell me the story. If I like it, we'll make the picture.'

Antonioni is a shy, laconic man. In his hesitant way, he duly told Dino of how the girl, Anna, disappears on an island, and how the rest of the film was a futile search to find her. At the end of the telling, Dino said, 'Well, what happened to Anna?'

Antonioni replied that he did not know.

'Who wrote the story?'

'I did,' said Antonioni.

'You wrote it and you don't know what happened to Anna?'

Antonioni admitted that that indeed was the case. Dino held out his hand. 'Give me back the price of the air ticket.'

L'Avventura became one of those rare transcendent films – poetic, mysterious, beguiling.

Broken Dream is a classic hero story, a variation on the Arthurian legend. A young, innocent boy is chosen for a great quest; the weight of the world falls on his shoulders. The wasteland is all about him. He must undergo painful ordeals to achieve his grail. A wise old man, the Merlin figure – his father, in this case – is his accomplice. As I pondered on *Broken Dream* as it waited to be born, my thoughts turned back to the great myth itself.

1978: *Excalibur*

Like so many others at the time, I had read Carl Jung's *Memories, Dreams, Reflections* and had been moved and excited by it. I was soon steeped in his other works, and was particularly taken with his theory of archetypes. He often alludes to the Grail legend although he never deals with it directly, since that was the life work of his wife, Emma.

Jung's archetype of the trickster, the magician, got me thinking about Merlin again. In the opening of *Hope and Glory*, the small boy, my surrogate, is playing in the suburban garden with mounted knights and a figure of Merlin. My childhood in river and oak forest had been steeped in the legend. John Cowper Powys's *A Glastonbury Romance* had reignited my interest with its intoxicating mysticism. That led me to T. S. Eliot's *The Waste Land*. In his notes, Eliot refers to Jessie L. Weston's 'The Grail in Myth and Romance', and I studied her theories as well. These Arthurian stories, 'The Matter of Britain', were passed down in an oral tradition, shaping the psyche of Europe. The invention of the printing press allowed them to be recorded. Thomas Malory was commissioned by William Caxton, who was searching for new books for his printing press, to write an English version of the 'French Book'. He wrote it in jail while serving a sentence for rape. Yet his *Morte d'Arthur* is so different from the French version by Chrétien de Troyes that he must certainly have drawn heavily on the stories he knew from the oral tradition. It also differs from the German version, *Parzival*, by Wolfram von Eschenbach. It is remarkable how these three versions reflect their several national characteristics. Malory's is eccentric but practical; Chrétien's is formal and romantic; Eschenbach's is about an idiot savant's destructive, ecstatic quest for spirituality.

I began to formulate the idea that the Grail cycle was a metaphor for the past, present and future of humanity. In the early chapters, the Uther Pendragon period, man is emerging. He still has an unconscious magical connection with nature, both in its violence and its harmony. That could be said to represent the deep past. What if Merlin were to summon Excalibur from the lake? The sword would focus the chaotic unconscious forces that lie beneath the surface. He could then give it to Uther, who would abuse it. Violence and anarchy reign. Merlin would arrange that the sword pass to Uther's son, Arthur, and its power allows him to impose his rule and make peace. As law and reason are imposed, Arthur gradually forfeits his connection with nature. Camelot is established, a place of learning and science and order. Man becomes the master of the world. He pillages the earth. He cuts down the sacred forest. He loses his way. Sadly, this feels like our present.

What of the future? What was once profusion becomes a wasteland. The King is sick from a wound that will not heal. The only way to cure the King and save the land is to find the Grail, the feminine symbol of wholeness and harmony, to find again a oneness with nature. This was my Jungian interpretation of the myth.

I was still smarting from the loss of *Broken Dream*, and wondering if I should even attempt another film, when the great legend caught me in its grip. The thought leapt at me – why not address my guiding myth head-on? I felt a surge of excitement. I tore up my earlier versions and started again. I laboured long over the script. I was determined to tell the whole span of the story although I was aware that it made better sense to tell some portion of .it – Merlin and the young Arthur, or the Arthur/Guinevere/Lancelot romantic tragedy, or the quest for the Grail. Nevertheless, I believed that the entire span of the legend revealed so much more, but how could I possibly achieve this in the context of a two- or three-hour movie?

The old overweening ambition took hold. There were huge problems of dramatisation. For instance, when Arthur sends his knights in search of the Grail – to atone for the sins committed against nature – he ceases to play an active role. Merlin also disappears much too early in the story. Then there was the sheer profusion of narrative events. I wrote a scenario which would have made for a four-and-a-half-hour film. It was constructed as a series of flashbacks centred on the character of Perceval. I sent it to Warners. Their response was predictable, but I could not see how to tell the story in less time. I'd encountered the same problem fifteen years before, when Rospo Pallenberg and I adapted Tolkien's *The Lord of the Rings*, for which the Arthurian legend was a primary source.

I persisted, for it was thrilling finally to address directly the myth that had inspired and underpinned my other films. The betrayal of Arthur by his wife and friend had always resonated with me, because of my father's friend who had loved my mother, and the recurring pattern of my own triangles with Barrie and Pat, Alison and Anthony, Rospo and Barbara.

The task seemed impossible, which filled me with reckless excitement, but it also swamped me. I asked Rospo to help me somehow condense, compress *Excalibur*.

He had several terrific ideas. The first was to tell the story chronologically but with major leaps between each stage. We cut from Arthur's birth directly to his youth, vaulting over his childhood, which forms the core of T. H. White's *The Once and Future King* (the basis of the musical *Camelot*). We cut directly from Arthur as the adolescent king to the mature, bearded, armour-clad king confronting Lancelot. In the same way, Mordred's mother kisses her young son, and as she draws back, he is ten years older. These leaps forward in time gave the story a dynamic narrative power. Pallenberg's other clever idea was to have the dying Uther Pendragon plunge Excalibur into the stone to prevent it falling into the hands of his enemies. Nowhere in the various versions of the myth is it explained how the sword came to be sticking out of a rock. In Malory the sword is embedded in a stone surmounted by an anvil which sits on the altar of a church. This was an attempt to Christianise a pagan legend and obfuscates its origins. We also found a way of making Arthur more present in the final section of the story, by making him also the Fisher King. Fusing two characters in this way made the story simpler and stronger.

We both felt that we were not inventing, but rather rediscovering lost fragments of the story, uncovering hidden truth. The Christian accretions had certainly confused the story. I considered telling it as a pagan legend, but I was simply the latest in a long line of minnesingers and storytellers, and my task was to pick up where the last man left off. People's expectations must be met. I had to take the Christian elements as a given. I decided to pitch the story between pagan and Christian, the one God replacing the many gods and Merlin's powers usurped and fading. A myth can be defined as a story that can be turned inside out, stood on its head and yet mysteriously remain itself. It's like a movie star who can play many different characters and yet is always himself. Rospo organised the material and wrote some beautiful scenes.

Merlin's ambiguity, the fact that he is both more and less than a man, his capacity to intervene in human affairs, albeit in an erratic and irrational fashion, and the gift he possesses of seeing into the future as well as understanding the past make him a representation of the unconscious. Jung tells us that the unconscious has to be confronted, since it represents the past of both the individual and the race. But engaging with the unconscious is a terrifying enterprise and may end with the destruction of the ego and madness. The Middle Ages, according to Jung, was something which, like the unconscious, we ought to study in order to gain a better understanding of ourselves. For a century now, we've been rushing headlong into the future; we've made a cult out of progress and we've forgotten our former selves, our former patterns of behaviour, whose origins can be traced to the Middle Ages. We no longer have roots; and today, in particular, when we contemplate the possible destruction of our planet, there is a pressing need to investigate the Matter of Britain.

We started at the beginning of things. We had Merlin say that Excalibur was 'forged when the world was young, when bird and beast and flower were one with man, and Death was but a dream'. The story, lying as it does between mythos and logos, is about people trying not to discover themselves, but to find their place in the world – a much humbler aspiration. Rather than our futile modern quest for self, they strive simply to learn their destiny.

I sent the script to the Hollywood studios and got the usual rejections. Only Mike Medavoy, of Orion Pictures, responded positively. He was a great admirer of the Errol Flynn *Robin Hood* and felt that *Excalibur* could have a similar appeal. I could see no similarities, but I felt it prudent not to argue the point. 'Promise me it won't be dark,' he said. I promised, but I had my fingers crossed. Orion was made up of the former management team that ran United Artists – Arthur Krim, Eric Plescow and Medavoy. Mike encountered strong resistance from his partners, but he was head of production and was prepared to go out on a limb. The budget was eleven million dollars.

Orion's policy was inherited from United Artists, which had been formed by Chaplin, Mary Pickford, D. W. Griffith and Douglas Fairbanks in order to give control to the artists. Like UA, Orion examined and considered each project cautiously and prudently, but once they gave it a green light, they allowed the film-maker complete freedom. Orion hesitated. There would be no stars in the film. It was expensive. Ireland's tax incentives were not yet in place. Out of the blue came a substantial offer for German distribution from Neue Constantin, a highly respected company. It was the encouragement Orion needed. They jumped.

As part of my preparations for the great endeavour, I went with my daughter Telsche to Bayreuth to see Patrice Chéreau's production of the *Ring* cycle, whose Germanic myth has many elements in common with the Grail legend. Wagner's music is sublime, ineffable. It inspired my writing and eventually insinuated its way into the movie. The theme of

'Siegfried's death' from *Götterdämmerung* heralded Merlin's entrance and mourned Uther's bloody and primal battles; the prelude to *Tristan and Isolde* with its ever-rising erotic tension underscored the tryst of Lancelot and Guinevere; and the prelude to *Parsifal*, with those impossible chords that elevate the spirit, became the motif of the quest for the Grail.

Telsche and I would study the texts and score in the morning, then spend each afternoon and evening in thrall to the opera. Bayreuth is an insistently dull town embarrassed by this volcanic theatre in its midst. We stayed in an antiseptic guest house and were served *schwarzbrot* and *schinken* for breakfast. Telsche talked in her sleep to her lover – in French. This child, to whom I was so close, was slipping from me into another life, another language. Yet by day we still connected as we always had through the human comedy around us, the pompous opera snobs, the Ruritanian nobility, the congregation of oddballs. She would catch my eye and I hers. We recalled the mysterious falling leaves from the birch tree in Annamoe, our private epiphany.

The final part of the *Ring*, *Götterdämmerung*, is nearly five hours long. At its conclusion, the audience erupted in applause, standing, weeping, so deeply moved that it did not want this overwhelming experience to end. Our applause extended it. The curtain stayed down. We were baying for the performers to appear. There were some scattered boos from the traditionalists who believed the cycle should be performed strictly as Wagner had decreed and not in the postmodern mode of Chéreau. Five, ten minutes went by and finally the curtain rose to a wonderful *coup de théâtre*. Stacked up on the stage, holding their instruments, were the hundred and twenty members of the orchestra. The hundred-strong choir was arranged below them, and finally, the cast lined the foot of the stage. It was breathtaking. The applause continued for another forty minutes.

Tony Pratt built the sets for *Excalibur* at Ardmore Studios. They bulged out of the stages. He knocked out walls to extend them. The back lot was filled with the castle of Camelot. I chose locations close to my home where fragments of the primeval oak forests still remain. I have some of these noble trees on my own land, remnants of the forest that once covered Northern Europe.

In an undisturbed oak wood you can see deep into its heart. The canopy closes out the sky, allowing only fractured light to penetrate. It inhibits the humble under-plants that live in symbiosis with the great

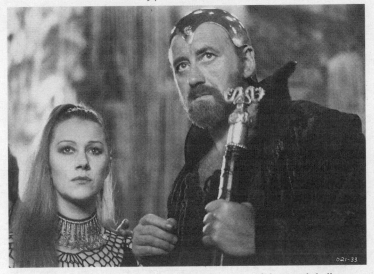

Excalibur: Helen Mirren and Nicol Williamson, with his metal skullcap

trees – bluebells, hazel, holly, mosses and lichens, bracken. They lie low. Inside the wood, the trees are pillars of a great natural temple. In this serene place, wind is baffled; it is rich with the scents of growth and decay, musky, fragrant. It is the atavistic homeland, the repository of fairy tales and myth. When the oaks ruled, there were no hurricanes, no floods, no extremes of climate. They held nature in balance.

It is dark in these woods. I told my cameraman, Alex Thompson, not to consider them as exteriors. I wanted to light them as though we were inside a building. We used green filters on the lamps. We pumped green light on to green moss to make it luminous. We shone emerald light at the oaks and on to the swords and armour, to enhance the mystical sense of the forest as a palpable living thing.

My concept of Merlin was not the conventional old bearded magician. Since he was 'not a man and not a god', I saw him as a kind of hermaphrodite. I wanted to cast Nicol Williamson and shave his head.

When I proposed casting Nicol, the executives at Orion were horrified. When they were at United Artists they had made several films with Nicol, all of which had failed. They begged me to cast anyone but Nicol. I trawled through other possibilities. What about Ralph Richardson?

they said. I tried, but could not imagine anyone else in the role. I wanted Merlin to be jagged, comic, melancholy, crazed. Because Orion had not insisted on having casting approval as most Hollywood studios would, I was more reluctant to oppose their wishes than if they had. I took my casting director, Mary Selway, to lunch. We ran over the possibilities. None worked for me. I said, 'Mary, I'm going to risk the wrath of Orion and cast Nicol.'

At that precise moment, Nicol walked into the restaurant. It was as though Merlin himself had intervened. I saw it as a sign, although later I suspected Mary of arranging the encounter. She swears her innocence. Nicol came to the table. Mary said, 'Nicol, John wants to offer you the part.' Nicol looked deeply melancholic. He said, 'Who will play Morgana?' I told him, Helen Mirren. 'Then I can't possibly do Merlin.' I knew they had done the notoriously unlucky *Macbeth* together, and it had been a disaster, but surely . . . 'Why not?' I asked. 'What is the problem?' Nicol flared up. 'If you must know, she wanted me to fuck her and I wouldn't.'

That afternoon I called Helen. She had heard I was thinking of casting Nicol. If that was the case, she couldn't possibly play Morgana. She explained that they had had a huge row. 'What was it about?' I asked. 'He wanted to fuck me, and I wouldn't.' I was nonplussed. Neither had a reputation as a reluctant lover.

'I'll tell you how bad it is,' said Helen. 'The other day I was at the airport and Nicol got into a cab ahead of me. I thought, it's time we made up. I told the cab driver to catch up with Nicol's. We came up alongside and I wound down the window. I smiled and waved. Nicol stared at me with those cold eyes and without expression, then turned away without a word.'

I cast them both, calculating that an awkward tension between them would work for the story.

Nicol was a notorious hypochondriac. He had two fatal diseases during the course of the picture. Although I specified that his head would be shaved, at the last moment he baulked. He feared it would not grow back. In an attempt to solve the problem, I did a U-turn and gave him a long wig and beard. It was a disaster. His expressive face was buried under the hair. He had no purchase on the character. I showed him the first two days' rushes. I said, 'It's not working.' He agreed. 'I'll step down,' he said gloomily. 'Send for Ralph.' He still would not cut his hair.

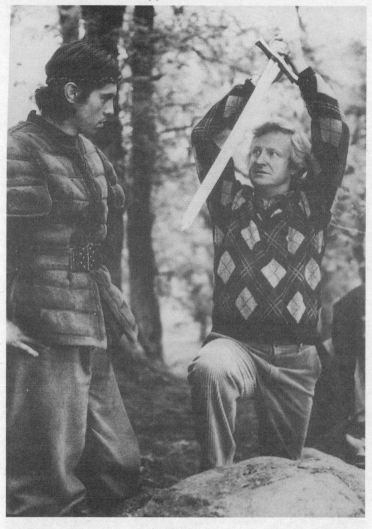

Pulling the Excalibur from the stone, with Nigel Terry as the young Arthur

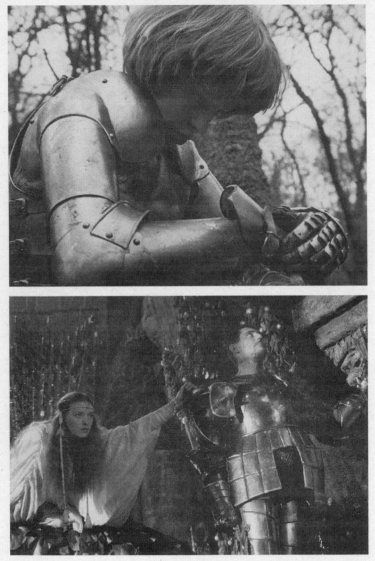

Excalibur: Charley (above) as young Mordred; Katrine (below with Gabriel Byrne) as Igraine

Terry English, who made the armour, had an idea. He fashioned a shiny metal skullcap and fitted it on Nicol. It not only solved the problem of the hair, it also enabled Nicol to find the character. We reshot the first two days. He was brilliant. The helmet gave him the man.

Huge sets, battle scenes, hundreds of extras, horses, armour, special effects. I was once again plunged into the maelstrom. My daughter Telsche did continuity and it is her hand that rises from the lake offering Excalibur. Her sister Katrine played Igraine, who is seduced by Uther and bears his son, Arthur. My son, Charley, at fourteen, was young Mordred. Nigel Terry played King Arthur, convincingly, from ages sixteen to sixty. It was a first film for Liam Neeson and Gabriel Byrne. I assembled a cast of young actors and put them into training. We had to find a suitable horse for each of them, one that matched their riding ability. Casting the horses was nearly as difficult as casting the actors. We had a long period of training. The actors had to muck out and groom their horses each day, and get the animals used to the clanking sounds of armour.

When you direct a film in which there's an abundance of elements it takes a considerable time to assemble and control them. Even if you have twenty weeks of shooting instead of the six or seven for a modestly budgeted film, ninety per cent of your time is spent preparing shots, not directing the actors on camera. As a result, you have, in fact, far less time to shoot intimate scenes than in an inexpensive film, where the director is better able to focus his attention on that essential aspect of the work. That's why, in so many epics, the performances are inadequate. The fact is, quite simply, that the director hasn't had time to concentrate on them, which is why I insisted on an extended rehearsal period. The actors did their horsemanship and swordsmanship in the mornings, then worked on the scenes with me in the afternoons. I drilled them in the rhythms of the dialogue to ensure a consistency of style. We analysed the scenes. We worked on the characters, trying to make them real as well as archetypal.

The Irish climate is heartbreaking to a film-maker – unpredictable, constantly changing, but mostly raining. There was a lot of grey, flat light, but then the moist air would become magically luminous as a low sun broke through cloud, and we would try to snatch the shot. That mystical fleeting light felt like a metaphor for the film itself. I was trying to grasp the ineffable, to capture spirit. I applied the skill I had acquired in shooting landscapes on the stages for *The Heretic*. I decided to shoot

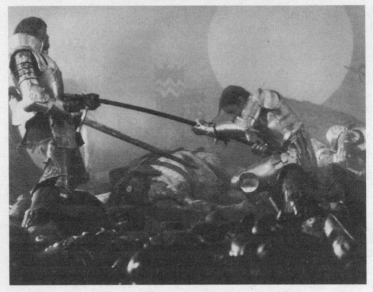

The climactic battle in front of the artificial setting sun

the final battle with Mordred and the death of Arthur as an interior, even though it takes place on an open plain. A huge artificial sun is setting behind them. It is the climax of the movie. It is clearly unrealistic. I had to hope that what had gone before would justify this twilight of the gods, this sense of Arthur moving beyond our world and into the realm of myth.

We laboured for sixteen weeks. Once again there was no room in the budget for a fee for me. I worked for three years on the film. However, I owned fifty per cent of the equity.

Excalibur was a success everywhere it played. I saw it in Westwood, LA, in the third week. The audience was cheering; addicts were chanting the 'charm of making', Merlin's magical incantation. Shortly after the opening, Orion filed for bankruptcy. Warners took over their films and their debts. When my lawyer, Ed Gross, asked Warners for our share of the profits, he was told that we were ordinary creditors and that it would take years to sort out Orion's books. They estimated that we would not receive more than five cents on the dollar.

Ed pointed to the millions Warners had earned in distribution fees across the world. Was it equitable that I had written, directed and produced a film, had devoted three years of my life to it, and had earned not a penny? Eventually, Warners gave me an ex gratia payment of two hundred and fifty thousand dollars. The film has gathered devotees over the years and is one of Warners' biggest sellers in the video and DVD market.

Excalibur may be flawed, it may not be the transcendent movie I had striven for, but its great power derives from the myth it retells, and it improves with the years. I felt great satisfaction in having made it against all the odds. It was a lifelong quest: I had found the Grail. As a matter of fact, I have it sitting on the piano as I write, and the sword, Excalibur, rests against the wall.

A Chinese-American rode up to my house on a bicycle. He was a devotee of *Excalibur*. He wanted to visit the locations of the film. I told him what he needed to know. 'Would you like to see the sword?' He held it in his hands, eyes shining. He was overcome. In a low voice, I said, 'Would you like a glimpse of the Grail?' It was too much for him. Like many a knight before him, he could not bring himself to look upon it. He rode away on his bike.

1981: *Angel*

Channel Four was starting up. Jeremy Isaacs, who founded it, told me he wanted to make proper movies for the new channel, and asked whether I would help to get them started. It was an important initiative for British film. Neil Jordan had written a screenplay, *Angel*, which he had submitted to Channel Four with my recommendation. It was heavily influenced by *Point Blank*. They would allow him to direct, but only if I would produce it. I agreed, although much as I admired him as a writer, I was doubtful he would make a director. To give him experience I had commissioned him to make a documentary about the making of *Excalibur*. He struggled to overcome his difficulties in communicating but did a creditable job.

I obliged him to break down the script of *Angel* into shots, set-ups, storyboards. This is a sobering exercise. With proper time spent on rehearsal, preparation and lighting it is only possible to make an average of ten shots per day. With a modest budget like this, the picture had to be completed in thirty-five days.

I estimated that with Neil's inexperience and uncertainty he would be lucky to make three hundred and fifty shots in total. Neil's shot list was double that figure. I went through it with him, advising how he could economise and make cuts in the text and realise the scenes with fewer set-ups. All directors nurse a dream of an ultimate movie. At each stage, the realities of money and time, and the exigencies of casting, erode that ideal. But most of us – not just the inexperienced film-maker – hang on to an indeterminate beauty that no amount of time and money could ever realise. We put off as long as possible the brutal necessity of defining its reality. Directors are confronted with an endless succession of decisions and choices, and we avoid making them until the last possible moment. We hold on to the film in our head, because once we cast it, break it down into shots, we are giving bits of it away, and each bit will be altered by its new tenant – sometimes for the better, sometimes not.

It is a jolting experience when you lay out a schedule for the first time on a production board, with each scene represented by a strip of card and the strips juggled into the available days. Until now, each sequence has been worked on separately. But now we see the movie at a glance, as a whole, like a musical score. It was a shock for Neil to see how much he needed to shoot each day. That crucial moment of revelation in the preparation of a film always gives me a nasty shock.

He cast Stephen Rea as the lead, an actor he has subsequently worked with in most of his movies. I tried to persuade him to use Liam Neeson, but he was set on Stephen, who is very much his alter ego – they share a vague, enigmatic quality, and have the same bruised sensitivity.

I persuaded the great cameraman, Chris Menges, to shoot it. He gave technical help, always presenting Neil with the available options and careful not to push in a direction he favoured himself. He was not as unbiased politically. It was his sympathies for the Irish Republican cause that attracted him to the film. In a lapse from his neutral position, he persuaded Neil to shoot a scene of British soldiers brutalising civilians. What was distinctive about Neil's story was that it was a man's journey through a terrorist landscape. It did not take sides or make a political case. It was the one scene I insisted he reshoot so as to maintain his tone. A certain existential amorality is Neil's strength. Things happen. The other side of the same coin is his evasiveness, a reluctance to conclude.

I watched the rushes each day, but never went on the set. I talked to him in the evening as briefly as possible, knowing how exhausted a director is at the end of the day. His confidence grew. Although, like Stephen, he had the air of a little boy lost, there is also an underlying shrewdness, an artist's eye for impaling the truth.

I guided him in the cutting room. There is a sequence in *Angel* where Danny, the protagonist, pursues his suspect into a wood. Neil wrote and shot an elaborate scene in which Danny finds a revolver hidden inside a portable radio in a woodman's hut. He then conceals himself in the back of the antagonist's car and pops up and puts the revolver to the man's head. There follows a terrifying scene where the man drives faster and faster and challenges Danny to shoot and send them both to hell. I was always opposed to the scene of the finding of the revolver because I found it mechanical and laborious. It offered no insight into Danny's character, and slowed the narrative just at a point where it should be gathering pace and tension. Neil felt that since so much is made earlier in the story of Danny finding an automatic rifle, it was vital to show how he comes by a revolver. I pointed out that the film had moved on to another level by this point, that now it had to be driven forward by emotion and terror. The audience is involved and connected by this time, not needing to be convinced by the mechanics of the story. No one will ask where he got the gun as the car careens down an Irish road of madness and death.

I was able to show Neil that by cutting the scene of finding the revolver, and editing the scenes before and after so that they follow an emotional flow, not a single question would arise about the revolver. And so it turned out.

We took the film to Cannes and showed it in the market. It caused a stir. I hastily arranged a second midnight screening. It was packed. Critics love to discover a movie, to laud it in preference to the official selections. Alexander Walker, the brilliant and combative critic of the London *Evening Standard*, arrived in a white dinner jacket having come from a party given by MGM. There were no seats. I told him I would screen it for him in London. He said, 'I'm not going to go back to London as the only English critic who hasn't seen it.' I said, 'You're a Northern Irish Protestant. You're going to hate it, especially if you have to stand.' He stayed and stood, and wrote a rave review.

Although in *Zardoz* and *Excalibur* I had helped to train a new generation of Irish film technicians, *Angel* was the first film by an Irish writer-director to enjoy international success, and it launched the new Irish film industry. I was a member of the newly formed Irish Film Board at the time, which (in my absence) gave a small loan towards the budget of *Angel*. A number of older aspiring film-makers were incensed that Neil was given this money when, unlike them, he had not been making shorts and documentaries for years in order to earn such an opportunity. At the Celtic Film Festival in Wexford, they picketed the cinema and boycotted the picture. They launched a campaign of vilification against me. I had taken taxpayers' money to line my own pocket, they claimed. The fact that I took no fee for the picture, and had not even claimed out-of-pocket expenses, was an inconvenience that they were prepared to overlook. The *Tribune* newspaper published a diatribe attacking me with these accusations. I made a demand for a retraction which they ignored. I sued the paper for libel. After some weeks, when they realised I intended to go to court, the *Tribune* did a complete U-turn and published a hagiographic article about me: the wicked man was suddenly a saint. It was like reading a very flattering obituary of myself. They asked me if this made up for their mistake. I said it was three months too late. They asked whether I would accept shares in the newspaper as a settlement. No, I wouldn't. They responded with another offer. Would I accept the newspaper itself as payment? The snag was that it came with huge debts. Shortly afterwards, the paper folded. Some years later it was resuscitated, and now thrives as a vigorously independent journal, owned by the journalists who write it.

Angel launched Neil's career. He honed his craft over several films and finally, in *The Butcher Boy*, made a brilliant, if repellent, masterpiece.

I Hawk My Wares

Why are people so drawn to movie-making? Why are they ready to endure long hours, privations of cold, heat and boredom? Why do actors and crews embrace the harsh discipline of 5 a.m. starts and grinding workloads? I believe it is the same impulse that made my father welcome the war. We are escaping the vague dissatisfactions of safe and comfortable lives. We want to be extended, tested. We need to find the ends of ourselves. When a film is over, you return to your life like a sailor home from the sea. All the little domestic problems have been set aside in favour of the larger fictional ones. In the case of *Excalibur*, I had lived at home and my children were involved in the film, as they were in *Zardoz*, so it felt like an extension of family rather than an abandonment; Christel's seductive cooking had bonded cast, crew and kin. Now Telsche and Katrine had returned to their studies in Paris. Daisy and Charley were back at school in Banbury. There was a gaping hole where the children had been, a chasm.

Christel and I were face to face. I needed another movie to make, to escape my life, to find invented problems to replace the real ones. I started making notes towards what would become *Hope and Glory* – about the boy that I was caught up in the London Blitz, the dull suburban street torn apart by bombs, and my own family thrown into turmoil. It was a way of looking at my personal mythology.

I went back to LA and tested the idea around town. No interest. I pitched *Broken Dream* again. Futile. Everything had changed in Hollywood since *Star Wars*. The studios woke up to the realisation that the mass audience is made up mostly of young boys who want action-adventure movies with a style and pace as close as possible to the cartoons they grew up watching on television. The computer makes that possible. The speed and explosive movement of films like *The Matrix*, *Men in Black* and the latest *Star Wars* saga have become closer to that of animation. In fact, many modern mainstream movies are made with computer animation. Some of these movies have a computer effects budget of twenty million dollars. If all arts aspire to the condition of music, then all movies aspire to the condition of Tex Avery, the great animator. A new language is evolving. Film is a nineteenth-century technology and nothing had substantially changed since D. W. Griffith laid down the rules. Until now. Serious directors are recognising the magical, surreal possibilities. Films as diverse as *Crouching Tiger, Hidden Dragon*, *Amélie* and *The Lord of the Rings* itself are beguiling audiences with wonders fashioned in the computer. The poets of the new cinema are seated at consoles.

All that was yet to come. Nevertheless *Star Wars* had set a new agenda. Nothing would ever be the same. The power of the director would decline. Significantly, Lucas hired directors to make the subsequent episodes while he functioned as a controlling producer, implying that it was possible to be the 'author' of a film without directing it.

1983: *The Emerald Forest*

While I was in LA I had dinner with Rospo and we bemoaned these new trends in Hollywood. He fished out a cutting from the *Los Angeles Times*. He had shown it to me some years back when it first appeared. It concerned a seven-year-old boy snatched by Indians in Brazil. I was intrigued that his father, an engineer, would spend every vacation for ten years searching the rainforest for his abducted son. But even more extraordinary, when he found him, an integrated member of an Indian tribe, he elected to leave him there. What had each of them, father and son, become in those ten years? Ten thousand years of human progress divided them. Do blood and kin reach across such a divide?

Rospo could see that I was tempted. His real name is Robert. Rospo was a corruption by a mad aunt on the Roman side of his family. It means 'toad' in Italian – a manic insight, for so he looks. He sits with his hands folded across his large middle, a knowing smile on his face while I tour the studios and each of my projects founders. He knew that I would be fatally drawn by such a wild and dangerous enterprise. He called it *The Emerald Forest*.

Jake Eberts was in town for the opening of *Gandhi*, which he had helped to produce. He was then running Goldcrest, the great hope of British film-making. We pitched the story to him. Before we got to the end, he had to rush off to get his photo taken with Dickie Attenborough in front of a huge billboard on Sunset Strip. This was just as well, since our ending was sketchy, to say the least. Jake, euphoric with the success of *Gandhi*, agreed to finance the script and research. Rospo and I thrashed the story into some sort of shape. And while Rospo wrote the first draft, I set out for the great Amazonian rainforest. All my life I have loved rivers and trees, and here at last I came to the greatest river and the greatest forest of them all. It was perhaps the most profound experience of my life. I recorded it in my journal:

20 August 1983
I flew in a small plane into an airstrip deep in the heart of Amazonia where a mining project had opened up. An expert tree man, Carlindo took me into its depths.

    These particular hills have no navigable rivers to carry intruders, have been undisturbed since time immemorial. Here is the greatest variety of flora and fauna on the planet. Stepping into its jaws in the wake of the silent, watchful Carlindo, I witnessed primeval forest, unseen by man. The world in its beginning. It is wild, vibrant. Oaks are immensely slow, nursing old grudges and forgotten secrets. The rainforest is rampant, spiteful, tangled in angry knots, barbed thorns, spiked leaves, resins that burn, poisonous fruits, grasses that clutch you, huge ants that sting like snakes, caterpillars whose hair brings welts up on the skin, tarantulas a foot across wearing mink coats. It is so hot, so humid that growth is accelerated to a fever pitch. I stood in its midst and I could hear the roar of creation.

Carlindo checks me and stops. A thin shiny black snake slithers lazily across our way.

'The Indians call that a ten step.'

I laugh. It sounds like a dance from the forties.

'Because', he continues, 'if he bites you, you are dead before you can run ten steps.'

He glances up at the tree under which we are standing. He garners some yellow berries from it and urges me to consume them.

'If you eat these you will be able to make a baby when you are a hundred.'

I swallowed them down. One moment instant death, the next, immortality beckons.

We came to a big tree with buttresses splayed out on all sides supporting a hundred and twenty feet of trunk and branch in the shallow soil. It is thirty feet across at the base. In its upper branches a whole garden of satellites flourish. Vines hang sixty feet down from its branches, an irresistible invitation to swing on them. I grab one and it immediately snaps high up and drops around me in heavy lethal coils. I weave and dodge and somehow manage to evade it.

'How old would it be?' I ask Carlindo.

He explains that there is no way to tell. A tree will develop to a point, but if there is no gap in the canopy above, its growth will be arrested for years and as there are no winters on the Equator so there are no seasonal rings to count the years. When a big tree falls, a gap of sky appears and all the nearby trees start a race to claim it. The Amazon forest has almost no soil. Everything lives on the instant humus that the heat and constant rain produce. A big fallen tree is a bonus of nutrients and the competing trees shoot out roots to it. One will win and very quickly increase its growth and seize the piece of vacant sky.

'*How can they know where the fallen tree is?*' I ask. '*How can they tell where to send their roots?*'

Carlindo shrugs. He spends a lot of his time taking botanists and tree experts around these forests, but no one knows the answer to that, nor to a lot of other mysteries. For instance, stricken trees seem to be able to warn each other of an approaching disease, so that they can develop antibodies.

Inside the forest, it is dark and dank. The air is so rich in oxygen I am euphoric, it is fragrant with the scent of blossom and decay. You walk through subtle strata of the humid air: a current of hot air gives way to a cooler one, a juicy mango smell becomes the acrid, unmistakable whiff of snake. But under it all is the smell of death, sometimes concealed, sometimes raw and blatant. No wind penetrates. No leaf stirs. You strain to see and hear, every faculty alert, watchful. Never have I felt so intensely alive.

We stop and gaze about us. There is nowhere else I would rather be. It is alien, yet I feel an atavistic familiarity. I am anxious to keep going, and Carlindo's machete cuts a way for us. I have an urge to push further, to penetrate. Desert freaks describe this impulse, to walk on and on, never to turn back.

I need to find a way to contact one of these remote and hidden tribes which kidnapped the boy. Having made my version of a great European myth whose origins are lost in antiquity, I now want to travel back in time to the very beginning, to the primal source of human life.

The Zingu is a vast plateau the size of Sweden that was undiscovered until 1947, when an expedition led by an extraordinary man, Orlando Vilas Boas, managed to forge a route up a raging river and gain access. He found many Stone Age Amerindian tribes who had never had contact with the outside world. He devoted his life to protecting and caring for these people. Still today, no outsiders are allowed in unless they have a special purpose. I persuaded him to arrange for me to stay with a tribe so that I could study their ways and accurately reproduce them for the movie. He introduced me to Maureen Bisilliat who had photographed the Kamaira tribe and spent much time with them. She would go with me.

21 August 1983 Xingu
I am writing this by torchlight lying in a hammock in the house of Takuma, Shaman of the Kamaira tribe. It has been an extraordinary

day. Maureen and I left the hotel in Brasília at dawn for the airport. We reported to the office of the air-taxi company from which we were renting a plane. The arrangement was for them to fly us to the grass airstrip at the Posta Villas Boas, where the Funai (the Indian bureau) maintains an officer charged with taking care of one section of the Xingu Indians. The pilot would come back a week later to fetch us.

A situation developed that I am starting to recognise as characteristic in Brazil. First of all, no one seemed to know anything about our flight. After Maureen had bent a few ears, someone in authority emerged and demanded to see written evidence that we had permission to visit the Xingu. We produced our letters and papers, which they studied closely and laboriously. Gradually it emerged that they did not want to send a plane there at all. The Xingu tribes are very angry, almost in a state of war, with the Funai. The last plane that went in was captured and the pilot held hostage against various demands the tribes are making of the government, including the dismissal of the President of the Funai, no less. The plane was finally released after fourteen days and had arrived back in Brasília daubed all over with war paint. It is a dramatic emblem of Xingu hostility, sitting as it does in the heart of the capital.

Our pilot is a slight, thin man in his fifties who seems remote and nervous. He does not inspire confidence. Maureen harangues him mercilessly: if she, a mere woman, is ready to go, why not he?

Finally we set out, flying over the tundra almost due north for three hours. Down below fires raged across the dry bush. It was the burning season. Even at three thousand feet we could smell the smoke. As we got nearer, the pall of smoke began to obscure the topography. Our pilot, who was beginning to reveal a wry sense of humour, had not been there before and began to zig-zag, peering down none too hopefully. I took the map and he descended to two thousand feet. There was a river below us that we hoped was the Xingu; I tried to reconcile the twists and bends with the meandering blue line on the map. At this height and with such limited visibility, we could not see enough of it to be sure. He followed the flow of the river and we simply curved back and forth with it. At a certain point we would have to leave the river, which flowed south to north, and turn westwards towards the Funai Posta (the Indian department post). But, of course, if we did not turn at the right point we would miss it altogether. Just to make things more interesting, the fuel gauge was sinking at an alarming rate. The pilot

said, with a smile, that we had sprung a leak and would have to land
shortly with or without an airstrip.

I leaned over the side of the plane, trying to compare the map to the
terrain. When I looked back I saw that sweat was running down my
finger on to the paper. The river bends seemed to coincide with the map
and I said I thought we had reached the turning point. He said if we
don't turn now it will be too late, the fuel was sinking fast. So he
turned. The ground looked very rugged and broken, certainly there was
nowhere to land. When the pilot, Joao, calculated that the airstrip
should be below us, there was no sign of it. He started to fly in a big
circle. Suddenly, among the trees an Indian village appeared, like an
apparition from the stone age. A circle of nine domed, thatched huts,
each sixty to ninety feet long and perhaps half as wide. I saw figures
moving about, but none seemed to be interested in us. It was a thrilling
sight and I quite forgot the map as I craned back to keep the village in
my sightline as long as possible.

Joao nudged me and dipped the plane. Ahead was the airstrip. It was
overgrown and clearly not much in use. Near it were some shacks and a
single brick building with an antenna; they were clustered under some
shady trees along the bank of a small river, a tributary of the Xingu. We
landed on our last gallon of fuel. A young couple with a baby, the Funai
officer, came to greet us. In their wake, a straggle of Indians. Some with
T-shirts and jeans, others naked except for necklaces. They were a sorry
bunch, deformed, unprepossessing – I felt a stab of disappointment, but
we were still dazed from the flight and quite glad to be on solid ground
at all.

It turned out that these were the sick and crazy who drifted to the
post and hung out there. One man had been driven from his tribe
because he was too ugly. The young couple were hungry for news of the
outside world. Their generator was broken and they could not operate
the short-wave radio. A year ago on leave in São Paulo they had seen
Excalibur, so I had a calling card.

They gave us some fish and manioc, and we swam in the river. We
had brought soap and matches for the Kamaira Indians and we gave
some to them, which caused great delight. They ran to the river, soaped
themselves and took all their clothes with them and washed them too.

There was a barrel of aviation fuel at the post. The pilot said he
would first have to discover the fuel leak. If he could not repair it, he
would try to get the radio going and ask for a rescue plane.

It was a three-hour journey to the village where we were to stay and it was too hot to walk there in the middle of the day. We chatted and dozed in the shade of the trees. Taking Orlando's advice, I had brought nothing with me except a hammock, which I would leave as a present, plus the boxes of soap and matches, together with a fishing net – altogether a heavy burden.

The post owned an old tractor and trailer, which had gone off to fetch a group of warriors from the Kamaira tribe, who had been on a fishing trip. We could hitch a ride with them part of the way and then they would help us carry the presents.

They duly arrived. Thirty men, naked but heavily painted with their hair matted down with urucu, a red paste made from the dye of a vivid scarlet berry. They were pressed together and Maureen and I climbed up among them. Their catch of fish was wrapped in parcels of leaves bound with vines. They carried bows with long barbed arrows and harpoon spears. They smiled and fixed us with the strangest, seeking, probing eyes, open and innocent, yet infinitely mysterious. The urucu had a musky, fermented smell, but pressed together as we were, there was no discernible body odour from the men and their breath was sweet and fresh. A few spoke some Portuguese, learned at the Posta, and Maureen understood quite a bit of their language, Tupi. They knew her, of course, and soon began plying her with questions about me. How many children did I have? Don't tell them you have twins, she said, it is considered unlucky. They usually kill one at birth.

They became more excited and I found it difficult to gauge their mood, which was certainly teasing and provocative, and perhaps hostile.

Maureen translated bits and pieces. One man needed a wife and said he would take Maureen. They found this very funny. Another said, no, that was not possible because they were going to cook her and eat her since they had not caught enough fish for the tribe's needs.

When we arrived in the village – which was similar to the one I had seen from the air – there was great excitement. The Shaman, Takuma, was quite brusque. He knew from the various messages that had passed back and forth with Orlando that we had brought a net. He demanded to see it. It was unpacked and laid out near the men's house in the centre of the ring of domed houses. There were angry shouts and cries of dismay. Despite all our efforts, the net had the wrong gauge. We made strenuous promises to rectify it, which were greeted with great scepticism. The mention of promises sent Takuma off on an angry

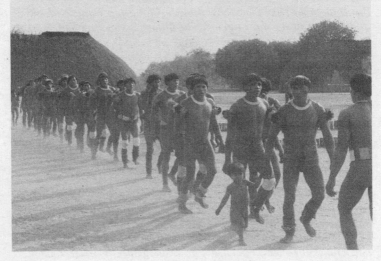

The village of the Kamaira Indians

tirade. The warriors began making a chilling clicking sound by rattling their bows against the arrows.

We judged it politic to display the cartons of soap and matches. These were greeted with enthusiasm, and diverted the general attention from Takuma's vehement speech. Seeing he was losing his audience, he abruptly turned on his heel and entered his house.

Even with the tribe in this volatile condition, their delicacy of behaviour was impressive. Nobody grabbed at the gifts. Instead, they were laid out in neat rows in the centre. The women and children, who had been very much shyly in the background, now edged forward. They paraded up and down looking at the presents, then they picked them up to examine them. Little by little they took up their portions and drifted back to their houses.

Maureen led me into Takuma's house. It is ninety feet long and perhaps forty feet wide and thirty feet high. There is an interior structure of crossed beams on which a woven lattice of vines and branches rests. Over it all is a thatch of leaves that curves down to the ground. There are no windows and only a tiny entrance, so the structure has a pleasing purity, being an unbroken elliptical dome.

It is dark inside, the only light coming from a number of fires and the daylight entering the two openings, which are opposite each other at the centre of the building. Between them is a large fire with a great flat griddle on which manioc pancakes are being made. There are perhaps ten families living within, each having a cluster of hammocks and its own cooking fire. They are all kin to Takuma. The smoke curls up into the high ceiling where there is a vent that allows most of it to escape. Takuma indicates a place near the entrance where we may hang our hammocks. We have brought cotton ones with us. The Indian hammock is made from fine woven vines and stained a dark red colour by the urucu and black dye, which rubs off from their bodies.

Takuma's seething anger over the Funai's treacherous behaviour soon surfaced. The Indians have become politically conscious. Some of the younger anthropologists have recruited civil-rights lawyers and the Indian cause is widely publicised. Takuma reminded Maureen of two men who had come to the village and had not fulfilled promises. He told each of them when and how they would die and they had duly obliged. It was a dark hint, I felt, about the fish net.

The sun is going down. Maureen says we should go to the lagoon to wash while there is still light. We take our soap and toothbrushes and head for the lagoon, which is two hundred yards away. The elders are smoking in the men's house and do not acknowledge us as we pass. The lagoon is limpid, the sun settling into a hazy mist at one end and a sharp crescent moon rising in the east at the other.

I wade into the water feeling reverence for the lagoon, which is held sacred, trying not to ripple the glassy surface. It recalled my journey up the Thames in a canoe. Camping on Runnymede Island, awaking to a dawn of such stillness as this. Stepping into the water, I had felt conscious that it was a place of power, not chosen by chance for the Magna Carta ceremony. It made me aware of the spirit of place. As I did then, I enter the water with great care so as not to ripple its perfect smoothness. I swim far out into the lagoon. Thirsty from the hot journey, I open my mouth and drink with each stroke, fish-like. The warning voices, 'Never touch the water,' seem distant, irrelevant. I feel quite safe. I know now, as I knew then at Runnymede, that if I am in such harmony, no harm can befall me. I am drinking the Amazon, but it is drinking me too. We are the same. And I am filled with grace, as I was then, at sixteen.

Soon the water is fractured by the villagers. They are washing with our soap.

Back in Takuma's house, we are given some fish and manioc. It is fresh river fish cooked in leaves over an open wood fire. The manioc is crisp, and quite tasteless. It serves as a plate for the fish. We eat it with our fingers. Dietitians are baffled as to why these people are robust and healthy when their diet is so restricted. No vegetables – no meat – just an endless repetition of fish and manioc; a few berries if they find them by chance in the jungle – nothing else. Other tribes in the Xingu eat monkey and other meat, but not this one.

It is all Maureen and I have eaten today, first at the Posta, now here. It will be interesting to see how one's system responds to it: no sugar, no coffee or tea, no alcohol, no fruit or vegetables.

So far I find the food is quite satisfying. I feel no hunger nor craving. What I do feel is awkward and uneasy. My clothes, albeit only shorts and T-shirt, seem an affront to their nudity. Both men and women are quite naked. All body hair, what little they have, is plucked or scraped, so as not to impede the application of body paint. The absence of pubic hair gives them an innocent, child-like vulnerability.

The Indians of the Americas, at least the ones from the tropical and subtropical regions, have been libelled. Their nakedness posed a theological problem to the Church and her missionaries. When we were cast out of the Garden of Eden, we were supposed to feel shame and cover ourselves. What could be concluded from the shamelessness of these Indians? Either they were not human, or they were still living before the Fall. With the handy excuse of not wishing to offend public sensibility, the nudity was hushed up and – as soon as possible – covered up.

Until that fateful expedition of 1947, the tribes of the Xingu were cut off from the world, so were spared the ministrations of the missionaries. The discreet artists of the past painted over the exposed genitals of primal people and the world never knew. By the time the Xingu Indians were found, the camera had taken the place of the paint brush, and the truth was out. Emerging from the Second World War, people were scarcely shocked by a few naked Indians, so the Xingu have kept their ways and still go without clothes.

I am embarrassed to know so much about these people. They have been studied in every aspect by anthropologists. Daily Life as Drama in a Brazilian Indian Village *gives a detailed account of these very people* with whom I am living, including a set of tables showing extra-marital sexual activities and the paths they use when they defecate. Many I know by sight from Maureen's photographs. Yet the essential mystery is more powerful than the specific knowledge. It is a time machine. I have stepped back into the Stone Age just as the boy did in our story.

When the sun is down, the air cools quickly. The men come in from their smoking and talking. The little fires cast moving shadows on the lofty roof. People lie in their hammocks or wander about talking softly. I noticed that there is almost no talk during the day. This is clearly the time.

Takuma came over and had a long talk with Maureen. The Indians have a catalogue of grievances. Only a portion of public money allocated to the Funai reaches the Indians. The rest goes on administration or is directed into the pockets of corrupt officials.

When the World Bank helped to finance a dam at Tucuruí, they gave money to resettle Indians displaced by the project. The help was bungled and inadequate and most of the money was embezzled.

Roads have been cut through the Xingu, contrary to the law protecting it. A well-placed bribe allows rangers to nibble at the perimeters of the reservations.

The most recent row concerned Jacques Cousteau, who has been shooting a big documentary series on the Amazon. He wanted to dredge and excavate their sacred lake in the hope of finding early Indian relics. This was vigorously opposed by the Indians. Since Cousteau was friendly with the President of Brazil, a lot of pressure was exerted. The head of the Funai arrived in the Xingu and made a threatening speech that inflamed tempers still more. The Indians decided to cut off all contacts with Brasília and all visits were banned and Cousteau never got to see the sacred lake. Killing interlopers and taking hostages is becoming widespread.

The Cousteau contretemps touches Takuma in a special way. Orlando Vilas Boas tells of learning from a chief, Tamapa, that their oral traditions spoke of a secret sacred pool that would be discovered only by a paje (shaman) of great spiritual strength who had the courage to dive into its waters. Many years later, Tamapa's own son found the lagoon and dived deep into the waters and brought up an object that has remained hidden and secret. The son's name was Takuma, now the greatest paje of all the Xingu, the very one who stands before us.

When you see the dignity and respect with which even the simplest tasks are accomplished, one can imagine their horror at having divers and dredgers in the sacred pool. Besides which, Maureen says that Takuma is very jealous of his reputation and prefers to be the only person courageous enough to dive into the pool.

The last few days had been so extraordinary I hardly knew how to express my feelings. I can't imagine ever seeing things quite the same again.

After Takuma's talk that first evening the house settled down for the night. A collective tiredness took over and the soft droning conversations petered out and we all feel asleep together. This experience was repeated each night, this drifting off in unison, and I slept deeply and dreamt old, mythic dreams, their dreams, perhaps. Apparently, a shared dream is common enough amongst the Indians. When I described my dream, they nodded. Yes, they knew that one.

The burning hot days give way to cool evenings and, finally, cold nights. The chill seeps through the thatch about four or five o'clock in the morning. It was still dark when I awoke. People were stirring out of their hammocks. Maureen and I followed them down to the lagoon. The morning sun made a thin red slash on the skyline. Shivering, they plunged into the water, which, having retained its heat, was like a hot bath. We splashed around waiting for the sun to come up. Big wood fires were lit on the beach and we gathered round them drying ourselves. How else? No towels, of course. The absence of things is what strikes an outsider, and the happy corollary: a total lack of litter.

We went back to the house and as the orange light of the sun slanted through the entrance, a lovely girl came in wet from bathing. She stood by the fire and swung her mane of black hair in an arc, slapping it on to her back and then forward. Caught in the sunlight, the water drops took fire, hung in the air and then fell hissing into the flames. An image for the movie.

I was always asking what would happen next. What was planned for tomorrow? Would there be dancing tonight? They were perplexed by this thinking. At one level, life would go on as it always had, in unchanging patterns. It was simply obvious. The women would go off to the manioc patches and bring back the heavy roots that looked like turnips. They would boil them and then start the hypnotic scraping and grinding that painstakingly turns the manioc into flour and the juice into a delicious, slightly sweet soup. The men would go off to the river and fish, smoke and talk at night. All other time is spent in preparing feather ornaments, making necklaces from seeds and painting their bodies in elaborate patterns.

For no apparent reason, the mood would suddenly shift. Someone would start to chant. Sometimes it would simply peter out. At other times the chanting would be picked up, bare feet would beat a rhythm on the hard earth. Dancing would begin. An elaborate ritual would ensue.

One morning, two warriors blowing on seven-foot-long flutes and with rhythmic steps began to circumnavigate the village. Behind each man was a girl, one hand on the man's shoulder, keeping in step with him. They entered each house in turn playing continuously. The flutes make a deep, dark sound – no more than three notes. It is tedious to the Western ear, but its power lies in repetition. This ritual went on continuously for five hours, an astonishing physical feat. Little by little the flutes become hypnotic, possess the tribe, and yet everyone goes about his business. No one acknowledges the four figures, two men and two girls, going in and out of their houses. It has the discordance of dream.

My test came one day when Takuma came to me very early – it was still dark – and told me I could join him and the warriors on a journey to find logs for the quarup or ceremony of the dead. It would be very hard. It would be better for me to stay in the village with the women. Stung by the implied insult, I went with him. For three hours we tracked into the jungle at a fast lope. Takuma led the way, intense and very conscious of his importance.

Eventually, we came to a part of the forest which was where Takuma deemed the special trees could be found for the quarup. The men split up and searched. A wickedly funny old man who communicated with me in mime carried a length of twine and measured the girth of the trunks, which had to be exactly right. The first four we cut proved to be flawed. One had rot inside. Two more split as they fell and another was not perfectly smooth. We needed six of these, one for each of the people who had died during the year, and whose bodies were temporarily buried in the centre of the village. Each trunk would be decorated and the ceremony would release the souls to the stars, after which the bodies would be burnt.

The trek back with the logs in the blinding heat was almost unendurable. Nothing was eaten all day. We got back after nightfall.

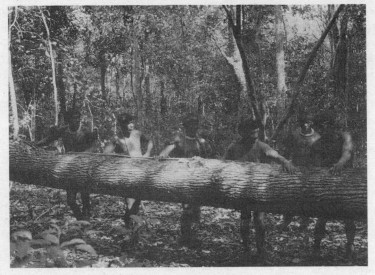

Choosing a log for the ceremony of the dead

There was no food on offer, only manioc, since there had been no one to fish that day. I began to realise how hand-to-mouth their existence was.

The next day the hostility towards me had melted away and I felt a great warmth. The couple from the Posta came up to visit and told the Indians what I did. Takuma was fascinated and insisted that I explain my work. It is not easy to describe a movie to a man who has never seen one or even watched television. I struggled and he listened intently. I told him how one scene would stop and another begin, in a different place and time as it does in a dream. He lit up, grasping that. I told him of some of the tricks and wonders we got up to. Finally he was satisfied. 'You make visions, magic. You are a paje like me.' After that, there was a sense of complicity. He would bring me a root or berry and show it to me, telling me of its properties. He had many ways to get into trance, some deeper and longer than others. The commonest way for the Kamaira is tobacco, which of course came from the South American Indians in the first place. They cure wild tobacco and roll it into long cheroots. They inhale the smoke violently, hyperventilating on it. It causes them to vomit. After two or three bouts of retching, trance is achieved. The chanting and dancing are often enough to induce trance, drugs merely kick-start the process.

Although their daily life is monotonous and unchanging, their spiritual life is an endless, unpredictable and sometimes dangerous adventure. There is no division between the material, the ritual and the spiritual worlds. It is all one, a continuum. Living with them was like a dream, shifting and changing. They believe they are connected to all the animals and plants that share their environment. In the trance state, they visit them at night, watching their movies of the spirit.

Takuma was clearly in possession of a body of knowledge hidden or lost by us. A closeness grew between us, an affinity. I began to sense his thoughts and feelings. I had the distinct conviction that he could project them into my mind. I would sense him calling to me and know where he was. I would go to him unerringly and he would show me something that he was doing or berries he wanted me to eat. When we left he pronounced us brothers in a simple and moving moment. I could return whenever I wished and when I did he would give me a bench carved in the shape of my animal. Everyone is connected with the spirit of a particular creature.

'What is my animal?' I asked.

'Your animal is your animal,' he replied as though it was perfectly obvious and he did not deign to name it. The only intimation I have is that when they painted me it was with the markings of an eagle. This was a strange moment. Just as they prepared to cut the quarup trees they told me that I should not witness this naked. Since I was the only person with clothes, it was puzzling. To them, someone without ritual paint is considered naked. So I was painted and I was allowed to see.

I made no further entries in my journal after this. Writing just seemed antithetical to life there. I tried to be inconspicuous, practising a self-effacing technique I learned in my documentary days. I took no photographs until they invited me to do so, and then only very few.

The pilot, Joao, could not contact Brasília for help so he set about trying to repair the plane himself. Fortunately, he was a trained engineer as well as a pilot. It took him some time, but he fixed it. He was a keen fisherman and had brought his rod with him. He caught many fish and the degenerates at the Posta came to rely on him for food so he decided to stay on and wait for us. All three of us were quite relieved to be leaving safely, what with the faulty plane, the incipient violence, and the inherent dangers of such a journey. It had been one of the great experiences of my life. Whatever else happened, the movie would have been worthwhile for this alone.

Just when we were feeling we had made it, Joao said he was beginning to feel feverish. Last night, he said, a bat bit him in the neck. He shows me two puncture marks. It was a scene from a *Dracula* movie: we all knew how it went on from there. He slumped over the controls and I had to land the plane. Then we found there was a killer bat inside the cockpit. Maureen tried to fight it off as the plane lurched towards the airfield. We were going to crash. I woke up with a start as we landed in Brasília. It was hard to remember where the dream had begun. I looked across at Joao and the puncture marks were indeed on his neck and he was still very feverish. The air-taxi company were glad to see their plane.

For the purposes of the film we recruited detribalised Indians from Rio and Belem and, with the help of experts, we retrained them and developed our own tribes. Many of the images I saw with the Kamaira are reproduced in the movie.

Jake, having persuaded the board of Goldcrest to finance our movie, was lured away to join a new US company, Embassy. His successors at Goldcrest sent out an emissary to Brazil. When he saw the vast scale of the picture, the remote locations, witnessed the tropical rainstorms and got a taste of the endemic violence, he hastened back to London to report. David Puttnam was on the board of Goldcrest. He said that when a director is his own producer, the director wins all the arguments. They predicted that the picture's budget would run out of control. They decided to cut their losses and cancel the picture. The cast and crew were already assembled and we were constructing sets. I was enraged, but from this distance in time I have to say I would probably have shared their view had I been on their board.

Jake was mortified, felt he had let me down. Had he stayed at Goldcrest he would have seen it through. My daring, or recklessness, touched a chord in him. He found it irresistible. Embassy had already bought the US rights of the film, so he hastened to persuade them to take over the whole thing before it collapsed. Embassy was reluctant for all kinds of reasons. It was a new company. They were feeling their way. They reasoned that Goldcrest must have had good reasons for pulling out. Not least, their bank insisted that they must carry a completion bond on all pictures that they made. There was simply no time for a bond company to tour the locations and study our budget and schedule unless we delayed our start. Since we were carrying a full complement of crew, delay would be costly. There were also weather and contractual factors that compelled us to start on time. For instance, the climax of the film occurred at a dam which we could only shoot at a specified date.

Embassy was the plaything of Norman Lear and Jerry Perenchio. Both were successful entrepreneurs with strong nerves and deep pockets, tsars of capitalism. Example: Jerry and his wife took their private plane to London. On impulse they decided to go to New York. They took the Concorde and had their own plane follow them. I had met them in Cannes when they threw a lavish party at the Hotel du Cap for Lew Grade, whom they had rescued from the debacle of his own film adventures, surely the first octogenarian to get a new job in this youth-oriented business. Lew duly danced the Charleston and we all cheered. I was sitting next to Lew's down-to-earth wife as fireworks lit up the sky. 'Haven't they gone to a lot of trouble?' she said.

Norman and Jerry had wooed Jake away from Goldcrest to run their new company. They felt obliged to follow his judgement despite their reservations. When it came to negotiating a deal with Embassy, I was in a hopelessly weak position. They took everything. Jake solved the problem of the completion bond. He said to the bond company, you take it on and Embassy will undertake not to call on you under any circumstance. Nobly, they agreed to a reduced fee.

I cast my son Charley to play the kidnapped boy. Rospo was bitterly opposed to this and told me that if I insisted he would advise Embassy to abandon the picture. I had auditioned dozens of boys and they were the pick of hundreds seen by my casting directors. I tested four of the best on film, including Charley. I sent the tests to Embassy without revealing the names. They all voted for Charley. Nevertheless, Rospo's call unnerved them. They sent people down to check up on me. Our equipment was stuck in customs and we could not find out whom we had to bribe to get it out. We started shooting with just a camera and a tripod. Disastrous weather put us behind schedule in the first week. The Indian village set we had built was destroyed by a storm. We were attacked by a particularly voracious species of mosquito and several crew members could not endure the welts and fevers and had to be shipped home. It seemed that Goldcrest's fears were justified.

Why do I relish this kind of adversity and thrive under it? What unconscious impulse makes me court danger? Why do I drive myself and

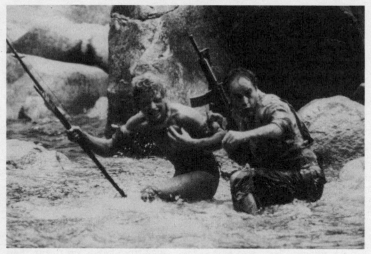

The Emerald Forest: Charley as the kidnapped boy
with his father, Powers Boothe

others to the edge? Does it go back to my childhood in the war? Am I
somehow contriving to repeat the conditions of the Blitz when I was in
the midst of chaos and fear and falling bombs?

Somehow or other, after enduring every kind of hazard imaginable,
we finished the picture and actually came in under budget. I cannot
take the credit for this. We were cash-flowing the movie by buying
'frozen' Brazilian *cruzeiros*, profits made in Brazil by American companies which they were not allowed to repatriate. Inflation was so
rampant that goods in the supermarket would cost more in the afternoon than in the morning. One day my accountant came to me in
despair. He said, 'I can't figure it out, but it seems that the longer you
go on shooting, the cheaper the picture will be.'

'Well, that's not so bad,' I replied, trying to console him.

'But it makes a mockery of everything I stand for,' he said, shaking
his head.

I had lived with a Stone Age tribe. I had witnessed the malevolence
and glory of the great rainforest. I had taken a boat to the middle of the
mouth of the Amazon where it is seventy miles wide, and plunged into
its waters. I had felt its power as it swept me out to sea. I had been with

my son on a great adventure. But alas, my friendship with Rospo was damaged beyond repair.

Just as the mountain men in *Deliverance* represented the malevolence of nature, so the tribe in this film personified the forest. When they witness bulldozers clear-felling the giant trees, the chief says, 'They are taking the skin off the earth, how will she breathe?'

The Emerald Forest inspired many young people to devote their lives to conservation. It persuaded the Brazilian government to legalise organisations trying to protect the rainforest that had hitherto been banned. It made me realise that this is a tree planet, and trees are its architecture. Our survival depends on them. It sent me back to Ireland determined to plant as many as I could.

Back to Cannes

We took *The Emerald Forest* to the Cannes Film Festival where it was the closing film, out of competition. After *Leo the Last* and *Excalibur*, this was my third picture at the Festival. In other years I had taken part in seminars, hunted for finance or tried to raise money from distributors. For the fortieth anniversary of the Festival they gave a special prize to directors who had been honoured there in the past. Billy Wilder and I walked down the Croissette to the Grand Salle for a rehearsal of the ceremony. He had just finished shooting what turned out to be his last movie, *Buddy Buddy*. I asked him how it had gone. He said, 'John, our pictures are our children. When you have a kid you hope he will grow up to be Einstein, but sometimes they turn out to be congenital idiots.'

We were the first directors to arrive. The flustered lady organising the event asked us if we would mind waiting. 'Do I mind waiting?' said Billy. 'I spent my life waiting. Waiting for the money, waiting for actors [two pictures with the notoriously tardy Monroe], waiting for the lighting, waiting for the sun to come out, waiting for the sun to go in. In fifty years of movie making, you know how long the camera was running? Maybe two weeks.' We were to come on stage in alphabetical order: Antonioni, Bergman (didn't show), Boorman – so Wilder, of course, was the last man. He said, 'I'm always last unless Fred Zinnemann is there.'

The year after *The Emerald Forest* there was a tribute to David Lean at Cannes, and he asked that I deliver the homily. The sponsors chartered a beautiful yacht, the *Fair Lady*, for David and me to live on. David had a horror of yachts, having been trapped on Sam Spiegel's boat on several occasions when, he claimed, Sam had developed stratagems for cheating him. So I had the *Fair Lady* all to myself. It was particularly useful since Jake Eberts and I were trying to raise money for my next film, and we were able to invite distributors to lunch on the boat, which had an excellent chef. When the Italians saw my yacht they asked me why I didn't simply finance the picture myself. David Lean, Omar Sharif and I sat at the top table while four hundred doyens of the film industry – producers, directors, distributors, actors, critics – ate and drank at the expense of British Petroleum. An orchestra played selections of music from David's films. It put him in a reflective mood. He looked back over his career. Sam Spiegel still rankled. He recalled how J. Arthur Rank had allowed him to make whatever he pleased. He began to muse about his love life, even though his sixth wife, recently married, was at his side. 'My problem,' he said, 'is that I always took the women who wanted me. I never had the courage to go after the women I wanted.' Omar, one of the world's most desired men, said to my astonishment, 'Same with me.'

1985: *Hope and Glory*

Home from the turbulent heat of the Amazon, in the deep Irish midwinter of gaunt leafless trees when all life is buried in the cold earth, I set out to write *Hope and Glory*, a recreation of my childhood in the London Blitz. This respite from life, this winter death has always inspired me, and watching the solstice sun creep low over the hill outside my window has summoned many an idea from the dark well.

Why did I feel impelled to write this now? My time with the Kamaira tribe in the Xingu had taught me more about our society than theirs. I had stepped out of my life and time and seen myself for what I was – or at least, what I was not. When I saw how harmoniously they related to the world about them, I realised how disconnected was my own tribe. Witnessing the origins of human society caused me to reach back to my own beginnings. As I wrote the script, the kingfisher reproached me from its glass case, a reminder of my fall from grace, and the moments of recovered grace I had experienced from time to time. The episode in which I shot the kingfisher did not get into the script. It was too far-fetched for fiction. Nevertheless this sacred bird, the spirit of the river, God's messenger, pervaded the whole story. I replaced it with a scene, also true, of a stray bomb dropping into the Thames and killing hundreds of fish, fracturing the boy's Thames idyll.

In the script I named my mother Grace. Did I identify with my father's loss of her to his friend, the losing of grace?

I completed the first draft script during that midwinter and the two-week doldrums that followed Christmas. Given its nature, the parochial Englishness of it, I was not at all sanguine about getting financial backing. I showed it to Jake Eberts, who liked it, but predicted it would be a 'tough sell'. He agreed to pay for the preparation of a budget and some initial design work, which was necessary to get the information to make a budget. I sent it to my agent, Jeff Berg, at ICM in Los Angeles. His response was enthusiastic and he pledged himself to getting a deal made.

Our first budget came in at around ten million dollars, to the shock and horror of some studio assessors, who got the impression from the script of a rather small, intimate picture. I had never seen it or intended it in this way. I wanted the family story to be set against the larger world of the Blitz.

The script was liked and admired by many of the major studios, but it was considered commercially dubious. Fox came very close, but finally backed away. Warners felt it conflicted with *Empire of the Sun*, a Spielberg project about a small boy during the fall of Singapore. One by one the 'passes' came in: Universal, MGM, UA, Tri-Star, Orion, Paramount.

The first glimmer of hope came from France: Paul Rassam, head of AMLF Distributors in Paris, had had a huge success with *The Emerald Forest* and without a moment's hesitation pledged half a million US dollars. This was very important for us. Paul's judgement is greatly respected and many distributors around the world would follow his lead.

We approached Simon Relph at British Screen. He liked the project, but after examining the budget felt he could not support it unless it was 'costed down' to the level of a 'British' picture, as against an 'international' one.

Jake's next target was Channel Four. They had achieved one of their best audience figures when they showed *Excalibur*, and I had produced one of their first successes in the 'Film on Four' series, Neil Jordan's *Angel*. Jeremy Isaacs' policy has rescued and revived British films. His judicious backing had made possible films like Tarkovsky's *The Sacrifice*, *Paris, Texas*, *My Beautiful Laundrette* and *Room with a View*. Calling in my credit and his own, Jake pleaded our case and prised out a promise of three hundred and fifty thousand dollars. Unfortunately, the money would not be paid over until they were able to show the film, two years after its cinema release. Nevertheless we could enter it in the ledger.

Jake's major play had to be the United States market, which – if video, TV and cable is included – then represented seventy per cent of the world income of an English-language movie. He went to André Blay, Head of Embassy Home Entertainment. They had made considerable profits on the video sale of *The Emerald Forest*, of which, because of the unfortunate deal, we received no part. Jake was not slow to suggest to André that he had a moral debt to pay. Blay expressed interest and talked of a million-dollar advance, escalating to match the prints and advertising budget of a US distributor up to a maximum of three and a half million dollars. The trouble was that we had no US distributor, so all we could rely on out of the US was a million dollars.

While Jake was battling away in Los Angeles, a new possibility arose in London. Golan and Globus, owners of the Cannon Group, had bought EMI. The acquisition was greeted with suspicion, anger and chauvinism, as the only major film-making and exhibition force in the UK fell out of British control. When Cannon announced it would make thirty films a year, most of the barking dogs rolled on to their backs or at least wagged their tails.

I phoned Menahem Golan and told him I had a project. 'Come and talk to me,' he said. 'When?' 'When you like.' 'I'll be there in an hour.' It was only their second day in charge. The switchboard receptionist had not yet worked out the difference between Menahem Golan and Yoram Globus. 'Both names sound the same to me,' she complained. I gave her some helpful advice. 'Globus is the plump one, Golan the fat one.'

As I was shown in, Menahem was conducting at least four meetings simultaneously. Supplicants were hunched or cramped in every corner and crevice. EMI employees with stunned expressions wandered past – fired, or rehired, or transferred. Michael Winner sat at Menahem's elbow offering witty and scabrous interpretations of the local natives' behaviour. I looked out of the window and there was producer Jeremy Thomas standing across the street, looking up at us with a wry expression – wondering, I expect, if Cannon would honour the deal he had forged with EMI.

I made several attempts to tell my story, but each one was frustrated by the intervention of other burning issues requiring the great man's judgement. I apologetically mentioned the parochial Englishness of the piece. Suddenly I found myself with his full attention. The very thing that put off all the others made it attractive to Menahem. It was the perfect project to confound those critics who were predicting Cannon would make only crass multinational movies. What better subject to proclaim his commitment to British films?

'Listen,' he said, 'I don't have time to read it, but if you like it, I like it. You don't want to make a flop, nor do I. How much?' 'Nine point five,' I said. 'Do it for seven and a half and we have a deal.' I winced and shook my head. He took that as an affront to his integrity.

'I'll tell you how we work. Directors love us. You become one of the family. Yoram and I will be the producers. We give you everything you want as long as it's not more than seven.' I had just lost another half a million dollars. I must have looked glum. He tried to convince me. He reached for the phone. 'Zeffirelli will tell you. He never wants to work for another producer, only us. Franco will tell you.' He started to dial, but Globus rushed in, waving a sheaf of papers.

'Worse. Much worse,' he groaned. 'Their books smell bad. These are not good people, Menahem.' He wafted the papers at Golan, who sniffed them. 'Forget it,' he said. 'We just made a deal for John Boorman's picture.' He turned to me. 'What's it called again? He's going to make it for seven – max.' He looked me in the eye. 'We've got to get it under seven. Talk to Goram.' Goram led me into the next room. He looked at me sorrowfully. 'Menahem gets carried away. We can't spend seven on your movie. I know you can do it for six.' I gulped. I protested. He looked offended. 'Everyone comes in here trying to rip us off.' He pushed me into the next office. 'We're leaving in the morning. Talk to Otto Plaschkes. He's going to look after creative matters for us in London.' Otto looked shell-shocked. 'Otto, we've made a deal to do Boorman's picture as long as it's no more than five and a half million.'

They announced their intention of making *Hope and Glory* in Cannes, along with thirty other projects. I wrote a new draft of the script, eliminating two expensive set-piece scenes; I reduced the amount of night work, and effected other economies. In this way, and by deferring my fees as writer, director and producer, we managed to squeeze the budget down to seven and a half million dollars, although Michael Dryhurst and I both felt uneasy about being able to hold to this figure.

I duly reported this to Otto, who had read, and professed to love, my orphan script. He sent his recommendation to Menahem in Los Angeles, who promptly telexed his reply: 'We'll go ahead if you can make it for five million dollars.'

Meanwhile Jake was making better progress with André Blay at Embassy. I was summoned to Cannes. I proceeded to the Hôtel du Cap in nearby Antibes, where Blay and his lieutenants were living in pampered purdah from the vulgar Festival down the coast. André had an air of decency about him, of detached amusement and quiet intelligence. Jake arrived looking his most wolfish. André and his men were slightly off guard, taking it easy after the rigours of the management buy-out they had just negotiated with Coca-Cola, the owners of the company. Jake proposed that Embassy should put up the whole budget, and he demonstrated how foreign sales and a US distribution deal would pay off most of their investment, leaving them with the video rights at a bargain price, plus the lion's share of profit-points in the picture.

Jake juggled the figures, making lightning calculations in his head. André would not commit, but came very close. He was hovering, wavering, tempted. After all, the video rights of most important films are tied to a major distributor. The independent video distributor must invest in films up front to ensure a flow of product. He was clearly enchanted with Jake's acrobatic arithmetic. Finally, he agreed to come to London after Cannes and take a look at our designs and plans.

He duly arrived at Twickenham Studios, saw our sketches and layouts, listened to my predictions about what the film would be and, still harbouring reservations about its commercial prospects, he pledged his troth. There was one reservation: he was obliged to seek the approval of Coca-Cola. However, since the company would be his in a couple of weeks this was a formality that could be overlooked. He agreed to fund the pre-production right away. It was just in the nick of time. It was mid-May. Since there were so many children in the movie, it was essential to shoot during the school holidays. We also needed summer for the river scenes. Construction of the sets had to begin right away if we were to start in late July. Had André hesitated or procrastinated another couple of weeks, I would have been obliged to delay the film until the following year. A movie gathers a certain momentum, which, if checked, is almost impossible to regain.

We had already made the momentous decision to build Rosehill Avenue, the street of semis in which I was born. When Michael Dryhurst gave the go-ahead to Syd Nightingale, our construction manager, an army of men descended on the deserted airfield at Wisley where we proposed to build it. André Blay had baulked at the cost of this massive construction. Surely, he protested, we could find a street of thirties semis where we could shoot the picture. We had looked. Existing streets were bristling with TV aerials, the kerbs were jammed with cars, and they were festooned with modern accretions like double glazing and metal garage doors. All that aside, the occupants might not have taken kindly to their houses being bombed and burned. The only hope was a street that was abandoned, or about to be demolished to make way for a motorway. But no such situation occurred, nor would it quite have worked if it had. Building the street allowed us to express its raw newness and absolute monotony. It would be one of the two central metaphors of the movie. The Street. The River.

Tony Pratt contrived a triumphant concept. On each side of the road we built the facades of six pairs of semis on a framework of scaffolding. Cut-outs of further houses painted in perspective suggested a child's remembrance of a street that reached into infinity. In the apparent far distance were further cut-outs of the skyline of London, including a movable St Paul's Cathedral. My fictional family's house was built properly of brick and wood, since it had to be burned, which would of course reveal what lay behind the facade. A range of back gardens extended on one side, leading to allotments and an abandoned building site. We used the backs of the houses on the other side as a backdrop for an area of bombed ruins.

All in all, the multiple set covered more than fifty acres, making it probably the largest set built in Britain since the war. Four weeks into construction Jake called with shocking news. Coca-Cola had decided not to sell Embassy Home Entertainment to André Blay after all, and had castigated him for entering into my deal without their approval. Blay sued Coke; Coke sued him. There was deadlock. Embassy ground to a standstill and our weekly cash flow abruptly stopped. There was insufficient money to cover the wage bill at the end of the week. Jake

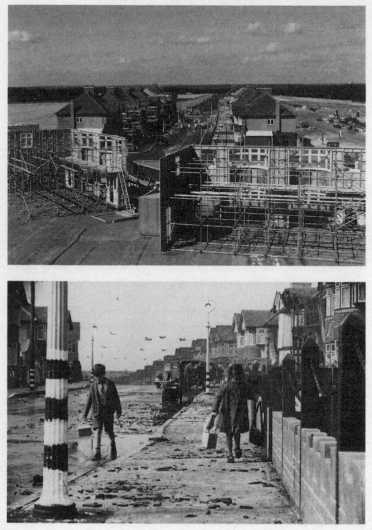

Before and After: the street in *Hope and Glory*

stepped forward with a cheque from Allied to tide us over, and Michael Dryhurst dashed down to Wisley and gave two weeks' notice to the men.

In Los Angeles, my agent, Jeff Berg, and the redoubtable Ed Gross, who handles my business affairs, laid siege to Embassy and Coca-Cola. Two weeks later, just as the notices were expiring, the matter had still not been settled, although Jeff had persuaded Coca-Cola director Frank Biondi that they had a moral obligation to fund us.

We calculated that I would have to find some thirty-five thousand dollars out of my own pocket in winding-up costs to cancel the picture; Jake would lose his sixty-five thousand dollar advance too.

At 11 p.m. on Thursday, Jeff called to say that Coca-Cola would resume payments. At eight o'clock the next morning we had been going to close down the picture.

Coca-Cola subsequently sold Embassy to another group, and part of that deal was that Columbia (which Coke also owned) would undertake to distribute the film theatrically in the States. At the very last gasp, the movie was saved. We re-engaged the men and started up again. There was a loss of momentum. Suspicion and uncertainty were hard to dispel and some men deserted. Hearing of our troubles, the various unions insisted that we deposit substantial bonds with them as a condition of continuing. All in all, it put us back a week or more and cost us around sixty thousand dollars.

David Puttnam's appointment as the new chief of Columbia Pictures brought a fresh confidence and stability. He gave *Hope and Glory* his full backing and stepped up his investment to take the UK rights as well as the US. So as it turned out, this most English of subjects was financed by some twenty distributors around the world, the exception being Britain.

We commenced photography on 4 August 1986 and shot for fifty-five days, with the final wrap on 21 October. Post-production was completed on 14 February 1987. Making the film was the happiest of times. My daughter Telsche coached the child actors and she infused them with her own joy and wit. Their fresh and truthful performances were more her doing than mine. My daughter Katrine played one of my aunts and accurately reproduced their oohing and cooing and aaghing. Charley was a German pilot who parachutes on to our suburban allotment. An ageing and nervous constable leads him away through the vegetable patch, and has one of the best lines – 'Mind the Brussels sprouts.'

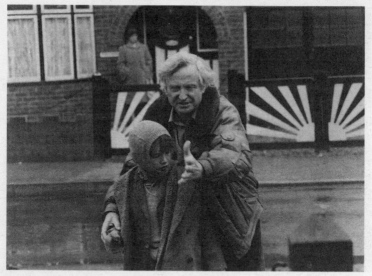

Hope and Glory: watching my childhood come to life
(with Sebastian Rice-Edwards)

Bemused, I watched my childhood come to life. It was as though dim black-and-white memories had burst into colour and solid life. Yet of course, I was in the process of converting them into ephemeral light, which would flicker on a screen, as insubstantial as memory itself.

While I was doing the editing at Twickenham Studios, my mother was knocked down by a car. She was eighty-four years old. As she lay in the road, she believed her time had come, but she wanted to see *Hope and Glory* and so she decided to live. Her body was a mass of bruises. My sister Angela cared for her but I would go to her flat after work, peel off her clothes and lift her gently into the bath tub. Her slender legs were still shapely. Her pale blue eyes were wide and bright from pain. One of the breasts I had sucked on was severed, the skin gathered together to a point like a parody of a nipple. At seventy-six she had developed a lump. The specialist recommended removing the breast and lymph glands. I argued against it. What was her life expectancy anyway? And wasn't it true that cancers developed more slowly in old people whose metabolism had slowed? He said, 'Everyone has a theory about cancer except someone like me who works with them every day.

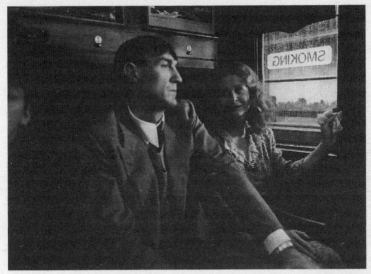

Hope and Glory: the Mother (Sarah Miles) and the Next-Door-Neighbour
(Derrick O'Connor) – conflicts long buried

There are so many variations. You can never tell how a tumour will
develop.' Reluctantly, I agreed to the mastectomy. When I visited her
after the operation I was appalled. This beautiful vigorous woman had
shrunk into a little old lady. But to my great joy she recovered her vitality and lived another twenty years.

Necessity brought us into intimacy. I bathed her as she had bathed me
half a century before. As I sponged her body I wept for the cruel ruin
time wreaks on beauty. She chided me for my tears. She relished life. She
had survived two wars, fire and flood, had lost all her possessions and
the two men she had loved. She had worked all her life and brought up
three children. She was looking forward to the premiere in the Odeon
Leicester Square where her son would be celebrating her life. I made her
a cup of tea. It did not please her. 'Get me a gin and tonic.'

As the crowd poured out from the premiere, press and television
surrounded my mother, demanding to know how she felt about seeing
her life on the screen. 'It was quite good in its way,' was her faint
praise, 'but personally I prefer a good thriller.' It was her way of
guarding her true feelings. She was pleased with the idea of the film,

but it stirred up conflicts in her which she had long buried. She enjoyed the attention, but – like Marion Knight and Alison – felt I had stolen something from her. She never said as much, but I knew it was so. Even though I had celebrated her, I had taken something from her, and I felt like a thief.

The UK critics voted it Best Picture of the year. It won the *Evening Standard* Best British Picture award. The LA critics made it Best Picture, Best Director and Best Screenplay. As I went up each time to collect these awards I said that as the writer, I felt the director had not done full justice to the script. As the director I blamed the producer (also me) for not finding me sufficient resources. I said this was the one occasion when a recipient was justified in thanking his mother. A Best Picture Golden Globe came our way and awards continued to flow; the US National Critics gave it Best Director. I was nominated for Academy Awards as director, writer and producer. Philippe Rousselot was nominated for photography and Tony Pratt for art direction. We had thirteen BAFTA nominations, a record.

1987: The Academy Awards

I was urged by Columbia to attend the awards. Los Angeles, the whore city, had put on her prettiest frock when the jumbo carrying Christel and me flopped on to the runway after eleven hours aloft – Hockney-blue skies, palms a-flutter, none of the grey heat haze of bilious smog that is more common. This is the way California is supposed to be and seldom is. Everyone was having a nice day, not just wishing it on others. The usually frosty immigration officer smiled us through in a trice. 'Purpose of visit?' 'I've come for the Oscars.' 'You're due one,' he said, stamping my passport.

In the grounds of the Beverly Hills Hotel is a cluster of bungalows. Like Marie Antoinette, the rich can play house here. There is a little kitchen and a porch, and for four hundred and fifty dollars a night you can pretend to be early homesteaders. The rainforests of the world may be disappearing, but they are alive and well in Beverly Hills. It is so lush around the bungalow that you almost need a machete to cut a path to the Polo Lounge.

On 29 March the Academy gave a lunch for the nominees, and we dutifully went along and lined up for a group photograph and then traipsed up on stage to be given our certificates by Robert Wise, the eponymously sage president of the Academy. It was like prize-giving at school. We were jolly and well behaved. After all, many members had yet to vote and we wished to be seen at our very best.

Sam Goldwyn Jr, who produced the Oscar show, extended the school analogy with his headmasterly tone. He lectured us about the etiquette of the occasion. 'Don't thank the cast and crew. There are a billion people watching who don't know them and don't care about them. What we want is a moment of wit or emotion. At thirty seconds a red light will flash at you. At forty-five seconds it will be solid. At one minute the orchestra will drown you out and we'll take a commercial break.'

So there it was laid on the line: we were playing bit parts in a TV spectacular. They showed us a round-up film of past Oscar winners, the ones who rambled and thanked too many people, and the ones to be emulated, who got on and got off fast with a merry quip or a tear hastily shed.

There was a lot of kissing and hugging, but the prevalence of contagious diseases has modified Hollywood behaviour – now the air is kissed rather than cheeks, and there is a technique of hugging which clasps the partner in the arms, but holds the bodies apart. But the beautiful Sherry Lansing, producer of the mega-hit *Fatal Attraction*, and fatally attractive herself, retained her siren status. With her it was lips and the press of correctly curving flesh separated only by a film of silk. She reminded me that she offered me *Fatal Attraction* to direct. She was wearing a heady perfume. I think it was the smell of money.

The voting would close on 5 April, so the next few days saw the final intensive advertising in the trade press. A film needs a lot of money to run a successful campaign. It divides into two parts; the first and more expensive is to get nominations. The biggest slice of money goes on running ads in *Variety* and the *Hollywood Reporter*. These quote favourable reviews and cite other awards already garnered.

The first problem is simply to get those four thousand-odd Academy members to see your film, to be aware of its existence. To this end, a programme of screenings is arranged so that the members do not have to suffer the inconvenience of going to a regular movie theatre. There are some five hundred films released in America each year. How many can one person see? Even newspapers use several critics to cover them.

Academy voters tend to be older, since it takes some years of distinctive work to be elected a member (although a nomination earns automatic entry). Many are very old, tired and conservative, and to lure them away from their swimming pools and golf clubs taxes the invention of studio publicists. It is ironic that as the movie-going audience gets younger, the Academy membership gets more ancient, and the gap between box-office hits and Oscar pictures grows wider.

In between are the critics. They are obliged to see everything and they too vote for awards at the end of the year, and they seldom coincide either with the box-office hits or the Academy choices.

Soundtrack albums are mailed to Academy members, while information sheets, scripts, videotapes and DVDs of the film itself arrive by Federal Express. It probably costs eighty thousand dollars to send a videotape of a film to all the members.

Some of my competitors had spent four hundred thousand dollars to promote their claims. Since then, the budgets have escalated. Lobbying for votes has become more than unseemly. Nominees are urged to visit the Actors' Home, where five hundred geriatric members of the Academy can be wooed.

We had the added problem of struggling with a crippled and depleted Columbia Pictures. David Puttnam resigned at this stage after a brief and contentious stewardship. Columbia was swallowed by Tri-Star. There were mass firings and reorganisation.

To find success in the Oscars, a picture needs the enthusiastic backing of the studio and a readiness to spend. Given the Columbia situation, this seemed unlikely, and so it proved. Jake Eberts pitched in money to supplement the meagre budget assigned by Columbia for the campaign. After some arm-twisting, Nelson Entertainment, which had the video rights, also made a contribution. Even so, it left us with only a third, or perhaps a quarter of what other pictures were spending.

In another part of the rainforest, Dawn Steel, Puttnam's successor at Columbia, gave an eve-of-Oscar party in her Bel Air home. In her jungle garden, movie stars – that endangered species – could be seen in the wild. Glenn Close, who got pregnant in *Fatal Attraction*, was heavily and eerily pregnant in real life. As if her liaison with Michael Douglas was not dangerous enough, she was to film *Dangerous Liaisons* after the baby was born. She asked me to introduce her to my cameraman, Philippe Rousselot, who was to shoot the film for Stephen Frears. I presented him. She offered him her face. He surveyed it. The appraisal was technical, but the moment was potently sexual at the same time.

Sean Connery was celebrating the achievement of his fellow Scot, Sandy Lyle, in winning the Masters. Sean said he would trade an Oscar any time to play golf like that. Shirley MacLaine could not recall an encounter we had in Dublin. I suggested that now that she had taken to peering into the future she was perhaps forgetting the past. I tried again with Tatum O'Neal. 'You won't remember me, but we met when you had just done *Paper Moon*. It was in your father's house.' 'I remember what we said, what I wore, what you wore. I remember everything. That's my problem. I can't forget anything.'

One could not remember meeting me, the other wished she could forget. With a crumpled ego I turned to Kathleen Turner who told me, in pealing tones that penetrated five neighbouring conversations and stopped them dead, that, 'I have a five-thirty call tomorrow morning. I only came by because I heard you'd be here.' She flitted away leaving me feeling much better, but I saw her speaking to Bernardo Bertolucci. I asked him jealously what Kathleen had said to him. He would only smile enigmatically, but confessed to me that he had been in analysis for fifteen years. 'Why?' I asked. 'I made beautiful movies, but people did not want to see them.' 'Have you stopped now everyone is seeing *The Last Emperor*?' 'Yes,' he said with a grin.

Sean Connery was listening agog. I could see him doing silent mental arithmetic, totting up all those fees Bertolucci paid out over fifteen years.

The Los Angeles Psychotherapists' Association gave me its 'Courage in Film Making' Award. I hoped a course of treatment might go with it, but alas, no – I will have to pay like Bertolucci.

At three-thirty in the afternoon, a scalding sun burned out of a white-hot sky on the throng of people in the lobby of the Beverly Hills Hotel. They were all in dinner jackets and ball gowns. It was all so bizarre, it was hard to take it seriously. The hysteria surrounding the Oscars has come about only since it became a great television event.

The limos stretched back in a two-mile jam and crawled to the Shrine Auditorium in downtown LA where the Oscar ceremony was to be held. We edged through a wilderness of dereliction and decay with every window and door fortified by metal grilles. Black youths stared at us. Thankfully, the tinted windows precluded them from seeing us in all our finery, and we hoped that the slowness of our progress might persuade them that it was a funeral procession.

Everyone's secret fear is that their limousine will break down in the middle of the ghetto.

It was ninety degrees. The air was more suitable for chewing than breathing. The smoggy sunlight did nothing for the glitzy dresses as the stars alighted to an hysterical welcome from fans and media.

The show opened with Sean Connery making a magnificent entrance. He stood stock still, centre stage, head raised, no longer the man who would be king, but finally the crowned monarch. His subjects rose as one to pay him homage.

Cher arrived late and all heads turned to see what she was wearing. She was also nominated. Her seat was next to mine. Behind me, I heard the voice of the demon in *The Exorcist*, Mercedes McCambridge, growl: 'That's her thing. Good luck to her, but would you like her to be your mother?'

During the commercial breaks I dashed out to the bar and once got locked out until the next break, missing some of the action. I was driven away by the musical numbers. From the second row I found myself learning more about the dancers' crotches than I wished to know. As soon as a seat is vacated a 'seat filler' occupies it so that the camera will never witness anything but a full house.

Pee Wee Herman was suspended on a wire, kicking his feet, and he hung out over us in the front rows. Mercedes' voice rasped out again: 'What a way to go, crushed to death by Pee Wee Herman.'

All the nominees were in the front half-dozen rows, but the very front row was reserved for trained extras, their leaders wired up to receive radio instructions from TV control. These were the cheerleaders. They started the applause and we all followed suit. If the control room felt that a standing ovation was appropriate, they signalled, and up jumped row one. We in row two now could not see, so we stood too. The wave spread back, and there you had it, a standing ovation.

When Cher got up to collect her award it seemed I was standing on her dress. It was a tarantula spider's web spun out of beads. A piece ripped off and she threw me a look so lethal that it stopped my heart. I was mortified. I made a dash for the bar. I stepped on the loose beads, losing my footing. I flailed my arms to keep my balance. A grim security man started towards me. His thoughts were clear from his eyes: 'If this drunken limey starts a scene, boy, will I fix him.'

The Last Emperor swept the Oscars. My role was to applaud bravely as other men took my Academy Awards. Those cameras are always in tight on the faces of the losers, searching for glimmers of pain, envy, tears. We all affect a little rueful smile which says, 'It's just a game. We play along but don't really take it seriously. We're above all this sort of thing.' The notes for my acceptance speech were screwed up in my fist, burning a hole in my hand.

Afterwards there was a media feeding frenzy. We, the losers, the sacrificial victims of a spectator blood sport, were brutally elbowed aside as press and TV converged on the winners. Most people tried to avoid my eye. I was contaminated by failure. A few brave friends offered condolences. They wore funereal faces. I searched for a waste bin where I could bury my notes with my hopes. I felt humiliated.

We had endured the three-and-a-half hour ritual. From leaving the hotel to the end of the Governors' Ball nine hours had elapsed. Losing gracefully is incredibly exhausting, but Meryl Streep looked radiant right to the end. She even does losing better than anyone else.

The headlong success of *Hope and Glory* was thus checked, but the story of this anonymous lower-middle-class family became celebrated around the world. I was astonished at how many Englishmen I had marked out as aristocratic, or at least, upper-middle, came forward to confess that they too were boys from the semi-suburbs.

I had thought of ending this memoir at this point with a kind of happy ending, with my life come full circle, but as Orson Welles said, 'There are no happy endings if you tell the rest of the story.'

Death of a Hero

At the time of the Oscars, Lee Marvin became seriously ill. I went to Tucson to see him. He was gaunt and wasted. He rallied for my visit. His wife, Pam, cooked dinner and he made a brave attempt to eat. He was all charm but the old mockery was present too. I took a picture of him by his pool, the arid desert stretching out behind him with the crazed sequoia cactus, arms akimbo. I looked into his eyes. He knew. And he knew that I knew. He did not flinch. He died in intensive care, strapped down. Pam was with him. He watched the screens recording his vital signs. He saw them run down. He faced the truth.

When I heard the news, a memory, an image sprung to mind – the serene smile on Lee's face as our Cessna fell towards the lava beds of the volcano on Maui. Then I thought of all those villains he had played and how he had succeeded in obliging us to connect with them. The profound unease we experience in identifying with an evil character in a movie is the recognition that we may be capable of such evil. Conversely, identifying with a hero elevates us, leads us to believe ourselves capable of sacrifice, honour and courage. So many actors, when required to play bad guys, cannot resist some coded plea to the audience for sympathy. Lee never did, which is why his villains were so shocking. He knew the depth of our capacity for cruelty and depravity from his war experiences. He had committed such deeds, had plumbed the depths, and was prepared to recount what he had seen down there. His performances were unflinching and sometimes almost unbearable. He knew this stuff was hard to take. But he also had to live in the world, the Hollywood world. Just as alcohol offered him an escape from unbearable reality, so his other acting persona, the bumbling drunk, released him from his obligation to truth-telling. The two manifestations are perfectly paired in *Cat Ballou*, where he played the dual roles of deadly killer and hopeless drunk.

He was a young boy when he witnessed and perpetrated the atrocities of war. His wounds never healed. They left him raw. All life was salt rubbed into them.

A lot of that experience found its way into *Point Blank*. Lee was hypersensitive to everything going on around him. He could walk into a room of people and feel all the pain. His mind was still on combat alert. Drink desensitised him, but he always carried America's guilt in his heart. He felt America was doomed because it was founded on the genocide of the Indian nations. He believed, therefore, that America could only express itself through violence. America was war, and he was a helpless conscript. My camera held Lee at arm's length in *Point Blank*. It framed him in stark compositions. He was beyond human help, beyond redemption. The audience could feel compassion for his isolation, for a condemned man, but at a distance. A man, a nation, in violent and hopeless pursuit of destiny.

Is there a celestial accountant somewhere, totting up the sum of human misery, back to the beginning of time? The suffering inflicted on man by man accumulates. It passes down the generations, lying dormant then erupting to seek redress and vengeance for past ills. Hostility and vengeance had lost their focus. They searched for a new home and landed in Afghanistan. The satire paper, *The Onion*, put it well: 'Our long nightmare of peace and prosperity is finally over.' The

Americans have unleashed their weapons of destruction with a kind of relief, as though having them with no prospect of using them built up a massive craving, such as an addict might feel. The release of all those bombs and missiles was morphine to our psychic ache. Are war and conflict the natural condition of man, and times of peace merely a brief aberration?

Something had to be done that would be appropriate to the man he was. I called Pam. I said Lee should be buried in Arlington. He was a decorated Marine. It was an entitlement.

His friends and family gathered there. The National Cemetery now has the marble Vietnam wall, with its list of the fallen tidily arranged in alphabetical order, and we watched the relatives of the dead, mostly black, making rubbings from the raised names.

There was a service for Lee in the chapel. I gave the funeral oration. I said Lee was a spiritual warrior whose war wounds had never healed. He was the Fisher King. He felt damned by what he had done in the war, yet longed for redemption. The flag covering his ashes was ceremonially folded and given to Pam. The officer in charge spoke quietly to her of the nation's gratitude. The Marine guard fired a fusillade. The last post sounded. He was buried just below the Tomb of the Unknown Warrior between the great boxer, Joe Louis, and a twenty-one-year-old soldier who had died in Vietnam.

Ours was an unlikely friendship, coming, as we did, from such different places, yet I knew his mind, and he mine. We trusted each other to go on hazardous journeys together, which we narrowly survived. As large as he was in life, so also was his absence. He left a great gap in the world, as an actor and a friend. As we get older, more and more of these holes begin to appear in the fabric, until our own lives hang on the few threads that remain.

Returning home to Ireland, seeking solace, I walked to Glendalough, close to my home, where steep hills enclose a black lake. It is a sacred place, and I contemplated St Kevin's cell, a cave perched over the water. I have stood there many times, pondering the mystery of what brought a solitary monk to this remote place and why disciples flocked to join him. I have always sensed power flowing from that lake. It is a blind power without purpose. Perhaps St Kevin felt this too. His patient prayer was intended to funnel that power towards good ends. Before the monks, the druids were in these same places, drawing the power to their own uses. As I stood there I had a vision that, in our godless times, that power is running wild, untended, undirected, bent on destruction. Is it fanciful to believe that there are places where man and earth can connect and interact, as the Indians of the Xingu appeared to do?

This last autumn the holly was thick with berries, beech trees richer in nuts than I have ever seen. Indeed, every tree was heavy with fruit. Owners of orchards use a cruel technique. They tighten wire around their trees, cutting through the bark. The tree believes that it is dying and produces a massive quantity of fruit in order to ensure its perpetuation. Nature seemed to suspect that the last summer had come, or at least, that great forces of destruction were abroad. Hurricane winds and floods seem to confirm that fear.

1988: *Where the Heart Is*

I was emboldened by the success of *Hope and Glory* to attempt another personal film. *Hope and Glory* was about being a son; this one would be about being a father, drawing on the lives of my four growing-up children and their friends. There would be an irascible father trying to get his children to leave home, to grow up, to take life seriously. It would be a comment on London in the eighties. I asked Telsche, my oldest daughter, who was an amused observer of her siblings' irresponsible adventures and mishaps, to write it with me. She was living in Paris, married and pregnant, and already had a reputation as a screenwriter, often working with French directors who wanted to make films in English.

I had been nursing the idea of a modern Lear, master of a business empire, who walks out, dividing it among his offspring. I had Sean Connery in mind and he and I had chewed it over from time to time. Telsche's idea was more a state of being, a condition rather than a story. She was interested in how her sisters and brother and their friends were in a permanent state of preparation, getting ready, living in a tumescence of anticipation – we had a fine time pillaging the family history and scavenging the lives of friends. We made the father, Stewart McBain, the owner of a demolition company. He has acquired a house which, frustratingly, has a preservation order, and he is not allowed to knock down. He drives his three grown-up children out from the family home and

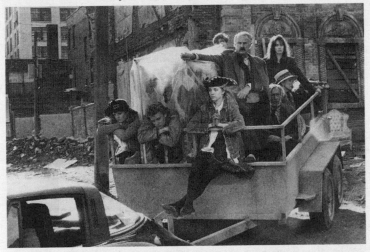

Where the Heart Is: material comforts snatched away

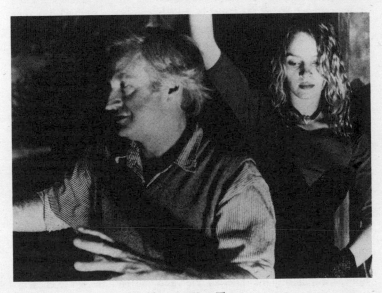

Me, directing Uma Thurman

obliges them to live in it, rent rooms and make their own livings. In the vacuum left by their children, the parents find themselves strangers to each other, echoing my own marriage.

We aimed to make a diversion, an entertainment that turned on certain social observations, but darker issues, serious matters, inevitably intruded. Our comedy held them at bay but they hovered at the edge of things. The shadow that fell across this sunny romp was the fear of all of us who enjoy material comforts – possessions, houses, cars, chattels – the fear that this good life might some day be snatched from us. Lear gives up power, authority, position, and becomes the lowest of creatures – spurned, mad. The father, Stewart, is ruined by the system, plumbs the depths, joins the homeless, tastes despair and madness. Now that the Third World is on every street corner of our cities, the cold fingers of that fear creep up on us. I look into the faces of street people and I see men like myself. As I shamefully spurn their pleas or guiltily shower them with money, I recognise my own frailty in their eyes. I reflect that we might all be homeless soon, in the most terminal way, if the planet can no longer endure our demands and excesses.

We called it *Where the Heart Is*. Jake Eberts began to market it as he had *Hope and Glory*, going to the same buyers. We began pre-production. Then Sean Connery defected. His agent persuaded him that he should not be making little English movies. Spielberg offered him a role in the third *Indiana Jones* film (and he was wonderful in it). Our finance fell out. We had to abort the picture. All our efforts to revive it came to nothing. But the clever men at Disney, Jeffrey Katzenberg and Michael Eisner, got a whiff of it. They said they would do it if we would transpose it to America. After some misgivings Telsche and I decided to give it a try and I set out for LA once again.

I stepped off the 747 and took a deep lungful of the smog-baked yellow gas that has long since replaced the stuff we were designed to breathe. When Bob Hope came to Ireland he said, 'It makes me nervous to breathe air I can't see.'

On the San Diego freeway, the black taxi driver told me he was a minister in a sect that speaks in tongues. English wasn't one of them. As he rambled on, my mind drifted off: all the while I've been absent from LA, these eight lanes of traffic have been running non-stop, twenty-four hours a day, at fifty-five miles an hour, and will until the world ends.

Disney agreed to distribute the film in the US, but only if we could twist the script into a shape that would satisfy them; and so after this wearisome journey my fate was to be decided on Dopey Drive where the almost infallible priests of popular taste sat in judgement. They presented me with several pages of notes, all aimed at making the script more American. I told them I would give them consideration. Telsche was to join me a day or two later to start on the rewrite.

I lay awake half that night in the throes of jet lag, the Disney notes spinning in my head. When I did drop off, I was awoken by an earthquake. The Evian water, hauled all the way from France, now spilt uselessly on to the hotel carpet. Concern for the fate of the planet was a theme of the movie. Was this the earth giving a warning elbow nudge, I wondered?

The people at Mouseville were distressed that we planned to reset the film in New York, where they said it was much too expensive to film. The unions mug you. If we insisted, they demanded that we shoot the interiors and some of the locations in Toronto, drastically reducing the number of days we absolutely had to shoot in New York.

So, still awaiting Telsche, I found myself flying over the eerily dead Lake Erie, and the equally lifeless Lake Ontario, to see Toronto announce itself with a cluster of blazing skyscrapers. The sameness of North American cities has been relieved in recent years by the fanciful phallic towers that billionaires build to confirm their manhood. Everyone wants to trump Trump. Toronto has sprouted its own defiant downtown skyline. It sends a message to the US: we can do it too, but better – some of ours were designed by the genius of the Bauhaus, Mies van der Rohe.

I found the town jam-packed with invading film-makers from across the border. I was soon in a struggle for possession of draughty warehouses to build our sets, but wasn't able to make firm commitments until I had satisfied Disney's script demands.

I rented a place on the beach in Malibu. Telsche arrived with her baby, Daphne. We did several drafts of the script. The dynamic of our group of characters did not translate easily to America. We had to adapt the characters to the new environment. It began to emerge that Disney's veiled agenda was to turn it into a dopey farce. We resisted staunchly, but there was a process of erosion.

After several drafts, we took our compromised script to Toronto, itself a compromised New York, and made the movie. I edited it at home in Ireland, then took it back to LA to preview it. We used to call them 'sneaks'. The market research companies that organise them today dignify them as 'recruited public previews'.

In the old days they simply put an ad in the paper: 'Major Studio Sneak Preview Tonight' (all studios are major studios – at least I never heard one claiming it was minor), and people would simply turn up. Louis Mayer's great film editor Margaret Booth (she who defended *Point Blank*) once told me about sneaking *Gone with the Wind*. Someone got up to warn the audience that the movie was three hours long. Such was the pre-publicity surrounding it that they knew instantly it had to be *Gone with the Wind*. They stood up and cheered: a standing ovation before the first frame was shown. 'I had a feeling then,' Margaret drawled 'that we had a hit on our hands.'

D. W. Griffith would edit all day and then throw the cans into the car and drive out to a movie house and show what he had. He would do that three times a week, having audiences edit with him as he went along. It was easier with silent movies. Today we are obliged to do 'temporary sound mixes', a painfully unsatisfactory process: the music score has yet to be recorded, the dialogue is still to be post-synchronised, sound effects are only roughly laid in. We slap in scraps of music off commercial discs, and do a rough mix of dialogue and sound effects. This half-cooked dinner is set before the sceptical and ill-prepared in the hope that they will understand what a wonderful soufflé this indigestible, soggy pudding will eventually become.

For two years we had laboured to make the movie as good as we could make it, polishing every nuance. The audience in my head is witty, warm and receptive, responsive to ambiguity and irony, quick to catch the resonances of myth and fable, alert or at least awake – but here we were in a shopping mall in the San Fernando Valley. I scrutinised their faces as they filed in, the bored, glazed eyes. Most seemed overweight. They were laden with buckets of popcorn and pint-sized cartons of Coke. They yawned, they scratched, they chewed gum. Were these the people I had made the movie for? They had been 'scientifically' recruited. Interviewers had been out on the street, quizzing them – age, level of education, the kind of movies they go and see. This was an 'up-scale' audience, they assured me. In practice, people are given passes which go from hand to hand, and you get what you get.

I sat among them, my nervous system invisibly wired to each member of the audience. Every sigh or inappropriate giggle sent a stab of pain to my brain. A man walked out – five hundred volts. Then a surge of joy as he came back with popcorn. A slow passage set off squirming and murmuring – must speed up that scene – then utter silence and stillness as a sequence engaged them fully.

As the lights went up there was light applause. Cards and pencils were distributed and they all scribbled away, every one a movie critic. We paced the foyer while the marketing people counted up the scores. My insecurity tempted me to tell my colleagues how absurdly inaccurate these score cards are, how often they are wrong, but I said nothing in case the results were good. I contented myself by complaining about how in Hollywood the marketing tail is wagging the movie dog. Now they even test movies before they are made. They go out and ask people if they would go see a film with such-and-such a title, with this-or-that kind of story. This may be helpful in relieving movie executives from the irksome task of deciding what should or should not be made, but it certainly works against movie ideas that are complex or original. Inevitably the stories that are liked best are the ones that are similar to other movies people have seen – much easier for them to visualise, hence the proliferation of sequels. Or very simple ideas.

Michael Eisner, when he was running Paramount, coined the phrase 'high concept', meaning a strong story that can be expressed in a few words, like 'Danny de Vito and Arnold Schwarzenegger are twins'. Orwell showed us how words could be made to mean their opposite. 'High concept' of course usually means 'low concept'. One studio head, to whom I was pitching a story, interrupted my rambling narrative with a brutal question: 'Just tell me how you would express this in a thirty-second TV ad. That's how we sell pictures today, and if a story won't make an ad, then I'd be crazy to make the movie.'

Another 'major' studio was testing titles and the marketing people put down the titles they wanted to test, then added a few extra ones, like placebos, to give some choice. A bright young employee, thinking up movies he would like to see, put down 'Roger Corman's *Frankenstein*'. It came out top. They tested it a few more times. Bingo every time. What did they do? They asked Roger Corman to make the movie. He had not directed for twenty years, too busy running his own studio. The offer did not offend him. On the contrary, in making and distributing twenty or so low-budget movies a year, he was way ahead of the majors. Roger shamelessly does the whole process back-to-front. He tests titles and, when he finds one people like, he has his art department make up an exciting poster. If that appeals, he gets his trailer people to devise a

TV ad. He then hires a writer and bids him concoct a screenplay based on these artefacts.

At last the marketing team came back to the foyer with the preview scores. The studio executives, my editor and I gathered in a tight knot around the man with the numbers. People are asked to rate the movie: excellent, very good, good, fair, or poor. The critical number is the percentage you get in the top two categories. The other significant indicator comes from the question: 'Would you recommend it to your friends? – definitely, probably, probably not, definitely not.'

We did fairly well, but the movie clearly divided the audience. Those who liked it liked it a lot. The ones who didn't get it, who couldn't see it as a sort of a comic fable, absolutely rejected it. The next day I perused the cards and mulled over the comments. One question went: 'How would you describe the movie to your friends?' The first one I looked at said: 'I couldn't, I fell asleep.' The next wrote: 'Uma Thurman is the most beautiful creature alive in the world today.' Some of the others: 'It is completely enchanting. I didn't want it to end.' 'It is boring, stupid and unrealistic.' 'A great movie so go see it or I'll never talk to you again.' 'Only go and see it if you can get in for free.'

Were they all watching the same movie? The structuralists could make something of this, but it did not much help me. I resolved to make the film more like itself, rather than twist it into a shape that might convert the doubters.

I went back to the cutting room, made changes, got actors to re-record the lines that were not clearly understood, remixed the soundtracks, and a few weeks later we were back previewing again. Disney insisted that this process went on for six weeks. Each time our scores crept up a little. Our alterations were quite marginal, but it has become common to shoot whole new scenes for movies after previews – particularly endings, the most notorious being *Fatal Attraction*. In the original version Michael Douglas and his wife watch the tragic finale of *Madam Butterfly* while his mistress, Glenn Close, maliciously kills herself with a knife we know has Michael Douglas's fingerprints on it. The preview audiences would have none of it. 'Kill the bitch,' they screamed. The film-makers dutifully got Glenn Close back, put her in a bath tub, killed her off as messily as possible, and the rest is box-office history.

In the seventies, the studios believed in directors. They left it to us. When Michael Eisner and Jeffrey Katzenberg took over the flaccid and ailing Disney studio they applied the methods they had learnt in television. They set up stringent controls at all stages of film-making, particularly the scripting and casting. All the major studios have now adopted their methods, wresting control back from the film-makers. They all have 'creative groups' which make detailed notes on each draft of the script so that anything illogical or quirky or irrational is rooted out at an early stage. They press for a conventional three-act structure. The victim of this system is originality. Elements that cannot be recognised as familiar from previously successful films are ruthlessly eliminated. The new Disney understood that audiences are bottle-fed and weaned on television. They correctly concluded that movie audiences would respond to films that follow the rigid formulae so insistently applied by the networks.

After our final preview, a young man came up to me in the parking lot and told me he went to the movies every night and saw at least three sneak previews a week. He knew people who worked for the marketing companies and they tipped him off. This was the third time he had seen *Where the Heart Is*. He had his own rating system: 'First time out I gave you a 6 out of 10, but you're up to an 8 now. It gets better. I'll see it again. It's like a friend now.'

Late at night, back in my hotel, I went through the cards again. Despite my efforts, an awful lot of people still hated it. I remember that David Lean once gave the advice: 'Make your movies to please yourself and if they don't please the audience, then get out of the business.' Perhaps I should. Then I turned up a card that said: 'John Boorman's movies are unpredictable, subversive and crazed. Tell him to keep making them no matter what.' Perhaps I should.

I think it was Auden who said, 'Poems are never finished, only abandoned.' Likewise, movies are never finished, only released. I'd done what I could. It was time to let go. Jet-lagged, I fell asleep in the chair, preview cards scattered all over the floor. I dreamt I had made the ultimate movie. I was showing it to a preview audience. As it ended, the crowd leapt to its feet, cheering, weeping, laughing. Then I saw that one man was still in his seat, shaking his head sceptically. I went over to him and he looked up at me and I saw that he had my face. He said, 'Aren't you ashamed of yourself?'

The studios use preview audiences to clobber directors. They interpret the results to suit their own ends. Disney always wanted *Where the Heart Is* to be a teen comedy, and despite all the evidence to the contrary, they advertised it as such, thus putting off the people who might have liked it, and disappointing those attracted by the ads.

It opened poorly in the States in February 1990, and throughout the year in other territories, without much more success. Somehow it mutated into a creature that was not quite mine and not quite theirs. As Jeffrey Katzenberg put it when our horns were locked over the script, 'The trouble is, it's still a Boorman film. It's not yet a Disney film.' Afterwards, he lamented, 'I guess if you ask Hockney to paint a Renoir, however hard he tries, it will still come out looking like a Hockney.' I had to agree with him.

Perhaps it suffered from being based on my own unresolved marriage. There were areas that Telsche and I had to skirt around. Christel had been loyal and true, and I had not. Trust was lost. I lived on sufferance, closely watched. When I finally broke away, the severance was wrenchingly painful for all the family.

Endings

After *Zardoz*, the last of our collaborations, Bill Stair had gone back to Bristol. He taught art and film and dabbled in animation. He called me to announce that he had prostate cancer. As a hypochondriac, he had contracted numerous imaginary diseases in the past and been scorned. Now he felt vindicated. He had a real, measurable disease. He said it was terminal, and would I like to come down and say goodbye – or we could do it over the phone if I was tied up. I said of course I'll come. 'Oh, good,' he said, 'I'm dying to see you.' I took the train to Bristol. He was in top form, doing death jokes. He was giving audiences to all his friends. He had been shopping around the religions for a funeral to his taste and had finally settled on the Quakers.

I asked him whether there was anything he wanted, anything I could do for him. 'I'd like to see the sea one last time,' he said. I hired a car and took him to Weston-super-Mare. The tide in Weston goes out for more than a mile. It was at its lowest ebb. The sea was a grey sliver in the far distance. 'Story of my life,' he said. 'Everything I wanted was always out of reach.' We talked about *Point Blank* and Lee Marvin and *Leo the Last* and Marcello. We laughed and laughed.

'They tell me I won't see Christmas. Perfect excuse to get out of those family gatherings. They always bored me to death. Whoops!' The jokes were getting forced. His bones were aching. He was shrinking back into his pain, his only constant companion. He was done with me. I had an impulse to slip silently from the room without a word, and should have done, but instead I tried to conduct a final goodbye. All the ameliorating cliches – 'keep in touch,' 'see you soon,' 'take care' – sprang uselessly to mind. I embraced him, but he pushed me away. I said, 'Goodbye.' The word felt hopelessly inadequate, incapable of expressing finality. He nodded, looked away. I left. I ran all the way to the railway station, exulting in being alive.

I waited word of his death. Christmas came and went. I called his number. I got his answering machine. Had his voice survived him? Then he picked up. 'I'm still alive. Do you realise how embarrassing that is? I suppose you wouldn't feel like coming down again? Too much of an anti-climax? After all, we've played the big scene.' I went. He was weaker but still managed to be funny. He was in a hospice. We were much more at ease, expecting less of each other. He died shortly after.

A Quaker funeral consists simply of an hour's silence then a joining of hands. I never knew he had so many friends. Most were students and past students. They were all branded for life from the Bill Stair experience. We entered the silence together, all thinking of our times with Bill, how he had forged his neurosis into an art form – the frantic, comic chronicler of his own desperate life – and how he had made us aware of our own absurdities. His mind seemed to be among us, spinning above our heads like a balloon you inflate and let go and it farts around the room in all directions. After what seemed only five or six minutes, the hour was up.

David Lean

Woes seldom come singly, and shortly after Bill's funeral, I saw a report in the paper that David Lean had been taken seriously ill, a month before he was due to start shooting *Nostromo*. I called and a very careful man answered, took my message, but would not say where I could reach David. The next morning David called back. Through a croaking voice the old spirit burned. I said those silly things we say to the sick: 'David, what is all this? You have to shoot your movie, I want to see it.' He said he'd been suffering from a sore throat and that it had turned out to be cancer. He told me he was having radiation treatment. He took heart from the fact that the insurance company had agreed to postpone the picture for nine weeks rather than cancel it. He was very moved at the calls he had received. 'I didn't know so many people cared about me,' he said. I promised to visit him in London.

A few weeks before, he had invited me to his wedding. At eighty-three he was starting out on his sixth marriage and his seventeenth film. He had a lot more left to do. The lives of great men are too short. I had read a quote from him in which he said he had no interest in naturalism any more. He wanted to make transcendent cinema. In his combination of image and emotion he has occasionally done just that. There are no great movies, as there are no great lives – only great moments. By anchoring himself to simple, even trite, stories he has often been able to achieve those transcendent moments without losing his mass audience. But he dreamt, as we all do, of a movie made up entirely of those moments.

He was staying in the home of his new wife in South Kensington. When I got there a blizzard was raging and London was coated in several inches of powder snow. His secretary, a male assistant and his driver were busy clearing a path from the front door to the car. They were working with exaggerated fervour. Devoted to David, helpless in the face of his cancer, they seized on a small task, something they could do, something that would at least smooth his way. The house was very feminine, even exotic, quite different from David's sturdy warehouse in the Docks with its ocean-liner interior. I found him sunk in a sofa in the company of cushions. The great frame had collapsed. He looked frail. His impaired speech made it hard to make out what he was saying, but as he spoke the old fire flared up.

He told me the history of his cancer in detail and described his radiation treatment. He said the tumour was regressing, responding well, and he had received hopeful signals from the doctors. He told me of a dream he had had. 'It was more than a dream,' he said. 'It was so real, so sharply focused, almost a vision.' He dreamt that he woke up with the feeling that there was someone in the house. He went downstairs and there he sensed that this dread thing was in the basement. He walked down the dark stairs and opened the door. There was a burglar. He stood there with an insolent grin on his face and David said, 'I know who you are.' 'Who am I?' the man asked. 'You are cancer,' said David, 'and I am going to beat you.'

We had the most sweet and intimate conversation. The urgent sounds of the city were muffled by the snow. We sat there snug and warm with all barriers breached. 'I was always so stupidly shy,' he said. 'We should have had lots of talks like this.'

David turned to his wife, Sandra, and told her how he had seen *Point Blank* and told Bob O'Brien that he should hang on to me (which he did not), and I related to her how David's opportune phone call to O'Brien had saved the picture from extinction. Sandra brought in camomile tea. Through the window, powdery snow drifted down in slow motion. It felt as though we were inside the ice house in *Dr Zhivago*. His head suddenly dropped, and Sandra called his name sharply. He woke up. 'Damn radiation. The other day I was giving an interview – to prove I was still alive – and I nodded off in the middle of it. The poor journalist had to sit there watching me sleep.' He laughed, then his eyes drifted off a little, not to sleep but towards the past. He looked up and said:

> I started out editing silent pictures, John. When sound came in, it slowed everything down. Soundtrack became a tyrant. Having to lace up and run track and picture together. Bloody cumbersome. You need rhythm to edit well. So I used to learn the dialogue by heart and lip-read the actors. Didn't need the soundtrack then. So I could throw the film about with the old abandon.

He said that all his best ideas had been irrational and intuitive, and that he wished he had followed them with more conviction, defended them against the opposition of others. I suspect that it was the other side of David, the rational, meticulous side, that had opposed them.

I had read Robert Bolt's wonderful script, *The Bounty*, which, alas, David never made. At the tribute to David in Cannes I suggested that the conflict between Captain Bligh, the rigid disciplinarian, and Mr Christian, the man of feeling who embraces the sybaritic life, represented the two sides of David. It is when those two elements are in creative conflict in his films that they are at their best.

Sandra came back into the room. David and I had allowed our talk to wander where it would as we sat in our silent winter cocoon. It was time for him to go to the hospital. His loyal familiars had cleared his path to the car. I rose to leave. He looked up at me and said, 'Haven't we been lucky, John? They let us make movies.' I said, 'They tried to stop us.' His face creased into a grin, the suburban boy from Croydon breaking cover. 'Yes, but we fooled them.'

His memorial service in St. Paul's was so magnificently and expertly staged that many of us afterwards found we had had the same thought: the master had directed it himself from the grave. The great organ, the St. Paul's choir, and a full orchestra opened up with 'Sunrise' from Richard Strauss's *Also Sprach Zarathustra*, forgivably borrowed from Kubrick's epic *chef d'œuvre*, and a suitably cosmic comment on David's work and life. There were readings by John Mills, Peter O'Toole, Omar Sharif, Sarah Miles, Tom Courtenay and, most powerfully of all, by the actor George Correface, who was to have played the title role in *Nostromo*, the last in the long line of Lean's leading men. He read the opening and conclusion of the script and did enough to convince us that David would have launched another career.

The readings, mostly from his films, were interspersed with soaring anthems from the choir and the secular film music of Maurice Jarre, who was conducting the orchestra himself. Melvyn Bragg gave a warm and incisive account of David's work. As the television torchbearer of the arts, Melvyn is destined to bury the men whose lives he has celebrated. Robert Bolt limped bravely to the microphone and spoke with his stroke-impaired, computer-like voice, each word a staccato stab of pain. He said, 'Dav-id – I – am – here. Every-thing – I – know – about – film – you – taught – me.' John Box, Lean's designer, spoke of David as a great architect – he compared him to Christopher Wren and his films to the cathedral in which we stood.

Even the sun broke free of a grey sky, just for a moment, and sent a shaft of light through the stained glass, like a benediction. I imagine David watching the rushes and saying, 'Bit over-the-top, that shaft of light. Oh, bugger it, leave it in, it works.'

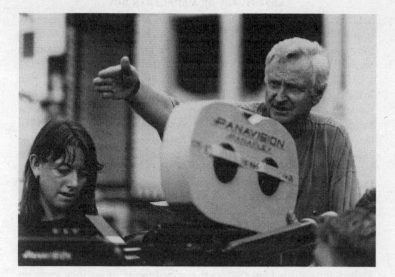

Among Trees

Deeply saddened by the loss of friends and the end of a marriage, I made *I Dreamt I Woke Up* for the BBC, a film about the outer and inner landscapes of my life, my dreams and obsessions, an ironic dissertation on life and death. With great trepidation I acted the role of myself while John Hurt played my alter ego. Parts of it were dramatised. Merlin appeared, as did the Lady of the Lake, and John Hurt confronted them on my behalf. It was about trees, the mature ones I inherited here and the young ones I am planting. It has sketches of my friends and neighbours, a tour of my sacred places: St Kevin's bed at Glendalough, the primal oak woods where I filmed *Excalibur*, the river that runs through my land. Other ideas insinuated themselves: the ghosts haunting this house; J. M. Synge, who wrote in this room where I now write; the druids, the Dark Ages, the monks in the monastery up the way; the cruelty of man and nature; and the quest for harmony, for an end to the endless conflict.

I suppose the only completely satisfactory ending to an autobiography would be a suicide note. Or as Sam Goldwyn is supposed to have said, 'No one should write their autobiography until they are dead.' I am not prepared to go that far in order to find a conclusion, but where and how to stop? There are a dozen more years too recent to write about, and still some years of life left to live; another life, in fact, in which the Dark Lady plays the central role. My daughter Telsche died five years since and I grieve for her still, and always will.

During those years I made several more films: *Beyond Rangoon*, *Two Nudes Bathing*, *The General* and *The Tailor of Panama*. I am in the final stages of *Country of my Skull*. I have plans to make several others, work that would take me into my eighties. I am conscious that I have left loose ends dangling, but that just happens to be the way things are, for the real world lacks dramatic shape.

Perhaps that is why it is so hard to find endings for movies. Imposing solutions on the messy business of life often feels forced. The studios are always urging us to make endings that are 'uplifting'. The great director, Sam Fuller, was more practical with his advice: 'Spend your money on the ending and shoot it early in the schedule. If you wait until the end, the money has usually run out and you are too exhausted to get it right.' That might also apply to the larger world. Politicians are too caught up in crisis management to think of long-term endings, but economists have taken to discussing the future in terms of 'possible scenarios', and given the momentous problems that beset our battered little planet, none of them can come up with a plot twist that will make everything come right in the end. The trivial tribulations of a film director are certainly small beer when seen in the wider context.

So what of the future? Nothing will stop the all-conquering advance of the moving image. High-definition television will bring more vivid images into the home. Omnimax and virtual reality will strive to match the veracity of the human eye. The camera has tamed our planet, domesticated its dangers and wonders, diminished its mysteries. F. Scott Fitzgerald wrote, 'The movies have taken away our dreams. Of all betrayals, this is the worst.' For we have been everywhere, seen everything. There is no experience that we can approach in innocence. We have lived it all out at the movies. We have made love in every possible way, died a thousand different deaths. We have scaled all the mountains, dived in the deepest oceans, closely observed all the creatures of the earth. T. S. Eliot's Prufrock, reaching for the remotest form of life as a metaphor for his degradation, said, 'I should have been a pair of ragged claws scuttling across the floors of silent seas.' We've been there, Tom, with the underwater camera.

Movie-makers search frantically for unused locations, for corners of the earth that have never been seen on film, only to discover a piece of gaffer-tape or, that ethnographical mark of movie-image culture, the polystyrene cup. We are second-hand people. How often, in emotional situations, do we say, 'It was like a bad movie'?

When Buñuel was preparing *The Discreet Charm of the Bourgeoisie*, he chose a tree-lined avenue for the recurring shot of his characters endlessly traipsing. The tree-lined avenue was strangely stranded in open country and it perfectly suggested the idea of these people coming from nowhere and going nowhere. Buñuel's assistant said, 'You can't use that road. It's been in at least ten other movies.' 'Ten other movies?' said Buñuel, impressed. 'Then it must be good.'

Buñuel's image will always be with me, but who remembers the other ten movies? Only the artist's metaphor can transcend the banality of the physical world, pierce the veil, uncover the mystery that lies hidden beneath.

My eye keeps drifting over to the script of *Broken Dream*. I picked it up the other day, did some revisions and left it on my desk. Of all the enthusiasms that come and go, it is the only script that lives on in my mind, rounded and complete, alive and alight.

The old illusionist discovers the ultimate trick – to make objects disappear. He teaches it to his son, and when the boy has grown strong in it, the old man asks his son to make his body disappear. He wants to follow the objects across, for the present world is fading away, coming to an end. Once he is on the other side, the old man hopes to make a bridge so that the other characters can cross too. When we probe deeply enough, we finally see that our achingly beautiful and sorrowful world is made up of sub-atomic particles moving randomly in vast empty spaces. The world we perceive and that the camera records is a certain mathematical arrangement of these particles – which may, in truth, have no existence at all, but merely be echoes or shadows of their non-selves. So could not the imagination construct another world out of these ghostly fragments? *Broken Dream* is about making another reality, another world, out of magic, out of imagination.

David Lean's words echo in my mind: 'Haven't we been lucky, John? They let us make movies.' Directing films is one of the greatest adventures on offer in the modern world. How astonishing that a shy, suburban boy got to do it.

I turn more and more to the trees and the care of them. It is my small gift to the earth but also, selfishly, a curtain of privacy for my old age.

To end among trees, there's a fine thing. A great oak in its lifetime consumes little more than a cupful of nutrients. Everything else it needs to form its great bulk comes from the air and light and water. Light and water, light on water, have been my markers, my working companions.

I am seventy. I have lived in this house in the Wicklow Hills for thirty-three years. I inherited great trees. Some of them have died and fallen. I shall leave many more than I found. Some of my young oaks are now twenty-five feet high.

> I started planting too late in life
> But some acorns are now sturdy trees
> And I am not yet too old to climb them.
> I lie in their arms and watch the world
> Recede by one foot each year.

Annamoe, County Wicklow, Ireland

Index